T0334616

Information Security Governance

Framework and Toolset for CISOs and Decision Makers

Information Security Governance

Framework and Toolset for CISOs and Decision Makers

By
Andrej Volchkov

CRC Press
Taylor & Francis Group
Boca Raton London New York

CRC Press is an imprint of the
Taylor & Francis Group, an **informa** business

CRC Press
Taylor & Francis Group
6000 Broken Sound Parkway NW, Suite 300
Boca Raton, FL 33487-2742

International Standard Book Number-13: 978-0-8153-5644-8 (Hardback)

Visit the Taylor & Francis Web site at
http://www.taylorandfrancis.com

and the CRC Press Web site at
http://www.crcpress.com

To Beba

Contents

About the Author

 **Andrej Volchkov** is a consultant in the field of information security governance and program management. He has 30 years of experience as a security program manager and responsible for new technologies and IT change management at Pictet Group, a major financial institution based in Geneva, Switzerland. Within Pictet he was also in charge of compliance projects in the field of data privacy and data protection. Previously he served as a head of IT security, compliance and internal solutions unit in IT. He was also a project leader, likewise responsible for information technology architectures, introduction of new technologies, methods and standards. Previously he served as research assistant, business analyst and software developer.

Andrej is invited speaker at Geneva University School of Economics and Management in the domain of Security Governance and acknowledged speaker in some major international conferences. He graduated in Mathematics and IT, holds an MBA from Geneva School of Economics and Management and is member of major international IT and Security Associations.

Introduction

Why yet another book on the governance of information security?

Information security (IS) has become a major issue for businesses and communities in the context of digital transformation, business model changes, cyber threats, and compliance requirements. IS is on the agenda of decision-makers and is no longer considered solely a technical discipline. It has benefited in recent years from numerous recommendations regarding the importance of good governance. But governing IS is not easy for boards of directors and senior officials, and many of their questions remain unanswered. How can the adequacy of IS be evaluated considering the real needs of the company? How can different initiatives and investments be prioritized? How can the complex world of security controls be understood? And finally, what questions should management ask their security officer, and what are their respective duties in the context of governance?

Security officers are aware of the importance of governance and the role it must play in bringing operations and strategies closer together. Their duties today go beyond fighting cyber threats and repeated incidents with limited resources. They must become a major player in the development of their company in this new context and promote a new kind of security as a partner in the value chain. But dealing with strategic aspects while ensuring operations is an impossible mission without senior officials' support, involvement, and understanding of security issues.

This book helps fill the gap. Starting from a hierarchical approach with the division of IS governance and management activities into three levels (strategic, tactical, and operational), it becomes easier to understand the areas of responsibility of each one. Such a framework offers a reading grid that focuses immediately on the main areas of governance and asks the right questions.

The standards, such as International Organization for Standardization (ISO), National Institute of Standards and Technology (NIST), Control Objectives for Information and Related Technology (CobIT), Information Technology Infrastructure Library (ITIL), and others, note the good practices of IS management and governance and propose in particular controls or measures of protection that should be put in place, but with no advice as to how to implement them. This book fills this gap too. Based on modeling controls at three levels, the main areas of IS governance and management activities are grouped together, and then, their tools and methodical approaches are presented.

The following are major problems of security governance:

Responsibility: IS can no longer be delegated entirely to information technology (IT) services. Business leaders have become involved, not only because of cybersecurity threats, the theft of confidential data, or high operational costs, but also because of regulatory requirements. IS must therefore be properly managed, its contribution to the company measured, its accountabilities defined, and its cost maintained under control.

Positioning: Security must contribute to the strategic development of the company and its businesses. Yet, despite an awareness of the need for good governance, reality is often quite different: weak strategic alignment with business objectives, disinterested management, lack of risk-based investment decisions, and hasty implementation of technical solutions without further expectations from the return on investment.

Comprehension: Even though standards such as ISO 2700x note the requirements that a security management system must meet, they are not enough. Decision-makers need to be able to visualize security and its components in a more synthetic fashion, allowing them to ask the right questions and easily assess the adequacy of the controls in place.

This book presents a framework for modeling the main activities of IS management and governance. This same model can be used for any security subdomain, such as cybersecurity, data protection, access rights management, business continuity, and so on. It presents tools and examples allowing the various managers to take on their roles. Management and board members will find the elements to help them better understand IS, ask good questions, or require proper reporting. Security managers will find the necessary tools to assume their role and thus meet the needs of the company and its customers. The book is aimed primarily at information security managers (chief security officer [CSO], chief information security officer [CISO]), senior executives (chief executive officer [CEO], chief operating officer [COO]), IT managers (chief information officer [CIO]), chief risk officers (CRO), members of the board of directors, or any other business manager or project manager involved in the governance or management of the security program. It answers "How?" questions and is of interest as a repository of tools and pragmatic methods that are complementary to the standards. Many examples illustrate the concepts throughout the chapters that follow.

This book is not an explanatory guide to the standards. Other books are dedicated to them. It is not a technical reference either. It will not provide recommendations on the latest technologies or detailed explanations of the tools or operational controls to be implemented.

What is the structure of the book?

The book is divided into 12 chapters. Following are their summaries.

Chapter 1. Security Governance covers the principles and good practices of IS governance and management. The difference between management and governance is noted along with the division of responsibilities. The main activities are presented for which tools are developed in the following chapters.

Chapter 2. Security Governance Control Framework proposes a three-level security control positioning concept called the three-level control framework (TLCF): Strategic (governance), Tactical (management), and Operational (technical measures). The first two levels consist of building blocks or key control activities: Strategy, Policies, Organization, Risk Management, Program Management, Reporting, Asset Management, Compliance, and Metrics. The characteristics and purpose of each of these blocks are presented. The focus is on the usefulness of such a model, mapping this framework with the standards, including ISO 27001/2, and applying the framework to specific security domains such as cybersecurity or data privacy.

Chapter 3. Control Framework Use Cases presents examples of using TLCF as a tool to self-assess governance practices. It is shown how this same framework can be applied to different security domains and how to adapt it to the needs of every company.

Chapter 4. Strategy is devoted to strategy development methods and tools as the foundation of every security program. The following concepts are discussed in detail: the security strategy and its content; the process and tools to define a strategy aligned with business objectives; establishing and carrying out a strategy development project; and ways to present and use the strategy in the identification of security program improvement initiatives.

Chapter 5. Policies deals from a practical point of view with developing policies and the internal regulatory framework for IS. After noting the objectives of the internal regulatory framework, the chapter focuses on the different types of documents that compose it, the structure and content of policies, and the process of developing policies and documentation frameworks.

Chapter 6. Organization describes the principal functions, roles, and responsibilities that are part of an information security management system (ISMS). Today's context requires changes in the responsibilities and profiles of employees, security officers, and their teams. The most appropriate organizational structures are shown according to the characteristics of the company and the positioning of IS.

Chapter 7. Risk Management deals with the management of security risks. Risk mitigation is the raison d'être of every security program. It is therefore essential to be able to correctly identify, assess, and treat security risks. The methods and tools necessary for pragmatic and effective security risk management are presented with the following topics: the risk management process with practical recommendations; establishing the concept of risk management in a company; risk identification, analysis, evaluation, and treatment methodologies; and the best approaches to risk communication and reporting.

Chapter 8. Program Management discusses core governance and management activities. The management of the program must ensure an appropriate level of security as well as the execution of initiatives to achieve set objectives. Steering a security program or ISMS is the responsibility of the security officer but must be overseen by the governing body. Emphasis is placed on management methods and tools, how to elaborate a security program that meets the needs of the business, essential tools in program management, and the program review cycle. One of the vital tools in managing the program is the catalog of controls, which is discussed, presenting some recommendations and tools for its establishment.

Chapter 9. Security Metrics is devoted to the design and implementation of metrics and key point indicators (KPIs) that are used in the governance process. Metrics are indicators to assess the posture (capacity) of IS, its return on investment, or the security program's progress toward set objectives. Metrics have always been a challenge for the CISO, because the legitimate need to measure the effectiveness of investments is opposed by the difficult task of finding reliable indicators. This chapter presents the main types of metrics that can be used, along with tools or methods for their effective design.

Chapter 10. Reporting and Oversight addresses the topic of security communication for the needs of governance and for other stakeholders. The purpose of a report is to present the state of security and its evolution based on key indicators. An approach is presented to establishing a reporting system that is able to answer questions such as "How is our security?", "What is its evolution?", or "Are our expenses justified?" It also serves as a reference for establishing the objectives of the security program.

Chapter 11. Asset Management focuses on the management and protection of corporate information assets. There can be no effective governance or pragmatic management of a security program without knowing what to protect. This concerns not only data and their flows in the business processes but also all the other media and means of accessing information, such as the network, servers, or applications. This chapter presents methods and tools to effectively manage all the information assets, including how to develop and use an asset inventory.

Chapter 12. Compliance presents tools to manage security's compliance with the legal and regulatory framework. Knowing which legal and regulatory security framework applies to the business and how to comply with it is essential for governance. The legal and regulatory framework includes all the laws or regulations to which a company is bound by its activities. This chapter proposes an approach to creating a regulatory reference, compliance mapping, and gap analysis. It also addresses the management of compliance projects.

How should this book be read?

The best way to gain a broad view of all the tools and methods that can be used to govern and manage a security program is to read this book from beginning to end. Nevertheless, it is designed so that chapters can be read independently of each other. So, you can start with the topic that interests you the most and then go back to the others later on. We recommend reading Chapters 2 and 3 and Chapters 9 and 10 in that order to benefit from some prerequisite concepts.

The content of this book is designed to be accessible to a wide audience and immediately applicable in the governance and management of everyday security. Our goal is to make complex topics more accessible and above all, to guide the reader through the maze of security controls and benchmarks of good practices, which are often tedious. The methods, tools, and examples presented should not necessarily be reproduced per se. They are there to stimulate the creativity of security officers and the main actors in the governance process in their companies.

Chapter 1

Security Governance

As a vital resource in the digital economy, information must be protected. Companies realize the importance of being able to ensure its availability, confidentiality, and integrity. However, technical security measures alone are no longer sufficient. Senior managers are looking for ways to ensure a level of protection in line with the needs of their company. They must also have better control of the costs related to information security while remaining in compliance with legal and regulatory frameworks.

Security governance must be enforced at all levels of an organization. But many still do not understand quite what Security Governance is, what is its main objective and how it should be integrated within existing structures in an organization. This chapter provides answers to the following questions:

- What issues are behind information security in the global context?
- What questions should senior officials ask about security governance?
- What trends are we seeing today?
- Exactly what does information security governance include?
- How can inadequate security governance adversely affect a company?
- How is good security governance recognized?
- What is the difference between governance and management?
- Is there any specific standard for information security governance?

What issues are behind information security in the global context?

1.1 Information Security Is Important for Business

Information exists nowadays in multiple formats; it is stored on different media and exchanged through uncontrolled networks. Yet, it is a vital resource for the economy and for everyday transactions. Companies must therefore ensure information's availability (for its intended use), confidentiality (exploitable by those who are authorized), integrity (protected against unauthorized changes), and authenticity.

Information security (IS) is currently making a serious contribution to business development by ensuring not only reliable operations but also new opportunities for qualitative differentiation. It is increasingly seen as a value creator or facilitator of operations in new business models. Its added value includes providing reliable and secure exchanges, ensuring secure data transfers, enabling remote protected access, ensuring the availability of services, and offering the possibility of outsourcing processes in a controlled and secure manner. More traditionally, it protects a company's know-how and reputation, reduces operational risks, and ensures compliance with legal and regulatory frameworks. It is no longer considered a technical discipline that can be delegated to specialized services. Security is becoming an increasing matter of concern for top executives and is being supervised more and more at the highest level of company responsibility. This is not only required by laws and regulations but is also a reality in many companies anxious to improve cost controls and the return on their investment in protection systems. It is no longer an ancillary activity, as companies seek to optimize investments and ensure the adequacy of deployed IS measures. Management and the board of directors are additionally involved in developing IS objectives and supervising its added value to business objectives. Whether they are customers, partners, suppliers, employees, or shareholders, all stakeholders are concerned about security issues.

What should senior officials know about security governance?

Executives and board members must therefore be better acquainted with IS issues so that they can fully assume their new responsibilities. If they do not have answers to the following questions or if the answer is "no", then there is a real need to review the practices of IS governance within the organization:

- Is the board regularly informed about IS risks and measures taken?
- Are management or line managers involved in strategic decisions concerning the development of IS?
- Who defines IS strategy, policies, and guidelines?
- Who is responsible for data protection and associated measures?
- Do we know which business processes are threatened by high IS risks and whether anything is being done to mitigate them?
- Where is confidential data stored and how is it processed? Who is accountable for data privacy protection?

- Is our IS adapted to the real needs of the business?
- Are business units members of committees that decide about IS measures concerning their operations?
- Do our know whether IS expenses are justified and what is their return on investment?

If it can be shown that security plays a part in attaining strategic objectives and reducing the risks involved, then it can benefit from senior executives' attention and take its place as a link in the value chain. Security is essential, but the question is what level of maturity is needed: in other words, how much and what level of IS are enough? Its contribution margin, and especially its cost, must therefore be measurable. However, this cannot be achieved unless the board of directors and management are involved in setting objectives and monitoring the deliverables of the security program.

What trends are we seeing today?

Several studies have highlighted a positive evolution in management's awareness of the importance of IS. However, it is still noted that technical means are often deployed in a disorganized manner, in successive layers, to overcome visible threats. Boards and management are not involved or are unable to understand the real issues behind IS, and thus, they delegate this task to bodies with little decision-making power and therefore, few means to act. The return on IS investments is not evaluated systematically. Priority is being given to technical solutions without making the necessary organizational adjustments. Roles and responsibilities are often not well defined, resources are lacking, decisions are not made, objectives and information architectures are not clearly established, and this results in loss of energy, increased costs, and a sense of frustration by both management and the teams responsible for deploying protective measures. This, in turn, causes misunderstanding on the part of the governing bodies, which do not have sufficient visibility regarding the adequacy of the measures and the costs related to real risks, leading to a race to find technical solutions to counter visible threats, but without any real means of control.

The following observations may characterize many companies that have neglected the importance of governance in the field of IS:

- Lack of awareness of IS strategy and its degree of alignment with business strategies.
- Ignorance of the problems and concerns of the IS by senior executives.
- Lack of a formal evaluation process for IS performance or return on security investments (ROSI).
- Priority is often given to technical solutions without adjusting organizational structures.
- Lack of manager involvement in the prioritization of risk treatments.
- Lack of architectural design requirements for IS.

According to PwC (*The Global State of Information Security® Survey 2018*) [Source: PwC, CIO and CSO, The Global State of Information Security® Survey 2018, October 18, 2017]: "Most corporate boards are not proactively shaping their companies' security strategies or investment plans. Only 44% of respondents say their corporate boards actively participate in their companies' overall security strategy". The implication of the board in overall security is estimated as follows: 45% in the security budget, 44% in the overall security strategy, 39% in security policies, 36% in security technologies, and 1% in the review of current security and privacy risks.

According to EY's 19th Global Information Security Survey 2016–2017 [EY - 19th Global Information Security Survey 2016-2017], 73% of companies are concerned about poor user awareness and behavior around mobile devices, 86% say their cybersecurity function does not fully meet their organization's needs, and 86% of respondents say they need up to 50% more budget.

These observations lead us to believe that many companies have yet to establish real IS governance. There are many reasons behind this; our goal is not to list them but rather, to propose tools to facilitate the implementation of a governance process adapted to the realities of each company. But, first, let's take a closer look at governance and management activities to better understand what we are talking about and why it is important.

What does information security governance mean?

1.2 Information Security Governance

Security governance is an integral part of corporate governance. Remember that there is no single or commonly accepted definition of the term *governance*. It can be summarized as a set of activities and responsibilities aimed at achieving the objectives that a company has set by satisfying the needs of all stakeholders. From this point of view, we can obviously conclude that the same principles of governance can be applied to any other functional unit of a company, business line, or geographical unit. Consequently, we can talk about the governance of information systems and the governance of a specific sector of a company or of a subsidiary. IS and its governance system are therefore an integral part of a company's global governance system.

According to Control Objectives for Information and Related Technology (CobIT) 5, A Business Framework for the Governance and Management of Enterprise IT (Chapter 6), governance could be defined as follows:

> Governance ensures that stakeholder needs, conditions and options are evaluated to determine balanced, agreed-on enterprise objectives to be achieved; setting direction through prioritization and decision making; and monitoring performance and compliance against agreed-on direction and objectives.

It should be noted at this stage that for a company to benefit from appropriate governance, the board of directors and management need to adopt a strategy or define company objectives to involve all levels of responsibility, whether in the decision-making process or in conducting operations. In fact, governance is not just about the choices and decisions of the board of directors. It affects all levels of the hierarchy, allowing a company to make decisions quickly and apply them in business operations. Governance processes therefore traverse all company activities and spread at all levels, from strategic decisions at the top of the hierarchy to operations, going in both directions. Governance encompasses managerial conduct, decision-making structures, and processes that drive a business.

As with corporate governance, there are several definitions of IS governance. We will mention one here that we think is important because it stresses the mandatory nature of security governance:

> Information Security Governance is the process of directing and controlling an organization to establish and sustain a culture of security in the organization's conduct (beliefs, behaviors, capabilities, and actions), treating adequate security as a non-negotiable requirement of being in business. ["Governing for Enterprise Security (GES) Implementation Guide", Jody R. Westby, Julia H. Allen, SEI Carnegie Mellon University 2007]

Therefore, IS governance should be seen not as ancillary or an activity isolated from the rest of the company, but as an essential part of overall governance to preserve assets and mitigate risks. Stakeholders should look at security as a set of measures needed by the company to properly pursue its activities. This is not just a matter of skills, technologies, solutions, or plans and procedures; it must be a business objective and a permanent concern for every employee.

According to the Information Security Institute, Guidance for Information Security Managers, ITGI 2008, security governance must contribute to the following five objectives:

1. Strategic alignment of information security with business strategy to support organizational objectives.
2. Effective risk management by executing appropriate measures to manage and mitigate risks and reduce potential impacts on information resources to an acceptable level.
3. Value delivery by optimizing information security investments in support of organizational objectives.
4. Resource management by using information security knowledge and infrastructure efficiently and effectively.
5. Performance measurement by measuring, monitoring and reporting information security governance metrics to ensure achievement of organizational objectives.

The involvement and commitment of all the executives in a defined security program is obviously a *sine qua non* for a company to benefit from security tailored to its needs. So, the real question is how to manage IS issues by means of an appropriate organization and a governance system that meets its needs. IS can no longer be reduced to a mere set of technical measures. Security measures must be integrated into business processes, rely on a defined program, and be in compliance with legal and regulatory frameworks. This is not only good practice but also a requirement for company management, who are responsible for ensuring the adequate protection of company values (Figure 1.1).

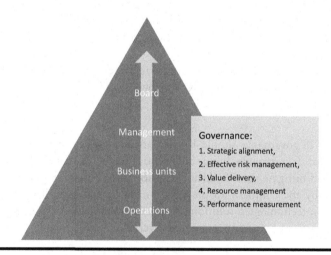

Figure 1.1 The five axes of security governance.

Complying with the requirements of the standards is not a guarantee of quality, by the way. A company where security decisions are made at an inadequate hierarchical level, where policies and directives are not applicable, where responsibilities are not exercised by persons with sufficient power to act, cannot pretend to have adequate governance and security. The following is a (nonexhaustive) list of examples of practices characteristic of inefficient or inappropriate IS governance:

■ Responsibility for deploying IS measures or controls is concentrated in a single department.
■ Business line managers consider IS to be the exclusive responsibility of the chief information security officer (CISO)/chief information officer (CIO), and it is up to them to ensure the right level of protection.
■ The board of directors does not get involved in strategic IS decisions and delegates this responsibility, considering itself not qualified to give an opinion.
■ The IS officer does not have the means to ensure the adequacy and application of security policies and directives.
■ Business initiatives and projects for change are not assessed to ensure their compliance with the security strategy or to identify security risks.
■ The board of directors does not have reports on the state of IS, its adequacy, and the effectiveness of the measures in place. It cannot evaluate the added value of security for the business.
■ The security officers feels that they are neither listened to nor supported by their superiors. Their prerogatives are reduced to actions to combat new threats or restore the situation after repeated incidents.
■ And so on.

Poor involvement by governing bodies in IS issues is a reflection of inadequate governance. The availability of efficient technical teams and sophisticated tools alone is not enough to ensure long-term protection. IS measures cannot be deployed without integrating them into business operations, without empowering all the employees, and without getting support from business unit managers. Without senior management support, the CISOs or senior information security executives and their teams will continue to fight visible threats with limited resources without being able to adopt a holistic and more proactive approach.

How can inadequate security governance adversely affect a company?

Finally, how can inadequate security governance affect corporate objectives? Senior executives need to ask themselves this question even if they think they are not concerned by IS. Table 1.1 summarizes some of the possible negative impacts on business objectives in the event of lack of adequate IS governance.

Governing well means considering adequate security to be a prerequisite for company prosperity. If IS objectives are not defined, sufficient resources cannot be

Table 1.1   Negative Impacts on Business Objectives in the Event of Lack of Adequate IS Governance

Business Objective	Possible Negative Impact in Case of Inadequate Security Governance
Developing a new business model	Inadequate level of protection required by operations
Protecting the company's reputation	Adverse opinion of customers aware of the importance of security for transaction and data privacy
Compliance with legal and regulatory frameworks	Exposure to fines and loss of customers' and partners' confidence
Preserving the company's culture and value	Loss of security awareness and risk increase
Cost containment	Loss of control over security-related costs
Alignment of security measures with business needs	Inadequacy of implemented measures (too much or too little)
Operational risk management	Loss of control over security risks that may impact operations

allocated. Under these conditions, the desired level of protection cannot be achieved, measured, or supported. A certain level of maturity in governance requires that IS be directed by leaders with sufficient power and authority, including decision-making, accountability, and allocating the necessary resources. In such an environment, security can contribute to company objectives by strategically aligning with the business, implementing adequate measures (controls) to maintain asset-associated risks at an acceptable level, and managing the allocated resources effectively.

How is good security governance recognized?

Effective security governance has the following characteristics:

- *The whole company is involved*: The assets to be protected are known, and the level of security is defined. IS is considered indispensable by business units. Security measures support business operations.
- *Responsibilities are defined*: The board and management are involved in the security program decision-making process. Business unit managers validate

security measures that support their operations, projects, and development strategy. Data and process owners are identified and functioning. IS specialists implement the program according to defined strategies and policies.

▪ *The level of protection depends on risk appetite*: IS risks are assessed and systematically treated. Risk appetite is defined, and proactive risk management is in place concerning all company activities, both operations and projects for change. IS controls are managed and associated with risks.

▪ *Security is actively managed*: Security strategy, policies, and guidelines are established to serve the needs of the organization. The assets to be protected are identified, and responsibilities are defined. Management allocates adequate resources according to a repetitive evaluation and decision-making process. Responsibilities are defined at all levels. The reporting system supports the decision-making process and is based on key indicators. An incident management system is in place. Employees are trained and risk aware. The security program is supervised, audited, and adjusted to the needs of the company.

What is the difference between governance and management?

1.3 Information Security Management

When talking about security governance, we often tend to confuse it with management or operational management. Appointing a CISO, setting up an access rights management team, or convening a committee to decide on some issues related to IS activities planning does not constitute improving or establishing governance. Conversely, if policies and guidelines are established without requiring rigorous monitoring and management of their implementation, the desired level of security cannot be achieved. Therefore, a company must be able to set goals for its security program and ensure that they are met (governance) and at the same time ensure the means for the program's effective implementation (management).

The difference between security management and security governance is not very clear. To simplify, management encompasses the implementation and monitoring of the security program, while governance provides strategic orientations and ensures its proper execution.

To illustrate this, we can use the scheme proposed by the CobIT 5 framework (Figure 1.2). Governance includes activities called Evaluate (the state of security based on business needs and management feedback), Direct (provide orientations), and Monitor (oversight). The management part includes activities related to the security program: Plan, Build, Run, and Monitor. Management feedback to

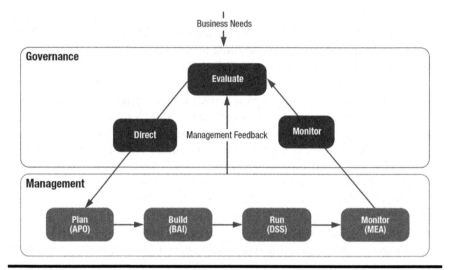

Figure 1.2   Distinction between governance and security management according to CobIT [CobIT5, "A Business Framework for the Governance and Management of Enterprise IT", ISACA, 2012].

governance is one of the key points in this process. It is indeed the CISO who should ensure the implementation of the program and reporting to governance bodies. He or she is also responsible for two-way communications with regard to strategic directions (or new business directions impacting security) as well as reporting operational indicators.

Function	Responsibilities	
Board	Define Strategy	
Management	Establish policies	
	Define risk appetite	Governance
Security Committees	Manage resources	
Business Unit Manager	Ensure adequacy of security measures	
	Manage risks	
CSO / CISO	Establish security controls	
Security Team	Communicate and educate	
Security Engeneers	Establish metrics and reporting	
	Establish architecture and standards	Management
Heads of operations	Secure applications, infrastructure, and operations	

Figure 1.3   Distribution of responsibilities between governance and management.

Generally speaking, governance includes decision-making, while management ensures the implementation of controls. An information security management system (ISMS) implements IS measures or controls and provides monitoring for reporting purposes to decision-making bodies. If we draw up a list of activities ranging from defining the strategy to carrying out security operations or controls, we will find that it is actually more appropriate to classify some in governance (e.g., strategy development) and others in management (e.g., monitoring or reporting). Considering the main activities of an ISMS such as those proposed by the standards, we can roughly schematize the areas of competence of governance and management as shown in Figure 1.3.

It is important to remember that governance and management responsibilities are found in nearly every security program activity.

EXAMPLE

A strategy cannot be validated solely by members of the board of directors or management without the involvement of the business managers, the CISO, and even the operations managers. For it to be applied, it must be accepted by everyone and considered as an indispensable part of the program. On the other hand, securing day-to-day operations also requires some involvement on the part of boards of directors to ensure that security measures have been adequately deployed (e.g., through audits). Between these two extremes, all other activities require attention from both those who govern and those who manage IS.

OK, but all of that is already well defined and explained in the standards!
Why not simply follow them?

1.4 Using Security Standards

We might ask: why not simply apply IS standards or best practice recommendations to establish good governance? Standards, guidelines, or benchmarks of good practices in the field of IS are indeed indispensable and extremely useful. However, they must be used for what they are: a set of recommendations to help build a security program. To draw a parallel with the field of construction, these standards can be compared to technical construction standards that provide the essential components of buildings but do not replace the work of the architect. A security program is a set of essential components, controls, or IS measures that are part of a defined architecture that meets the specific needs of a company.

Our goal here is not to explain the different standards in detail. Some excellent books have been published on standards, and the very explicit texts of the standards themselves can be referenced. The reader is invited to familiarize himself or herself with these, if they have not done so already; this will further facilitate their understanding of the rest of this book. Nevertheless, we will give brief explanations of some of the standards that may be useful in the development of an IS governance system.

The most widely used international IS standards are published by the following organizations: International Organization for Standardization (ISO), National Institute of Standards and Technology (NIST), Information Systems Audit and Control Association (ISACA) with its CobIT and Information Technology Infrastructure Library (ITIL). Other standards, recommendations, or benchmarks of good practice exist in some specific IS domains, such as the NIST Cyber Security Framework (CSF). The standards differ in their approach to presenting the recommendations: NIST presents and systematizes a catalog of controls, the ISO 2700x series is more process oriented in the development of an ISMS, and ITIL presents service-oriented security best practices in the form of specialized publications. Some directives or compliance frameworks may be issued by regulatory bodies (such as Finma in Switzerland, the Hong Kong Monetary Authority, or the Securities and Exchange Commission [SEC] in the United States for the financial sector) or by associations or interest groups in a given sector. Some regulations have been assimilated into laws directly impacting company IS processes (e.g., the General Data Protection Regulation [GDPR] in the European Union).

Almost every standard includes generic recommendations in different areas of IS, ranging from governance and technical infrastructure to more complex activities or controls such as risk management, access rights management, or incident management. They all mention the requirements that a security system must meet but do not specify how it should be constructed or guidelines for the realization of specific controls. In fact, there are many ways to meet the standard requirements: We will briefly introduce SABSA framework for establishing security architectures as well as the family of ISO 2700x standards that will often be referenced through this book.

Sherwood Applied Business Security Architecture (SABSA)

The SABSA approach [Enterprise Security Architecture, White Paper, John Sherwood, Andrew Clark & David Lynas, 2009] is not a standard in the sense previously mentioned. It does not offer a catalog or recommendations for operational controls. Its goal is to provide a framework for the establishment of a security architecture in accordance with business needs, which in turn makes it easier to design protection measures for critical business operations. To avoid building an IS system based on an accumulation of tactical controls or solutions without justification from above, SABSA proposes defining a security architecture based on strategic objectives. This allows operational controls to be defined based on the actual business needs.

Table 1.2 Architectures Based on Six Views

Views	Architecture
The business view	Contextual security architecture
The architect's view	Conceptual security architecture
The designer's view	Logical security architecture
The builder's view	Physical security architecture
The tradesman's view	Component security architecture
The service manager's view	Security service management architecture

The framework is comprised of six different Architectures based on six views in a layered approach (Table 1.2).

Each of these architectures is further formed while addressing process areas regarding what, why, how, who, where, and when, to understand the context of each of the layers and their relationships with other layers. This layered approached in combination with the process areas result in a business security architecture offering complete traceability in two ways:

1. From the Business Requirements to Security Controls (*Completeness: Did we identify everything we need*) and
2. From Component Architecture (Security Controls) to Business Requirements (*Business Justification: is every component traceably associated with a business requirement?*) (Figure 1.4).

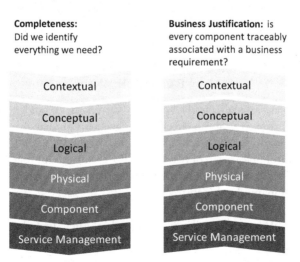

Figure 1.4 Traceability of controls.

ISO 2700x Family

The ISO/IEC 27000 family includes nearly 30 references in the field of IS. They are jointly published by the ISO and the International Electrotechnical Commission (CEI). Some of the main standards useful for IS governance are listed here:

ISO 2700x series (excerpt):
- ISO 27001 Information security management systems — Requirements
- ISO 27002 Code of practice for information security controls
- ISO 27004 Monitoring, measurement, analysis and evaluation
- ISO 27005 Information security risk management
- ISO 27014 Governance of information security

Other ISO standards dealing with information security (excerpt):
- ISO 15408 Evaluation criteria for IT security (Common Criteria)
- ISO 18045 Methodology for IT security evaluation
- ISO 15504 2013 Process assessment

The standard ISO 27001 can be used for the certification of an ISMS. However, compliance with the standards does not in itself guarantee adequate security. In addition to the recognition of security processes, certification could be credited with obliging a company to ask fundamental questions about its program, which would be beneficial if done with care and the desire to build a security program adapted to the context and needs of the company. By establishing fundamental IS processes based on a standard, the security officer can manage complexity better, improve communication, and reassure stakeholders.

To illustrate the use of the standards, let us take the example of recommendations in ISO 27001 applied in two different ways by two companies with different contexts. Both companies will reach the same level of maturity for the given process using completely different IS measures.

EXAMPLE

Two companies, a small family business (Company A) and a large bank (Company B), aim to establish effective management of their assets according to Recommendation A.8, "Asset Management," of the ISO 27001 standard.

In its control objective 8 of Annex A, ISO 27001 groups together recommendations for the establishment of an asset management system. It basically says that a company should (abstract):

1. Inventory all the assets and assign ownership. These include information (data), applications, servers, or data repositories.

2. Classify assets (in terms of value, legal requirements, sensitivity, and criticality) and take this into account while assigning access rights.
3. Define, document, and implement rules for the appropriate use of assets.

The two companies differ primarily in size and industry sector. Even without prior analysis, we can easily guess that only a few files or directories in Company A contain truly confidential data such as customer records or production secrets. There is no complex data processing involving confidential data. On the other hand, the production assets (machines or numerical control software) are critical for the survival of the company.

Company B has complex data processing involving both confidential and critical data. It must provide access to this data to different user profiles from inside and outside, as well as from many client applications. Different business operations also use the same data.

Company A made a relatively simple inventory of the few files or databases hosting confidential and critical data and assigned them a relatively high-level owner (chief operating officer [COO] or operational manager). The information was classified into two categories: (1) confidential and (2) nonconfidential. Access rights were given to a restricted group of people for Category 1 and to all staff for Category 2. The availability of data is ensured by a backup system and its confidentiality by an encryption system. Access to the applications processing this data was given to a restricted group of people.

For Company B, the inventory of assets was much more complete: it contains all the applications, servers, and main confidential data flows. The attributes of the items in the inventory are: owner and privacy class. The classification of data is more elaborate: (1) confidential, (2) limited (accessible by a certain group), and (3) public. Traditional banking applications will probably only rarely be associated with a single class of data, because they use both confidential and public data. The responsibility or ownership of the data is spread among several people, probably one person per business unit or geographical location. The access rights management system involves complex workflows to enable validation by multiple data owners. There is also a system for tracing the activity of those with access rights to a large amount of confidential data. Regulations probably prevent concurrent access to multiple applications or confidential data sources (segregation of duties). Security controls or measures also include data encryption systems not only at rest (databases) but also in transit.

This is just one example of different ways to meet the requirements of standards and regulations according to the specificities and real needs of each company. The complexity of an ISMS depends on many factors, including the industry sector, company size and complexity, and its risk appetite.

Is there any specific standard for information security governance?

ISO 27014 Governance of Information Security

(©ISO Adapted from ISO/IEC 27014:2013 with permission of the American National Standard Institute (ANSI) on behalf of the International Organization for Standardization. All rights reserved.) The ISO 27014 standard released in 2013 is dedicated entirely to the governance of IS. In its summary, it recalls the importance of good governance not only to ensure compliance with legal and regulatory frameworks but also to preserve an organization's assets and reputation. It refers to the governing body that is responsible for overseeing IS and ensuring that set objectives have been achieved. It also stresses the importance of links between the governing body, management, and those responsible for the implementation of operations: "Furthermore, an effective governance of information security ensures that the governing body receives relevant reporting—framed in a business context—about information security-related activities. This enables pertinent and timely decisions about information security issues in support of the strategic objectives of the organization."

According to this standard, the governing body is ultimately responsible for the decisions and performance of the organization. Its main objective must be to ensure that the security program is effective, is aligned with business objectives and strategy, and meets the needs of the stakeholders.

The standard first proposes some concepts, in which we find the abovementioned characteristics of good IS governance: strategic alignment, value creation, accountability, security adequacy, investment decision process, and compliance with standards. It then lists six principles that should guide organizations in establishing governance processes. These principles are the following:

■ *Principle 1*: Establish organization-wide information security.
■ *Principle 2*: Adopt a risk-based approach.
■ *Principle 3*: Set the direction of investment decisions.
■ *Principle 4*: Ensure conformance with internal and external requirements.
■ *Principle 5*: Foster a security-positive environment.
■ *Principle 6*: Review performance in relation to business outcomes.

These principles are finally translated into five governance processes with the participation of the governing body, executive management, and stakeholders. The flows and interdependence of these processes are presented in Figure 1.5.

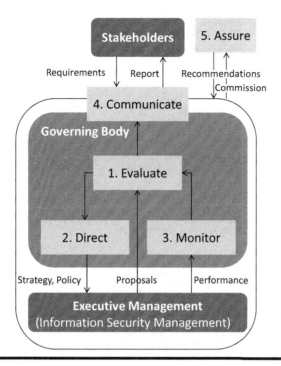

Figure 1.5   ISO 27014 processes.

The objectives of each of these processes can be summarized as follows:

1. *Evaluate*: Compare the current state of achievements in the security program with the objectives set. This allows the identification and communication of points of improvement and provides an orientation for the "Direct" process.
2. *Direct*: Issue guidelines with regard to strategy and security objectives. These guidelines may relate to resources, prioritizing activities, policies, and risk appetites.
3. *Monitor*: Enable the governing body to assess the degree of achievement of the strategic objectives.
4. *Communicate*: Based on the elements of the Evaluate process, this process allows information to be exchanged between the governing body and stakeholders.
5. *Assure*: Identify areas for improvement in governance and operations. The governing body may order independent audits or reviews.

The standard also mentions some essential elements for process entry to facilitate decision-making. Responsibility lies within the governing body and the IS management (Figure 1.6). Thus, for Process 1 (Evaluate), the governing

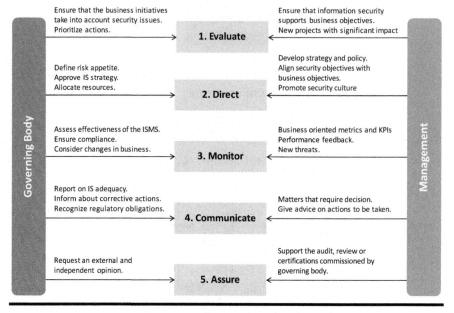

Figure 1.6 ISO 27014 processes with inputs from Governing Body and IS Management.

body must ensure that business initiatives take into account security imperatives (strategy, policies and guidelines), and IS management must ensure that ISMS supports business objectives and presents projects to improve the IS position.

The standard describes governance processes without going into too much detail, letting companies adopt them in their own way. It can therefore be used as a reference to identify potential gaps in company governance processes.

The chapter dedicated to metrics will show how a program or a governance system can be evaluated. Let us just mention that this is something critically desired by every business leader. The question should not be simply "Is our security adequate?" but also "How appropriate is our governance system?" Thus, there is no single or unanimously accepted model or methodology for IS governance, management, and program development. Such an objective requires thorough analysis of a company's specific features, its business model, and its context. The standards are very useful and can help define the scope of action, but it is ultimately up to the boards of directors, the management, and the CISO to find the best way to guide and supervise the IS program so that it is tailored to the specific needs of each organization.

1.5 Conclusion

Information security is an important part of business in today's environment. Despite this, we still see today that in some organizations the governance of the IS has not received the attention it deserves from the leaders and the board of directors. The responsibility is certainly shared between the different actors.

In this chapter, we have presented the essential elements of IS governance, its main issues and characteristics. Understanding the difference between governance and management helps to identify potential adjustments of responsibilities within the company.

The standards and benchmarks of good practices have not been presented in detail because many works already treat them in a very complete way. However, some of them deserve greater attention in governance and we have briefly presented them in this chapter. They will be used in the examples throughout especially in relation to the framework that will be presented in the next chapter.

Many books deal with the issue of governance of IS from different angles and it is certainly appropriate to consult them especially for the readers who are in charge of developing or reviewing processes in this field.

Chapter 2

Security Governance Control Framework

To establish effective governance and management processes, managerial controls should be modeled or grouped into easily recognizable blocks. Governance-specific activities are often presented alongside operational practices in the standards, which makes them difficult for senior executives to read. This is why it would be very useful to have a simple model presenting the main areas of management involvement when setting up an information security (IS) management system (ISMS). Such a model could also be useful in facilitating business leaders' involvement in the change management process, which impacts IS. Having such a model would make it easier to guide discussions with management, review practices in a structured manner, discuss new opportunities, and above all involve everyone, as well as security specialists, who has a role to play in setting up adequate security in an organization.

This chapter provides answers to the following questions:

- What do we mean by the term security "control"?
- How can managerial controls be presented and highlighted?
- How can controls be grouped by hierarchical responsibility?
- What are the characteristics of each level of a three-level control framework (TLCF)?
- What is the purpose of each building block and what do they contain?
- What is the mapping between TLCF and security standards?

How can managerial controls be presented and highlighted? How can controls be grouped by hierarchy of responsibility?

2.1 Three-Level Control Framework

Different terms designate the means that are deployed to protect information confidentiality, availability and integrity: measure, control, protection, countermeasure, and so on. We will use the term *control*, which, a priori, can be taken as a synonym for all the other terms commonly used.

Controls can be classified into different categories; for example:

- *By nature*: regulatory, physical, technical, human
- *By security domain*: information, physical (safety), human
- *By protected target*: information systems, physical premises, human integrity
- *By characteristics*: preventive, corrective, detective
- And so on.

When we look at security standards' recommendations, the immediate question that arises is: how can the various controls be broken down by level of responsibility? Board members cannot be expected to read the standards to identify the controls under their responsibility. So, we need a model that groups controls under different levels of responsibility, enabling the rapid identification of who is responsible for what in the governance process.

EXAMPLE

In ISO 27001, A.9 Access Control, the following control objectives can be considered from different levels regarding accountability:

- A.9.1.1 Access control policy (should be under the responsibility of the board of directors).
- A.9.2.5 Review of user access rights (should be under the responsibility of business units).
- A.9.2.2 User access provisioning (should be under the responsibility of IT operations).

Since security responsibility today is essentially shared by several actors in an organization, what we need is a model that allows us to quickly identify the following three classes of vertical controls: governance (orientations, assurance), management (steering, oversight), and operations (technical controls or processes). This makes it easier to identify the responsible authorities and any gaps in the governance and management process. It is still not uncommon today to see operational or technical controls put in place in response to incidents or to overcome a visible threat without worrying about the managerial- or governance-level impact. This usually leads to a waste of resources, misunderstanding among the different stakeholders, and poor alignment with business needs. The Sherwood Applied Business Security Architecture

(SABSA) framework mentioned in Chapter 1 can help set up security architecture that facilitates the implementation of operational controls in line with business needs. However, this approach also requires a high level of governance maturity.

EXAMPLE

Take the example of setting up a new system of identity and access management (IAM) based on business roles (role/rule-based access control [RBAC]). Setting up such a system means taking different levels of control into account, not just technical ones. It is not enough to simply install a software solution that automates the provisioning of user privileges from the human resources (HR) database on target platforms. The expected organization of responsibilities in role management must also be taken into account, along with elaborating specific policies in this field, defining the accountability of oversight or incident management. There is certainly a hierarchy of controls and a vertical distribution system that must be respected. This hierarchy of controls could be presented as follows (not exhaustive):

Level	Control (excerpt)	Responsibility
Governance	Policy, organizations	Governing body
Management	Risk management, program management	Chief information security officer (CISO) or IAM officer
Operations	Role and privilege management, periodic certifications of access	Business
Technical	Incident management, monitoring	IT operations

This vertical distribution of the control groups is of paramount importance in setting up IS governance and management. It emphasizes the need to share responsibility at different levels, which is a prerequisite for establishing adequate security. Every level of responsibility must be concerned by IS. In this context, any significant adaptation of the system, such as the one just observed, can have repercussions on governance, managerial, operational, or technical controls. Some changes in technical controls, however, such as replacing one intrusion detection system with another, will most likely have little or no impact on guidelines or risk management. Nevertheless, the scope of any change to IS governance and management should always be reviewed.

Why not use the standards?

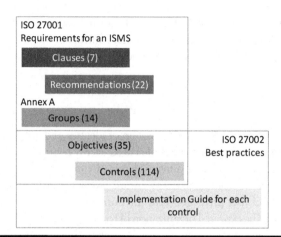

Figure 2.1   Structure of ISO 27001/2 standards.

Each of the standards has adopted a system of grouping and distributing controls in sets of its own. The NIST 800-53 standard presents a catalog of controls and classifies them into 18 families and three classes: managerial, operational, and technical. ISO 27001 groups the requirements that an ISMS must meet into seven clauses containing 22 recommendations. In its appendix it presents 14 Groups containing 25 Control Objectives with 114 controls. The ISO 27002 standard (Code of practice for information security controls) reiterates the Objectives and Controls and adds, for each control, a guide to good practices (Figure 2.1).

The following observations can be made:

- The grouping and naming of groups, control objectives, and the controls themselves evolve from one version to another.
- Groups and objectives in ISO do not refer to the same level of responsibility. For example, A.5 "Information security policy"/A.5.1 "Management direction for information security" is not at the same level of responsibility as A.13 "Communication security"/A.13.1 "Network security management."
- Some groups refer to generic controls or processes (e.g., A.6 "Organization of information security"), while others mention controls linked to the means of protection (e.g., A.10 "Cryptography").

This is quite understandable. In fact, to avoid unnecessary complications, the standards seek to present the completeness of the controls in the smallest possible format, perhaps to the detriment of a certain vertical (hierarchy) and horizontal (domains) distribution of the control objectives. The formalism of presentation is not oriented toward governance but toward the completeness of the processes. Changes or adaptations to the content from one version to another are mainly due to evolution in the threats or protection techniques.

Therein lies the importance of proposing additional methods of grouping controls other than the standards. We need a simpler model allowing the consolidation of governance, management, and operational controls into building blocks for an entire ISMS or for a particular security domain (mobility, IAM, continuity) or technology (encryption, cloud). This will allow decision-makers to focus immediately on the sets of controls that affect them. Indeed, as we have just presented in the example of IAM, some control objectives have to be taken into account regardless of the scope of the system under observation. These control objectives are: strategy, policy and guidelines, security organization, risk management, security program management, reporting and oversight, asset management, compliance, and metrics.

What is the main purpose of such a framework?

Such a framework should allow management and security practitioners to ask pertinent questions about governance for IS as a whole, a specific security domain, or during major IS changes. These questions are the following:

1. Do we have a strategy?
2. Have we established our policies?
3. Is our security organization adequate?
4. What are the risks and how are they managed?
5. How is our IS program managed?
6. Is the reporting and oversight system adequate?
7. Which assets (data, applications, etc.) are impacted, and who is responsible for them?
8. Are we in compliance with the legal and regulatory framework?
9. Do we have metrics or key performance indicators (KPIs) to track the adequacy of our protection system?

EXAMPLE

Suppose a company wants to outsource some of the operations of a business line onto the cloud of an external provider. This initiative or project is obviously not only a technical matter and requires management approval. The security risks faced by the company must also be considered. The questions that management should ask are the following:

1. Do we have a strategy in the domain of cloud computing?
2. How should our security policy evolve following this change?
3. Is our security organization suitable? Who is responsible for it: IT or the business line?
4. What are the security risks that ensue?
5. What specific controls should be put in place or adapted?

6. Is there a need to review our system of monitoring the effectiveness of controls following this change?
7. What data or applications are involved?
8. What is the impact on our compliance with the legal and regulatory framework?
9. What indicators do we need to monitor the adequacy of the solution?

Other examples can easily be found of changes that raise the same questions, highlighting the key concerns of any responsible actor in the IS governance process.

What are the building blocks of the model?

Continuing our line of reasoning on the essential controls that governing bodies and security management must ensure, we can classify these controls into nine building blocks as follows (Figure 2.2):

1. Strategy
2. Policies
3. Organization
4. Risk management
5. IS program management
6. Reporting and oversight
7. Asset management
8. Compliance
9. Metrics

Figure 2.2 Building blocks of the information security governance framework.

A tenth block, Operations, could be added, despite the fact that they do not directly comprise the main activities of governance and management. The controls contained in this block provide essential elements for good governance, such as monitoring operations, metrics, the nature of the data processed, and so on. The operational level can be considered a functional instance of the security program.

Is there a hierarchy or functional dependency between these blocks?

Finally, is there a hierarchy between these blocks, and can we establish a functional interdependence? The answer is "yes." A security program cannot be managed without knowledge of the legal or regulatory framework, nor can a reporting system be developed without previously establishing a security metrics.

The primary interdependence between the model blocks is as follows:

1. Strategy is the prerequisite for a security program.
2. Policies and guidelines depend on strategic directions.
3. Organization (roles and responsibilities) is established to reflect the strategy and policies.
4. Managing risks requires knowing risk appetite as well as policies, strategic choices, and the assets to protect.
5. Reporting and oversight should be based on organization (or target audience). They use metrics and KPIs.
6. Operational processes provide essential knowledge needed to identify the assets to protect.
7. Compliance with the legal and regulatory framework depends on operational processes, the company context, data to be protected, and metrics.

Figure 2.3   Interdependence between building blocks.

8. Metrics and KPIs are identified by observing operations.
9. Finally, the security program is managed based on the strategy, risks, and report results and must be in compliance with the legal and regulatory framework.

This interdependence is schematized in Figure 2.3.

EXAMPLE

In the area of IAM, the *Strategy* sets out the objectives of the system that we want to build: for example, delegating the assignment of user access rights to business units provided that privileges are established based on business roles. This strategy will be used to develop *Policies* and access rights guidelines, including the role-based approach and the involvement of business units. The *Organization* describes the roles and responsibilities in the processes. *Operations* involves the effective implementation of the processes and mechanisms for granting access rights. These processes will enable us to identify the data to be protected (assets), exposure to the legal and regulatory framework (e.g., protection of personal data) (*Compliance*), as well as the *Metrics* that we will need. A *Reporting and Oversight* system will be set up for program management needs and will use the previously defined metrics. Finally, the *IS Program* will be managed by implementing and improving all the controls that are part of the system.

How can controls be classified according to hierarchical responsibility in a company?

There is also a hierarchical relationship between the building blocks in this model. A security strategy aligned with business is obviously the responsibility of senior management and the board. Risk management or the establishment of metrics will most likely be the responsibility of the security officer. Security operations or technical controls will be under the responsibility of the security or IT operations.

Controls at all levels help protect assets. These levels can thus be presented as follows (Figure 2.4):

Strategic: This level includes all governance controls intended to provide overall direction for the security program: Strategy, Policies, and Organization.

Tactical: This level includes all managerial controls aimed at setting up and managing a security program: Risk management, Program management, Reporting and oversight, Asset management, Compliance, and Metrics.

Operational: This level encompasses all the operational and technical controls within the security program.

Figure 2.4   Levels of control.

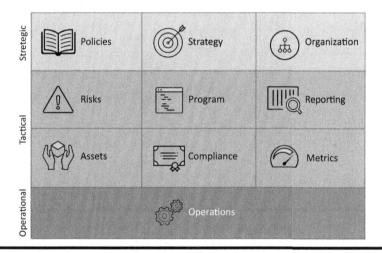

Figure 2.5   Breakdown of blocks into levels of control.

The model building blocks can thus be placed in the different levels as shown in Figure 2.5.

This three-level representation allows us to separate the families of controls by their nature and main level of responsibility: Governance, Management, and Operations. All the actors involved in setting up and running a security program can easily identify themselves in one of these three levels. The board of directors and business unit heads will be primarily involved at the strategic level, the CISO and the functional managers at the tactical level, and the security specialists at the operational level.

Observing the requirements of the standards and benchmarks of good practices, all the recommendations or controls could be placed in one of these levels (the controls recommended by ISO 27001 will be mapped with the blocks of the

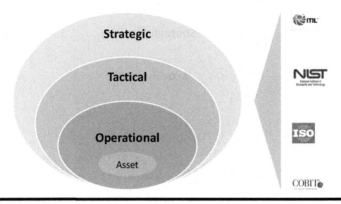

Figure 2.6   The recommendations of the standards fit into the levels of the model.

Figure 2.7   Specific controls for major security domains can also be distributed in three levels.

model at the end of this chapter) (Figure 2.6). This breakdown lets us propose a framework focusing on the main activities of each level, along with tools to analyze the adequacy of our practices in each block of the model.

Security controls in major areas such as human security, IAM, cybersecurity, mobility, data privacy, and so on can also be distributed in these three levels (Figure 2.7). Therefore, the model can be applied to the ISMS as a whole or to a specific security domain.

2.2 Strategic Level

The strategic level encompasses the three main building blocks of the model: Strategy, Policies, and Organization (Figure 2.8). These are the three areas where senior executives have the greatest responsibility.

Figure 2.8 Strategic level.

Changes at the strategic level directly affect processes and controls at tactical and operational level. The opposite is also true. Significant operational changes cannot be made without referring to the strategic level.

A new business strategy or changes in the business model (strategic level) require an adjustment of controls at the operational level. Technological evolution (e.g., in the context of process digitalization) or new security threats also require adaptations in operational controls, which in turn may require repositioning at the strategic level. Annual surveys of the large consulting firms indicate an almost systematic delay in the adjustment of controls at the strategic level, primarily due to inertia or the natural propensity of senior management to consider IS a purely technical discipline.

2.3 Tactical Level

The tactical level encompasses all the main activities and responsibilities that can be attributed to IS management. Since the implementation of a strategy and policies requires the deployment of various controls within an ISMS, the term *tactical* seems more appropriate than *managerial*. The grouping of activities into building blocks at this level makes it possible to highlight the main axes of security executive officers' activity either for the entire IS or for a specific domain (Figure 2.9).

All activities or controls at this level depend on the orientations given at the previous level. Once the strategic orientations have been taken, the security program will be reviewed or adapted according to a systematic approach. We should therefore talk about the repeated or renewable process of establishing and managing a security program. The opposite is also true. If management or the board do not have insight into tactical-level activities (such as risk management, the effectiveness of measures,

Figure 2.9 Tactical level.

asset management, compliance, or metrics), they will not be able to make educated decisions about investments, new projects, or the adjustment of controls. Good governance therefore needs a high-performing and transparent tactical level.

2.4 Operational Level

The operational level includes all operational security measures, processes, or controls. We often talk about the instantiation or functional realization of a security system. Standards, such as the National Institute of Standards and Technology (NIST), present a comprehensive catalog of all controls to be part of an operational system (Figure 2.10).

Controls at this level have been put in place to protect the company's assets in accordance with the strategy and internal regulatory framework and within a specific security organization (strategic level). Their main objective is to mitigate risks within the framework of an IS program; their effectiveness is measured; they are the subject of reporting and oversight; and they protect the assets in accordance with the legal and regulatory framework (tactical level). Operational controls should not be deployed in a disorganized manner by adding successive layers of highly innovative technical solutions. Company needs must be met at the best cost/performance ratio within the framework of an IS program and established plans.

Any operational measure or control must meet the following requirements:

- It is justified by the presence of a risk to which it responds.
- It is the responsibility of a specific person or entity.
- It responds to business strategy or need expressed by the business.
- It has been tested.
- Its effectiveness is measurable.

What is the purpose of the model blocks, and what do they contain?

2.5 Main Functions of the Model Building Blocks

Finally, what is the function of each building block, and how do they contribute to better IS governance? What do they contain? They will be analyzed in detail in the following chapters, and tools and methodical approaches will be presented to establish the controls that compose them. First of all, let us recall the role of each one in the IS governance system.

Figure 2.10 Operational level.

2.5.1 Strategy

The first block involves setting up a strategy for the entire security system. A specific security domain can also benefit from its own strategy aligned with the overall security strategy.

	◎ Strategy	

Having a vision for IS makes it easier for a company to choose among the different options available for the IS program and specific operational controls. All the actors should be familiar with the vision and align their efforts with objectives acknowledged as important for the organization. There are no alternatives to this approach. In fact, a security system without a strategy will be built by piling up protective techniques against new threats or ad hoc processes to comply with audit recommendations. This will ultimately have a negative impact on costs, will not be understood by management, and will not be efficient.

The security strategy includes the direction the company wants its IS program to take in the near future. It can also be established by major security domains (e.g., cybersecurity strategy, continuity, human resources, etc.). The strategies are entirely the responsibility of the company's management or its board, but proposals might be given by the security manager or a committee authorized for this purpose.

As with any strategy, a security strategy takes the form of a relatively short document that presents two essential elements: the vision or goal to be achieved in a period of a couple of years and initiatives that must be undertaken to achieve it.

EXAMPLE (SIMPLIFIED) OF A STRATEGY

International School of Management

IS must ensure the protection of our data and operations in the context of business development: offering courses of study adapted to new technologies in an international context, collaborating with experts and international institutions, outsourcing our IT operations (cloud), and opening new subsidiaries in European Union countries. To achieve this goal within 3 years, IS will be organized as an entity independent of IT with a CISO under the responsibility of the rector and board of directors. The following actions should be undertaken:

1. Development of a new charter, security policy, and organization
2. Revision of security guidelines and development of a new documentary framework
3. Implementation of security organization based on information ownership and risks associated with different units, including compliance and confidentiality requirements
4. Establishment of a central unit to monitor threats and manage incidents (Security Operations Center)

A business plan or project portfolio is often confused with a strategy. Just because a company has compiled a list of security projects for the coming period, often motivated by audit findings or foreseeable threats, it cannot boast of having a strategy. The strategy must be at the origin of the projects and not the other way around.

Strategic initiatives therefore remain objectives to be achieved over the more or less long term. It is obvious that resources will be primarily devoted to resolving incidents and restoring production. However, the realization of a strategy will lead to the progressive reduction of incidents and cost optimization.

Strategic initiatives serve as drivers for the establishment of roadmaps or more specific projects in annual plans (see more in Chapter 8, Program Management). These high-level initiatives or objectives have deadlines and need to be reviewed periodically. They mainly serve as support for the development of more specific programs or projects.

EXAMPLE

The objective "Inventory sensitive data and describe the missions of the data owners" could lead to several projects:

■ Development of a policy or guideline on the protection of sensitive data
■ Categorization and classification of corporate data
■ Transfer of data responsibility in business units
■ Development of a data inventory

The security strategy should explicitly include foreseeable changes in the conduct of business and new technologies, with defined roadmaps if possible.

The following elements should be part of the security strategy:

1. The external environment and business context.
   Recall the context and explain why the security strategy and positioning should be adjusted.
2. Legal and regulatory framework and its impact.
   Recall the main areas of compliance required and mention adjustment required to new regulations.
3. Changes in threats, vulnerabilities, technologies, and risk appetite.
   It is important to adopt a posture concerning threats, especially due to the evolution of technologies, business models, and risk appetite. The company can take a position in its strategy in the form of choices such as "no outsourcing of confidential data" or "waiting for the technology to mature," and so on.
4. Corporate culture.
   Recall the essential criteria that must drive IS decisions according to the company's culture and its position vis-à-vis competitors.

5. Requirements for explicit alignment with certain business initiatives or strategies.

When a company has to adapt quickly because of new directions in business strategies (such as new services, a new market, mergers or acquisitions, and so on), security must follow and adapt.

The IS strategy, promoted by the CISO, should enable governing bodies to obtain answers to these key questions:

■ Does IS strategy cover all the priorities of the business?
■ Is the security strategy well understood by business unit managers?

HOW IS STRATEGY REFERENCED IN THE STANDARDS

The term *strategy* is not used as such in the International Organization for Standardization (ISO) or NIST standards. The ISO speaks primarily about the "context of the organization," and in NIST it is "planning" (see the mapping of the model and the standards at the end of this chapter).

The strategy establishment will be discussed in Chapter 4 (Strategy).

2.5.2 Policies

The block called *Policies* is primarily about the internal regulatory framework. Policies are high-level internal regulatory documents. They translate the strategy into more restrictive terms. This block also deals with documents of the lowest level of the internal regulatory framework, such as guidelines, standards, or procedures.

The reasons why an internal regulatory framework is important are obvious. Let us recall some other arguments in favor of IS policies in the current context.

Support for the Extended Enterprise

An extended enterprise is understood to be an organization that is active in globalized markets and uses process digitization technologies. These processes are distributed among several actors in the value chain. Changes in business models, business diversity, geographical distribution, advanced outsourcing or delegation of activities, strong interaction, and sharing data with suppliers are just a few examples that characterize an extended enterprise. IS poses major challenges in this context and must be supported by a defined internal regulatory framework.

Governance and Management Component

The development of IS policy is a very effective way to put security on the agenda of decision-makers and other stakeholders in the organization. A policy that has been discussed, validated by line managers, and signed by the board of directors proves to be a very useful instrument for governance. All stakeholders are strongly interested in this, because it helps to anchor the IS program closer to their needs:

- The board may require periodic reports allowing it to make decisions regarding the evolution of the IS program and investments.
- Business unit managers can rely on the policies and guidelines to ensure that security meets their needs.
- Security officers will use the policies to strengthen controls and justify investments.
- Auditors will be able to rely on the policies to assess the compliance of operations.
- Teams responsible for implementing security controls need internal regulatory framework to guide their activities.
- Finally, the policies and guidelines can be used to raise awareness and as a code of conduct for all the employees.

Reflects the Needs of the Business

The policy is established with the business and for the business and its needs. It is validated, understood, and supported by management. Nevertheless, different business units with different business models might have different risk appetites and therefore need different security policies.

Imposes the Establishment of a Documentary Framework

Policies and the underlying documents that are guidelines and procedures must be part of a enterprise-wide documentary framework. This facilitates accessibility and an understanding of the internal regulations. Policies and internal regulatory documents will be available on the intranet pursuant to the graphic charter, comprehensible, and easily accessible and searchable.

Internal regulations, validated by all the stakeholders, should enable governing bodies to obtain answers to these key questions:

- Do we have security regulations in place that apply to all our activities?
- Are our internal regulations reviewed, and by whom, to ensure they are complete and accurate?
- Are our regulations adapted to the needs of the business units?
- Are policies and guidelines well understood by all the employees?
- Who is responsible for the evolution of our internal regulatory framework?

The following ISO 27001 recommendations are directly related to policies and the internal regulatory framework.

Requirements
5.2   Policy

Reference control objectives and controls (Annex A):
A.5   Information security policies
A.6.2.1   Mobile device policy
A.6.2.2   Teleworking
A.9.1.1   Access control policy
A.10.1.1   Policies on the use of cryptographic controls
A.13.2.1   Information transfer policies and procedures
A.14.2.1   Secure development policy
A.14.2.5   Secure system engineering principles
A.15.1.1   Information security policy for supplier relationships
A.17.2.1   Planning information security continuity

A method to develop policies and documents for the internal regulatory framework will be presented in Chapter 5 (Policies).

2.5.3 *Organization*

The term *organization* will be used to describe all the requirements related to responsibilities and functions in the context of an ISMS. This is not just about the governing body or executive management as specified in ISO 27014, but includes all the security functions, roles, and
responsibilities aimed at ensuring the operations of an IS program. Organization requirements must be formulated in the security policy.

EXAMPLE

A formalized incident management process is recommended by all the standards and also by numerous sectoral regulations, in particular in banking, through financial sector control and regulatory bodies in many countries. Almost all these regulations require the board and senior management to ensure that there is incident management process, that they are informed, and that they inform the regulators in the case of particularly important incidents.

Specific security organization should therefore be put in place to manage incidents with the following functions:

■ Central registration and incident dispatching service
■ Incident owner or responsible for the resolution and follow-up of corrective measures
■ Committee (if needed) to decide on the severity and follow-up of an incident (communication, crisis management)

Establishing security organization today is no longer limited to appointing a CISO. The responsibilities of different areas of security are scattered throughout the company. The role of a CISO has changed significantly in recent years. In the 1990s, they were the head of the user access rights team within IT departments with a technician's profile. Today, they lead multidisciplinary teams in charge of securing business processes and bringing added value. Their spectrum of activity is very broad, ranging from securing operations to communication, ensuring awareness, management of security risks, management of the overall program, and reporting to the board.

Modern security management means above all coordinating everyone's efforts. HR will most likely be responsible for monitoring and mitigating security risks related to human risks. Business units will be required to itemize the security risks specific to their operations. IT system engineers will be responsible for the basic configuration of equipment and the infrastructure. New security organization should take into account not only new needs, such as the integration of disaster recovery planning (DRP) in business continuity or the evolution of human and cyber threats, but also the overall problem of steering the IS program throughout the company.

Security organization can take different forms. There is no ideal model that fits every business. Nevertheless, it is important to recognize several functions that are needed to ensure good governance. The assignment of functions to individuals heavily depends on the size of the organization, its specificities, and the risks involved. The security executive officer or the CISO can be located inside or outside the IT department and may or may not direct a team of security specialists with some or all of the security functions under their responsibility.

Leaders will ensure that there is no conflict of interest and that decisions can be implemented with sufficient resources. One of the main mistakes is to mandate a CISO who does not have sufficient authority to make decisions without systematically consulting the board or management. Organizational changes have the same priority as projects. An effective security organization will contribute to the achievement of strategic objectives.

Although IS organizations can vary greatly from one company to another, a shift is being seen from operations toward governance, risk, and compliance (GRC). The positioning of the security team and the CISO has an important role in this evolution. IS organizations traditionally oriented toward operations, even with technology's extremely important role, are unable to effectively combat all the threats over the long run. On the other hand, an organization focusing on proactive risk management and business needs is more likely to bring perceived value and use available resources more effectively.

The establishment of adequate security organization will allow the governance bodies to obtain answers to these key questions:

- Do we have IS organization that covers all the necessary functions?
- Is the organization reviewed, and by whom, to ensure that there are no gaps?
- How does our organization compare with our competitors or similar companies?
- Is security organization well understood by business unit managers? Do they participate or are they represented in the different decision-making bodies?
- What are the main drawbacks in our organization, and how can they be fixed?

The ISO 27001 recommendations directly related to security organization are the following.

Requirements:
5.3   Organizational roles, responsibilities and authorities
7.2   Competence

Reference control objectives and controls (Annex A):
A.6. Organization of information security

The characteristics of different IS organizations, a method and tools to set up security organization, the best practices, and a pragmatic implementation approach will be developed in more detail in Chapter 6 (Organization).

2.5.4 Risk Management

Risk mitigation is the raison d'être of any security program. The activities grouped under this block will all be dedicated to the risk management process, including identification, analysis, treatment, and reporting as essential IS governance support.

Risk analysis allows security organization to fix priorities based on risk appetite, strategy, and policies. One of the main concerns of security governance must be to ensure the effective management of security risks, in particular their identification, analysis, and treatment. Ignoring risk or its implicit acceptance is one of the main dangers of any IS program.

The ultimate responsibility for security risks lies with the board of directors. Operational managers from different business units own the security risks in their operations. As the security operations manager, the CISO is also responsible for risks in their own department (e.g., the effectiveness of controls or failure of security operations). Their role is also to provide support for the identification and management of security risks in the business units.

Security risks are part of a company's operational risks, although they have some characteristics that must be taken into account. For example, quantitative evaluation methods are very often impossible to apply because of the difficulty of observing events within the organization. On the other hand, it is relatively easy for someone accustomed to observing security threat trends to qualify a risk on a simple scale such as small, medium, large. The chapter dedicated to IS risks will show a pragmatic way to analyze them.

Security risk assessment and emerging trends are key indicators for steering the IS program. An increasing risk for which mitigation measures are no longer sufficient or are poorly adapted must clearly be addressed as a priority.

EXAMPLE

If we discover that cybersecurity risk has been increasing over a period of time simultaneously with a decrease in the level of the effectiveness or maturity of security controls, such as "Intrusion Detection Systems" or "User Awareness," then these two indicators may be sufficient to make the decision to invest more in improving the intrusion detection systems to ensure a level of risk consistent with enterprises appetite. The IS program should then include an initiative to improve the efficiency or maturity of the associated controls to reduce risk.

Chapter 7: Risk Management will show in detail how to obtain these indicators.

The evolution of legal and regulatory requirements, as well as new threats, has made boards of directors aware of the need for good security risk management with their complete involvement as being ultimately accountable for the approval of reports and setting up mitigation measures. Therefore, they need to take an active stance in the risk management process to get answers to these key questions:

- Do we know what security risks can impact the business, how they are evaluated, and what are the priorities in their mitigation?
- How is IS risk management organized?
- How have risks evolved compared with the previous period and why? How have the associated controls evolved during the same period?

- Are security risks, the measures used for their mitigation, and periodic reports validated by the heads of business units or their risk managers?
- What constitutes high risk, and do we have a plan for its short-term mitigation?
- Are we doing everything necessary to facilitate mitigation of the most important risks?

The recommendations of ISO 27001 directly related to risk management are as follows:

Requirements:
6.1   Actions to address risks and opportunities
8.2   Information security risk assessment
8.3   Information security risk treatment

Chapter 7 (Risk Management) will focus on a method and tools to manage risk for IS governance purposes.

2.5.5 *Program Management*

Program management encompasses all the activities that ensure the effective deployment of security controls as part of an ISMS. Standards such as ISO 27001/2 or NIST (800-53) give a good summary of these controls.

According to Control Objectives for Information and Related Technology (CobIT) 5, management activities also applicable to security are defined as "*plans, builds, runs and monitors activities in alignment with the direction set by the governance body to achieve the enterprise objectives.*"

The main activities of the CISO and their teams consist of implementing and managing security controls. In addition to operational controls ("run" mode), a security program includes initiatives and projects that aim to improve the effectiveness of the controls in place or put in place new ones ("change" mode).

To be able to govern well, it is essential to know the controls in place and their usefulness (protection objective) as well as their effectiveness. Management and the governing body must be able to visualize all the controls in the form of a catalog or inventory containing the notions of responsibility and the level of maturity. This catalog is used as one of the main tools in the security program and risk management process and as support for internal and external auditors.

Operational measures or controls cannot be deployed without support from security strategy, policies, organization, and risk management and without a security program plan. The companies most successful in optimizing their security resources are those that implement operational controls based on their strategy and risk appetite and follow the policies and guidelines by first protecting data identified as critical or confidential in accordance with the legal and regulatory framework.

For a security program to be effective, the activities of this block must be based on the deliverables of all other blocks in the model. The strategy provides guidance on overall IS goals, allowing the program to stay focused on essentials; risk management pinpoints the main threats to be countered; reporting and oversight provide information on discrepancies between the current and desired states, as well as progress toward the goals set; and compliance provides information on developments in the legal and regulatory framework that must be addressed by the security program.

A steering committee or governing body, in collaboration with the security executive officer, must review the objectives and adapt the program at defined frequencies. Management of the IS program, which is the responsibility of the CISO, should enable governing bodies and management to obtain answers to these key questions:

- What security controls do we have in place, how do they contribute to the mitigation of our risks, and who is responsible for them?
- Is there a control monitoring process, and how are the results presented to management?
- How does the maturity of the controls evolve, and is it in line with the requirements of the risk treatment decisions?
- What is the roadmap for control improvement projects?
- How have security program priorities been validated by representatives of the business units?
- What can still be done at the management level to facilitate the implementation and improvement of the IS program?

The recommendations of ISO 27001 directly related to management of the security program are as follows:

Requirements:
4.4   Information security management system
6.2   Information security objectives and planning to achieve them
7.1   Resources
7.4   Communication
8.1   Operational planning and control
10   Improvement

Reference control objectives and controls (Annex A):
A.12.1.3   Capacity management
A.18.2.2   Compliance with security policies and standards
A.18.2.3   Technical compliance review

Chapter 8 (Program Management) will be devoted entirely to essential methods and tools to manage the IS program.

2.5.6 Security Metrics

IS governance needs reliable indicators as decision support. Metrics are used in reports; they quantify risks, evaluate trends and control effectiveness, calculate return on investment, and so on. They also make it possible to set thresholds to warn about trends and thus prevent incidents.

Nevertheless, measuring security is not easy, due primarily to the absence of measurable events or incidents. We cannot, for example, know exactly how many attempts have been made to break into companies similar to ours, their type, and especially whether they were successful or not. It is also difficult to know whether an intrusion protection system has captured all the attempts or not. There are many other examples like these. On the other hand, purely technical and widely available metrics, such as the number of viruses or attacks prevented or the number of servers configured with the latest updates, do not provide governing bodies with relevant information about the overall performance of the protection system. Basic metrics must generally be compiled or aggregated to convey useful information for the management, such as evolution of the level of protection compared with the evolution of risks, real return on recent investments to implement security solutions, the level of improved resilience against cyberattacks, the effectiveness of the awareness program, or the completeness of measures taken to fill gaps after the last penetration tests.

Security is one of the few areas that do not have their own standards or measurement techniques, as opposed to other well-known indicators such as consumption (kW/h), efficiency (price/earning ratio), yield, and so on. Senior managers are used to financial indicators or measuring the evolution of business turnover. Therefore, management and CISOs together must find a way to measure security for governance purposes.

The methods and tools to measure security developed in Chapter 9 will allow governing bodies and management to get answers to these key questions:

- What indicators do we have that allow us to measure security from the governance perspective?
- Are our metrics well suited to reporting purposes, and have they been validated by the stakeholders?
- Do we have metrics required by the legal and regulatory framework?
- How do we improve metrics to meet governance and management needs?
- How can we evaluate our security posture, and how do we compare with our competitors?

The recommendations of ISO 27001 directly related to security metrics and KPIs are as follows.

Requirements:
9   Performance evaluation
9.1   Monitoring, measurement, analysis and evaluation
9.2   Internal audit

Reference control objectives and controls (Annex A):
A.12.7.1   Information systems audit controls

Chapter 9 (Security Metrics) will be devoted entirely to methods and tools to elaborate security metrics from the governance perspective.

2.5.7 *Reporting and Oversight*

A reporting, oversight, or monitoring system is essential for good governance. Above all, it allows the security executive officer to present the state of IS from a holistic point of view; to relate investments, controls, and risks; and to use key indicators to explain how 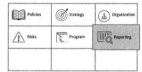 the security program contributes to business development and how resources are allocated.

This block groups methods and tools to develop IS reports for all the company stakeholders. Audit findings and recommendations, as well as specially commissioned reports, are also included.

The security reporting process is the responsibility of the CISO as instigated by the board of directors or governing body. It must provide decision support and allow the governing body to obtain answers to the following key questions:

■ How appropriate is our IS program?
■ How are risks evolving, and what are we doing to mitigate them?
■ How does the effectiveness of our controls evolve?
■ What are our key investments in IS?
■ What are the most important control change projects (new or improvements to existing controls), their objectives, and the roadmap of planned implementation?
■ How can management and the governing body help resolve IS problems (or pain-points)?
■ What are the costs related to security, and how do we control them?

As with all the rest, there is no single reporting template that can fit every business. The content and form will depend on the nature, size, and diversity of the business and the sector in which it operates. The regulatory framework requires security reporting to facilitate decision-making and enable the board to fulfill its responsibilities. Security reports and dashboards are not intended solely for the governing bodies. They also bring value to all stakeholders:

■ For the different business units, they must present the achievements of the various security projects aimed at contributing toward their objectives.
■ For customers and partners, they must convey information on the level of maturity of the controls.
■ For employees and security operations specialists, they must present a roadmap of strategic initiatives with priorities validated by the governing body.

The term *communication* is often used to emphasize the importance of disseminating information, raising awareness, or sharing information. Reporting, in our context, concerns and includes communication with the stakeholders to make security and its concomitant activities more visible. Communication in the sense of educating or raising awareness is part of security operations or operational controls.

The recommendations of the ISO 27001 standard directly related to the reporting process are as follows.

Requirements:
9.3   Management review

Reference control objectives and controls (Annex A):
AA.18.2   Information security reviews

Chapter 10 (Reporting and Oversights) will be devoted entirely to methods and tools to elaborate security reports.

2.5.8 Asset Management

Asset management within the wider security framework provides the basis for internal data protection policies and guidelines and for the assessment and treatment of associated risks. Risks involving data of different privacy classes will not have the same impact on the business.

Adequate security cannot be provided if protection priorities are not known. It is therefore important to classify assets, identify asset owners, establish protection rules for each class of assets, and establish an asset inventory.

Management knows the company's data but is perhaps not sufficiently aware of the risks related to how it is handled. IT asset management often involves inventorying hardware and software infrastructure components with specialized tools within a configuration management database (CMDB). Apart from the configuration tracking process, these inventories do not provide information on the nature, criticality, or confidentiality of the various components. The contents of databases or servers are often ignored by system administrators. These are mainly inventories of the technical layers of a system's architecture. The characteristics of the applications or functional levels, and especially the confidentiality of the data, are often not disclosed.

A company's asset management activities must provide decision support and enable governance bodies to obtain answers to these key questions:

- Do we know our assets?
- How are our assets classified?
- What are our policies and protection guidelines by class/asset/context?
- Who are our asset owners?
- How do various processes use confidential data, and what are the main flows of confidential data?

> The recommendations of ISO 27001 directly related to asset management are as follows:
>
> Reference control objectives and controls (Annex A):
> A.8 Asset management

Chapter 11 (Asset Management) will be entirely devoted to methods and tools required for asset management.

2.5.9 Compliance

Company activities are subject to global and sectoral laws and regulations. IS is particularly affected by this legal and regulatory framework, data protection above all. Therefore, one of the priorities of security governance is to understand this legal and regulatory framework and ensure the conformity of the security program. Collaboration with legal and compliance departments is particularly important in this area.

EXAMPLE

The European General Data Protection Regulation (GDPR) has requirements for all companies that process the personal data of European citizens. These requirements have a significant impact on IS programs.

Failure to comply with the legal and regulatory framework not only exposes a company to sanctions but may also have a negative impact on its reputation, overall security posture, and good business conduct. As with internal regulations, it is very important to raise employee awareness of the legal, regulatory, and normative requirements in their daily activities. An awareness of this framework facilitates an understanding and acceptance of IS constraints. For these reasons, it is essential to have a reference system of the laws and regulations in force (cartography, documentation, presentation, etc.) that can be made available to all staff members.

Compliance management activities enable governing bodies and management to get answers to these key questions:

- Do we know how legal and regulatory framework affects our information security program?
- Do we know the extent of our compliance and the gaps that need to be filled? Have we established an IS compliance map?
- Have our internal regulations adapted to the requirements of the legal and regulatory framework?
- How do we make employees aware of the legal and regulatory framework?

The recommendations of ISO 27001 directly related to compliance are as follows.

Requirements:
4.   Context of the organization
5.2 Policy (commitment to satisfy applicable requirements related to information security)
10.1 Nonconformity and corrective action

Reference control objectives and controls (Annex A):
A.18 Compliance

Chapter 12 (Compliance) will be entirely devoted to methods and tools for the compliance management process.

2.5.10 Operational Level

Finally, the operational level includes the technical controls put in place to prevent threats and mitigate risks. They are often considered company data's first line of defense. This is the set of controls that make a functional security system.

To take an example from the standards, NIST has released a best practice repository called Cyber Security Framework (CSF) that describes in detail the controls to be deployed in a cyber defense system. Controls are divided into five main functions (Figure 2.11). To simplify, we can say that the last four functions, which are Protect, Detect, Respond and Recover, cover controls or measures at the operational level, while the Identify function groups together the main governance and management activities related to strategic orientations.

Functions				
IDENTIFY	**PROTECT**	**DETECT**	**RESPOND**	**RECOVER**
Develop an organizational understanding to manage cybersecurity risk to systems, people, assets, data, and capabilities	*Develop and implement appropriate safeguards to ensure delivery of critical services*	*Develop and implement appropriate activities to identify the occurrence of a cybersecurity event*	*Develop and implement appropriate activities to take action regarding a detected cybersecurity incident*	*Develop and implement appropriate activities to maintain plans for resilience and to restore any capabilities or services that were impaired due to a cybersecurity incident*
Categories				
Asset Management	Identity Management	Anomalies and Events	Response Planning	Recovery Planning
Business Environment	and Access Control	Security Continuous	Communications	Improvements
Governance	Awareness and	Monitoring	Analysis	Communications
Risk Assessment	Training	Detection Processes	Mitigation	
Risk Management	Data Security		Improvements	
Strategy	Information			
Supply Chain Risk	Protection Processes			
Management	and Procedures			
	Maintenance			
	Protective Technology			

Figure 2.11   NIST Cyber Security Framework (CSF). (Framework for Improving Critical Infrastructure Cybersecurity, Version 1.1, National Institute of Standards and Technology. April 16, 2018.)

The recommendations of the ISO 27001 standard that directly concern the operational level are as follows.

Requirements:
7.3 Awareness
7.4 Communication
7.5 Documented information

Reference control objectives and controls (Annex A):
A.7   Human resource security
A.8.3 Media handling
A.9.2 User access management
A.9.3 User responsibilities
A.9.4 System and application access control
A.10 Cryptography
A.11 Physical and environmental security
A.12 Operations security
A.13 Communications security
A.14 System acquisition, development and maintenance
A.15 Supplier relationships
A.16 Information security incident management
A.17 Information security aspects of business continuity management
A.17.1.3 Verify, review and evaluate information security continuity
A.17.2 Redundancies

This level will not be further developed in the chapters that follow, because technical or operational controls are not part of the primary objectives of this book. Nevertheless, we will refer to operational controls when mentioning the importance of a catalog of controls as an essential tool for good IS program management.

What is the mapping between ISO 27001 and the TLCF?

2.6 Mapping between ISO 27001 and TLCF

Mapping between the standards does not really make sense, mainly because of the differences in their presentation, approach, and objectives. Many mapping tools between standards exist and can be consulted. NIST also publishes a mapping of controls between its standard and ISO.

Table 2.1 shows the correspondence between the blocks of the TLCF and the recommendations of ISO 27001. Since the TLCF is not a collection of good practices, the purpose of this mapping is to enable the reader to group the ISO control

Table 2.1 Mapping of TLCF—ISO 27001/2

Three-Layer Control Framework	ISO 27001 Requirements	ISO 27001 Control objectives and Controls (Annex A)
Strategy	4.1, 4.2, 4.3, 4.4	
Politicies	4.4 5.2	A.5 A.6.2.1, A.6.2.2 A.9.1.1 A.10.1.1 A.14.2.1, 1.14.2.5 A.15.1.1
Organization	5.1, 5.3 7.2, 7.3	A.6
Risk management	6.1.1, 6.1.2, 6.1.3 8.2, 8.3	A.6.2.1
Program management	6, 6.1, 6.2 7.1, 7.4 8.1 10	A.12.1.3 A.18.2.2, A.18.2.3
Reporting and oversight	9.3	A.18.2
Asset management		A.8
Compliance	4, 5.2, 10.1	A.18
Metrics	9, 9.1, 9.2	A.12.7.1
Operations	7.3 7.4 7.5	A.6.2.2 A.7 A.9.1.2, A.9.2, A.9.3, A.9.4 A.10.1.2 A.11.1, A.11.2 A.12 A.13 A.14 A.15 A.16 A.17

Table 2.2 Other Activities Related to IS Governance and Their Mapping to TLCF Blocks

Other Security Activities	Mapping to TLCF Blocs
Audit	Metrics
Training and awareness	Operations
Outsourcing	Vertical domain – all blocs
Human resource security	Vertical domain – all blocs
Security architecture	Operations
Application security	Policies Operations
Cybersecurity	Vertical domain – all blocs
Segregation of duties	Policies Organization
Change management (acquisition, development)	Policies Operations
Crisis management, communication	Organization Operations
Monitoring and supervision	Metrics Operations
Data Privacy	Vertical domain – all blocs

objectives into the blocks presented earlier. The reason why many of the ISO 27001 control objectives are found in the "Policies" block is because this is explicitly required in many control objectives.

Some of the standards' recommendations will be spread across all the blocks of the TLCF model because they relate to entire security domains (e.g., access control).

Other activities that may be thought of, but which are not explicitly mentioned in the standards, are listed in Table 2.2 with their mapping to TLCF's building blocks.

2.7 Conclusion

IS governance requires the involvement of management and boards of directors. To facilitate the understanding of the requirements of security standards, it is necessary to present them in a simplified form and grouped together in homogeneous blocks. In this chapter, we have presented a way to group security controls into blocks divided into three levels of responsibility. Each of the building blocks is presented with all the activities that constitute it and the objectives that these activities are intended to cover.

The TLCF model is not a benchmark of good practice and does not in itself make any recommendation that is not already present in the standards or reference works on security governance. Its main utility lies in the grouping and simplified presentation of the complex universe of activities related to the governance of IS.

In the following chapter, we will present the use cases of the three-level control framework. Methods and tools to achieve the objectives set out in each of the building blocks will be presented in the following chapters.

Chapter 3

Control Framework Use Cases

The three-level control framework (TLCF) is not intended to replace information security (IS) standards or any other inventory or benchmark of good practices. The recommendations of all the standards can fit into the model's building blocks, as seen in the previous chapter, but the model itself does not provide new recommendations. It should therefore be used as a complementary tool enabling decision-makers to focus on the essentials and ask the right questions about the IS governance process. The TLCF serves mainly as a support tool in the process of evaluating practices and as a grid to read recommendations from a governance point of view. Our primary intention is to make it easier for managers and governing bodies to read the standards by offering them a thought-provoking framework around the main blocks of the model.

This chapter provides answers to the following questions:

- What does the TLCF model provide, and what is its potential use?
- What are some typical use cases?

What is the model's potential benefit?

3.1 Model Use Cases

Governance and management practices can be schematized by applying the TLCF template to either an entire IS management system (ISMS) or a specific security domain. It can be used as an observation grid for the standards and as a model to group all the activities within the context of an ISMS, a specific security domain or a new technology or change. It can also be used to support discussions or brainstorming during change management or the self-assessment of governance practices.

The TLCF model can thus be used to observe security governance practices in various scenarios and from different angles. We have already seen some examples of its application, but remember that it can be used in all areas of security where governance practice is desirable. Generally speaking, security systems requiring a particular strategy, policy, or organization (roles and responsibilities), those with specific risks, and those having a particular legal and regulatory framework can be analyzed from the TLCF framework perspective (Figure 3.1).

Such systems can be grouped into the following categories (nonexhaustive list):

1. By security domain:
   Identity and access management
   Infrastructures, telecommunications and networks, applications
   Business continuity
   Physical security
   Human security

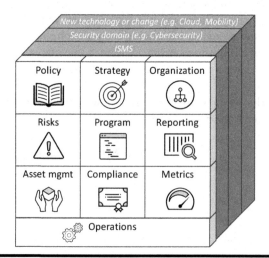

Figure 3.1   Areas of application of the TLCF model.

2. By the nature of the threat:
   Cybersecurity
   Data privacy
3. By technology:
   Cloud computing
   Virtualization
   Mobility
   Consumerization
   Digitalization of processes
4. By geographical or organizational units

The TLCF model can be used in these three situations:

1. *Governance self-assessment.* As the name suggests, its aim is to provide a synthetic view of how well governance practices are being implemented for a given system and suggest changes without necessarily going through an audit.

EXAMPLE

Cybersecurity posture can be the subject of self-assessing governance practices to ensure that operational controls benefit from all the necessary governance and management support: strategy, policies, organization, risks, program, asset management, compliance, metrics, and reporting.

2. *Impact on governance—a proactive approach.* This approach aims to establish good governance practices in anticipation of a new system or a major change.

EXAMPLE

When a new outsourced human resources management system is being set up, it is highly probable that governance aspects will need to be addressed: strategy, policies, organization, data protection, risks, program, and oversight. An analysis of the characteristics of the new system will then identify governance requirements and distribute them into the TLCF blocks.

3. *Impact on governance—a reactive approach.* This approach consists of reviewing practices in the model's nine building blocks as a result of changes in operational controls.

EXAMPLE

An office file encryption system as a means of protecting content (operational control) cannot be put in place properly without reviewing its impact on the model's nine blocks. A review will most likely be necessary of the guidelines, encryption key management organization, risks, the deployment schedule, office file classifications, and compliance with regulatory requirements.

3.2 Governance Self-Assessment

Self-assessment of governance practices can be done for an entire ISMS, for a specific security domain, or as part of a business or geographic entity. Such an analysis can obviously be made by using all the recommendations in the standards and then evaluating their level of maturity. This is done in audits, for example. However, we are looking for a less cumbersome and less restrictive way for management to judge the governance practices of a system based on a few key questions.

The template of the TLCF model makes such introspection possible and facilitates the task of identifying major points to improve. The model can be used in different ways: during brainstorming sessions, during the initial phase of major projects, within management security awareness seminars on security strategies, or during the meetings of committees in charge of planning major security initiatives.

Each model building block has a series of questions to focus discussion (Figure 3.2) adapted to the area under observation. A questionnaire that facilitates brainstorming can be made using recommendations from the standards, the regulations, the requirements of a maturity model, or any other document or study that deals with security governance good practices.

Using a model such as the TLCF to stimulate creative thinking or brainstorming about IS governance can be more beneficial than traditional methods such as maturity models (often based on one or more of the standards) or strengths, weaknesses, opportunities, and threats (SWOT) analyses. The proposed questions are meant to kindle thought processes and spark discussion on topics that are frequently not on decision-makers' agendas, because the model highlights key areas of responsibility at the strategic and tactical levels of IS. The outcome of such a discussion can be a report containing improvement proposals for each of the model's nine blocks.

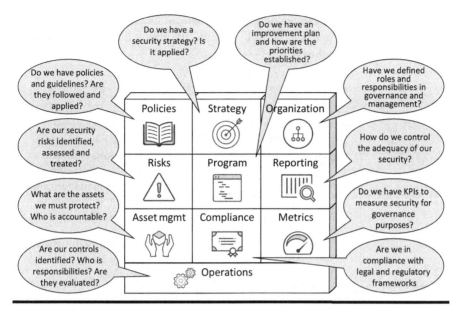

Figure 3.2 Questionnaire for each TLCF block.

During discussions, participants will be invited to comment on the possible weaknesses or gaps they see, along with proposals to resolve them. The different proposals will then be discussed, consolidated by model block, and presented as a future action plan (Figure 3.3).

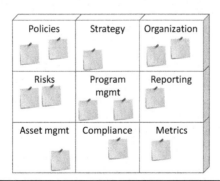

Figure 3.3 TLCF template as brainstorming tool.

The following is an example of questions that can be used to spur discussions about the governance practices of an IS system. The action plan for each block is presented in the third column.

Block	Questions	Action plan
Strategy	Do we have a security strategy aligned with business objectives? What is the level of management's understanding of security issues? How involved is the security executive manager in developing business strategies?	Review the security strategy based on discussions that will take place between business managers and the chief information security officer (CISO) Align security initiatives with business objectives
Policies	Do our security policies and guidelines correspond to the needs of the business units? Do we have the means to monitor the effective application of our guidelines? Do policies mention the responsibility of all the employees and the consequences of neglect? Have we established a documentary framework for internal regulations? Who is responsible for proposing adaptations to policies and guidelines? What is our security policy validation process?	Review the documentary framework of the policies and guidelines and provide better readability

| Organization | Have we delegated responsibilities in the governance of IS?

Does the position of the security officer and their team make it easier to take business unit needs into account?

Do we have a committee empowered to rule on exceptions and changes to security policies and directives?

How does the security officer communicate with the business units about security objectives (in both directions)? | Each business line must appoint a security delegate to participate in quarterly security project review meetings |
|---|---|---|
| Risks | Does security risk management fit into the company's operational risk management concept?

How involved are business unit risk managers in analyzing security risks?

Have we established a security risk inventory validated by all the business lines?

Do we have metrics and key performance indicators (KPIs) to measure the performance of our different security controls?

Have we established a security risk treatment plan? | No improvements needed |

Program management	How involved are the board, management, and business unit leaders in setting security priorities? How are operations managers involved in prioritizing security initiatives? Do business units participate in the development of the security business plan? Are all the expenses in technical solutions justified by a risk and cost–benefit analysis? Are the objectives clearly defined? Do we have an inventory of operational controls with responsibilities, maturity level, and validity test plans? Have we established an employee awareness program regarding the protection of our assets?	Set up a committee to validate IS initiatives and projects
Reporting	Do we have an IS reporting system for management, the board, and business units? Does the reporting system contain relevant information on the state of IS, high risks, compliance and maturity gaps, and the effectiveness of actions taken?	No improvements needed
Asset management	Have we identified, classified, and categorized our data? Do we know who the data owners are? How is it guaranteed that data owners' privacy, availability, and integrity requirements are integrated into the security program?	Define data classes and categories and inventory them in a catalog Identify data owners for each class/business line

Compliance	Do we know what laws and regulations apply to IS? How is the legal and regulatory framework communicated to employees? Have we established a compliance program?	Set up an employee awareness program regarding the legal and regulatory framework that impacts security
Metrics	Do we know the direct, indirect, and analytical (by activity) costs of information security? Do we have metrics to measure the performance of our various security controls? How do we measure the degree of employee training regarding threats and means of protection? How are business lines involved in validating security metrics?	No improvements needed

This process is an example of using the TLCF framework as part of self-assessment or brainstorming on security governance practices. This approach is based on answering a set of key questions that cover all the governance activities and then establishing recommendations for improvement.

3.3 Impact on Governance—a Proactive Approach

The proactive approach analyzes a specific domain (e.g., cybersecurity) from the viewpoint of all the model building blocks. To illustrate, let us take an example from the field of data privacy, although the same approach can be applied to any other domain.

The protection of personal data in the digital economy has become a subject of concern for many regulators. The European Community has adopted comprehensive guidelines to protect the personal data of the citizens of its countries—the General Data Protection Regulation (GDPR). Many other countries have similar regulations, such as the Swiss Data Protection Act or the Singapore Personal Data Protection Act, to name just two.

The GDPR requirements impacting IS are summarized in the following list. They should not be confused with other requirements, such as the right to be forgotten, the lawfulness of treatments, profiling, or explicit consent, that do not directly involve IS but rather, compliance and legal departments and therefore will not be taken into account in this example.

The GDPR recommendations on the protection of personal data that may impact IS or an ISMS are listed as follows.

1. **Personal data identification, categorization, and classification**

    Personal data are the data of customers, suppliers, employees, or any other person that a company uses and processes for its operations. Regulations require companies to identify such personal data, including the use and processing of "highly sensitive data" such as genetic, biometric, health related, and so on. It is therefore important to be able to categorize these data (customer, employee, supplier, etc.) and classify them according to the criteria of confidentiality (e.g., confidential, public), which will then allow adequate protections to be put in place.

    The internal regulatory framework then specifies how these data are protected according to their classification and the context in which they are processed or stored.

2. **Inventory of personal data**

    A company must have an inventory of personal data, the servers and applications that process these data, and a description of personal data flows (which process uses which data). These systems are classified according to the classification of the data they host or process, making it easier to set up specific risk management linked to these data and create the relevant indicators.

3. **Measures to protect personal data**

    A company must be able to demonstrate the existence of controls or measures to protect personal data according to data classification, storage mode, and treatment (access, transmission, destruction, change management, or backup).

    The data protection program put in place should include not only operational controls but also independent audits, privacy impact assessment (PIA) procedures, HR controls, and training and awareness plans. Protective technologies such as encryption should be used to avoid exposing data where this is not required (e.g., in development environments).

4. **Data protection by design**

    Personal data processing must be designed from the outset to provide functions such as the deletion of personal data at the request of the customer (right to be forgotten), access by customers to their personal data, and portability (data extraction in electronic form).

5. **Organization and responsibilities in data protection**

    Security organization must be in place and include data protection responsibilities in information technology (IT), HR, business units, decision-making bodies, management, and the board of directors. Specific functions should be defined, such as data processor, data controller, data owner, and data protection officer (DPO). A company must be able to demonstrate its compliance, and the board of directors must be held duly responsible for personal data protection with a direct line of reporting to it.

6. Risk management related to personal data

A company is required to manage the risks related to protecting personal data and report to the board of directors for decisions on the appropriate actions to take.

7. Liability of third parties

In the case of outsourcing, it is important to be able to ensure how personal data is secured from the viewpoint of both storage and processing. Regulations must also be respected by third parties.

8. Incident management

Incidents must be managed through a process that includes detection, remediation, and specific measures to prevent unauthorized access to data. A company is obliged to report incidents of a certain importance to supervisory authorities.

Based on these requirements, mandatory IS controls can be set up in all of the TLCF blocks. This makes it easier to plan the involvement of different profiles in the compliance project.

Strategy	Review security strategy to encompass data privacy rules for third parties, outsourcing and data transfers
	Define risk appetite regarding data privacy
Policies	Develop a data privacy policy or adapt existing data protection or security policies
	Include the definition of personal data, classification, categorization, and special categories of personal data (e.g., sensitive data)
	Specify what personally identifiable information (PII) is being processed
	Have written standards specifying minimum protection according to data classification, categorization, and context (data at rest, in transition, end-user access, transfer, mobility, etc.)
	Review and update HR policy regarding personal employee data

	Make sure there are policies and standards concerning personal data protection in the system life-cycle management process
	Include the "data protection by design" concept in development processes
	Update the externalization procedures, data sharing with third parties, and data transfers
Organization	Define security organization and establish responsibilities in data privacy protection (data processors, data controllers, data owners, governing bodies, management of the DP program, and DPO)
	Review or establish reporting lines to the board
Risk	Adapt the security risk catalog to include data privacy risk scenarios. This must include risks not only for the company but also for data owners (clients, employees, contractors, etc.).
	Carry out a PIA of the current security program, assess risks, and adapt priorities
Program management	Define the data privacy program's mission and goals. Adapt priorities for Data Protection/Data Privacy
	Specify in the catalog of controls who is responsible for which control and when effectiveness tests should take place
Reporting	Make sure there are sections in the reports concerning DP risks, the effectiveness of associated controls, and KPIs (incidents, breaches)
Asset management	Build/update the asset inventory to reflect the systems and applications hosting personal data
	Identify the major data flows of personal data
Compliance	Make a gap analysis with DP regulations
	Assess/update access rights management to comply with data privacy internal regulations on personal data
	Review data retention and disposal regulations for data privacy

Metrics	Update metrics and KPIs to facilitate data privacy risk assessment
Operations	Implement encryption where needed to protect personal data
	Adapt the Data Breach Incident Response Plan and associated procedures (responsibilities, reporting to data controllers by data processors, notification obligations to the authorities, etc.). Maintain an internal incident and breach register
	Update training and awareness programs for data privacy
	Implement controls to render data unintelligible in the case of unauthorized access

3.4 Impact on Governance—a Reactive Approach

Every time operational controls are changed, it is important to verify their interdependence with controls at the strategic and tactical levels. In other words, we have to ensure that governance activities and tools are adapted to the new operational controls. Requests for changes resulting from incidents, audit findings, or visible threats are often sent to operational managers who sometimes minimize the scope of change, ignore the imperatives of governance, or simply do not have the means to require that strategic or tactical-level controls be adapted accordingly.

EXAMPLE

The ISO 27001 standard recommends the following control:

A.13.1.3 Segregation in networks: "Groups of information services, users and information systems shall be segregated on networks."

For network segregation to add value to a company, it must address a business unit need or the need to separate assets or infrastructure from different confidentiality classes. This involves making strategic decisions and adapting security policies to take into account differences in the risk appetite of operators in different parts of the network.

Many operational controls cannot be implemented properly without strategic orientations or adjustments in the policies and guidelines. Even if not specified in the standards or audit findings, it is very important to examine the impact of operational changes on the governance process. Change managers could then use the TLCF template to present the impact of change on strategic and tactical controls.

EXAMPLE

Suppose an audit finding notes the lack of encryption solutions for USB flash drives. This is a weakness that could expose confidential data. After analysis, the company decides not to implement an encryption solution for USB devices, because it has other means of protection, including blocking USB ports on individual workstations and the obligation to pass by a support service if someone needs to store information on a USB device. This is considered sufficient to reduce the risk. Nevertheless, the company's regulatory framework does not mention this process clearly and must be adapted accordingly.

To illustrate this approach, which can be called *reactive* or *bottom-up* when using the model, we will take the example of cybersecurity.

Cybersecurity is a set of controls to fight malicious attack threats against infrastructure and corporate assets from cyberspace. Companies are much more vulnerable today due to their heavy dependence on information technologies, digitalization, national laws often unsuited to the international context, the very great availability of means for malicious attacks on the dark web, and the explosion of connected objects. The typology of the attacks is also changing: they are now more targeted, and malicious persons need less and less technical knowledge. The attacks are a set of operational risks that could threaten a company's very existence. Governing bodies must therefore remain sufficiently aware of their evolution.

As with any other security domain, the cyber-threat protection system must be integrated into the existing IS program. Cybersecurity should not be seen as a set of isolated technical measures. The fight against cyber threats requires the existence of a strategy, a policy, organization, risk management, a control management program, a reporting system, inventories of assets to protect, visibility regarding compliance with the legal and regulatory framework, and indicators and metrics to gauge the adequacy of the program.

The controls that a company implements to protect against cyber threats cover the capacity not only to detect and protect but also to recover after an attack. The context of rapidly changing threats means that the effectiveness of controls must be monitored so that they can be adapted accordingly. Management often asks whether their company is sufficiently protected, how their security compares with that of other companies in the same sector, and how to improve in the future. On the other hand, it is entirely legitimate for a company to consider installing a cyberdefense tactical domain with specific responsibilities to better manage its program.

Example of Adapting Governance Practices Following Changes in Operational Controls

Suppose a company wants to evaluate its protection capacity against cyber threats. The management has delegated this project to the IT department and expects to receive a report specifying the current level of maturity, the required level of maturity, and what actions should be taken to close the gaps.

The NIST Cyber Security Framework (CSF) standard can be used to assess the company's current cybersecurity posture. The primary purpose of this standard is to identify all essential operational controls in the field of cyberdefense. By assessing the maturity of its controls against the recommendations of the standard, the company will be able to propose improvement initiatives. The NIST CSF Framework Core containing all the controls consists of the following:

- Five major functions grouping cybersecurity protection controls called IDENTIFY, PROTECT, DETECT, RESPOND, AND RECOVER (Figure 2.11)
- Each function subdivided into many categories
- Each category encompassing a certain number of subcategories or requirements

The complete list of these subcategories is available in Annex A of the NIST publication Framework for Improving Critical Infrastructure Cybersecurity, Version 1.1, National Institute of Standards and Technology. April 16, 2018.

Purely governance and management controls are mentioned in the categories within the IDENTIFY function. The other functions primarily contain requirements for operational controls. At first glance, management has less insight into the impact of these controls on the governance process. Therefore, it is important to highlight the possible implications of operational controls at the strategic and tactical level.

Let us suppose that a maturity evaluation of the controls in place compared with the standard's requirements results in the six findings presented in Table 3.1 next to each subcategory.

The recommendations and their impact on practices in the blocks of the TLCF model are summarized in Table 3.2. Findings 1 and 2, which are directly related to the CSF's Asset Management and Risk Management Strategy categories, also concern the TLCF Strategy, Risks, and Asset Management blocks. Other recommendations have implications not only at operational level but also at the strategic and tactical levels in our model, including Strategy, Policies, and Program. We will not go into the details of the recommendations in this example, because they have to be worked out based on the company's context. Nevertheless, it is important to note that the findings, which are ultimately oriented toward operational controls, also have implications for strategic and tactical controls.

Table 3.1 Findings after Comparison with NIST CSF Framework

Function	Category	Subcategory	Findings
IDENTIFY	Asset Management	ID.AM-5: Resources (e.g., hardware, devices, data, time, personnel, and software) are prioritized based on their classification, criticality, and business value CIS	1. Not all systems are inventoried or classified
	Risk Management Strategy	ID.RM-2: Organizational risk tolerance is determined and clearly expressed	2. Risk appetite is not clearly defined or expressed in terms of factual indicators
PROTECT	Data Security	PR.DS-2: Data-in-transit is protected	3. Encryption is not used. Data flows are not classified
		PR.DS-5: Protections against data leaks are implemented	4. There is no automated data leak protection
	Information Protection Processes and Procedures	PR.IP-9: Response plans (Incident Response and Business Continuity) and recovery plans (Incident Recovery and Disaster Recovery) are in place and managed	5. There are no clear guidelines or service-level agreements on the time to recover critical processes. Tests are based solely on the restoration of all functionalities
RECOVER	Recovery Planning	RC.RP-1: Recovery plan is executed during or after a cybersecurity incident	6. There are no planned tests of large-scale cyberattacks

Table 3.2   Impact of the Recommendations on the TLCF Blocks

Findings	Recommendations	TLCF Impact
1. Not all systems are inventoried or classified	Define a classification and asset inventory. Include data flows	Asset management
2. Risk appetite is not clearly defined or expressed in terms of factual indicators	Define risk appetite and KRI for cyber risks	Risk
3. Encryption is not used. Data flows are not classified	Define an encryption policy based on confidentiality classifications. Install encryption protection for all flows that need to be protected according to the policy	Policies
4. There is no automated data leak protection	Depending on the risks and the return on investment, decide whether it is mandatory to install an automatic data leak protection system	Strategy
5. There is no clear direction or SLA on the time to recover critical processes. Tests are based solely on the restoration of all functionalities	Establish guidelines on the recovery requirements of processes deemed critical for the business. Schedule a regular time for recovery tests for critical processes	Policies
6. There are no planned tests of large-scale cyberattacks	Make a schedule for tests of the recovery from large-scale cyberattacks	Program

Therefore, any project aiming to change the operational level of controls must consider its impact on governance and the strategic and tactical level of controls. Only the vertical integration of governance controls and tools will provide a company with the information security it needs.

3.5 Conclusion

We presented the use cases of the TLCF model for the self-assessment of governance practices, for anticipating changes (proactive approach) and the impact of changes (reactive approach) on the strategic and tactical levels. Evaluating the impact of changes on governance, risk, and compliance activities should be a concern not only for security officers and management but also for all those responsible for changes in the field of security controls.

The model could also be used for all needs of simplified presentation of the controls at strategic and tactical level for the persons having a function in the governance of the IS and not very familiar with the standards and benchmarks of good practices.

Chapter 4

Strategy

New operational controls are often set up in the aftermath of incidents, new threats, new regulations, or audit findings. This reactive approach does not constitute a strategy. In the long run, stakeholders do not understand the role of security, its goals, and return on investment. The term *security strategy* is often confused with *project roadmap* or *business plan*, which usually consist of a list of projects aimed at mitigating risks. Although this is important, it is not a strategy, which is a set of projects that should reach a specific strategic goal. And what is this goal? What we need to understand is how and to what extent security activities contribute to business development.

A reactive stance marginalizes security executive managers and restricts them to their technical role outside of management. Aggravated by a jumble of expensive technical solutions, such an approach will not attract the attention of business unit managers. Without benchmarks showing progress toward commonly accepted goals, it is not sustainable in the long run. Security managers often have trouble drawing the attention of decision-makers and justifying their investments. If they cannot explain why and how security helps to reach business objectives, there is no reason to consider security efforts essential. Equally importantly, security executive managers and their teams must understand the objectives that are targeted by their efforts.

A security plan that supports business initiatives with a roadmap of projects heading toward them can catch decision-makers' attention and prevent security from being perceived as a necessary evil or cost center. Everyone is increasingly convinced today that security is essential for business development in a digital economy. Technologies and threats are changing; business models too. This evolution forces the chief information security officer (CISO) to solicit more resources, but such efforts do not seem to be appreciated at their full value. The reason is often the lack of a well-defined security strategy that has been circulated at the company-wide level.

This chapter provides answers to the following questions:

- What is a security strategy, and what is its purpose?
- What should a strategy include?
- What are the main steps in a strategy development project?
- How should a strategy be formulated?
- How should a strategy be presented?

What is a security strategy, and what is its purpose?

4.1 Security Strategy

In general, a strategy is the declaration of an objective, including ways to achieve it. A security strategy must therefore present the outline of a "new" security that will better contribute to business objectives. Without this aspect of its fundamental purpose, a security strategy will not be understood.

Every activity requires direction that gives meaning and purpose to what we do. Such purpose, along with coordinated actions to achieve it, is called a *strategy*. The term *strategy* is used in different contexts: military, political, business, gaming, and so on. They all encompass a specified purpose and the means to achieve it but are fundamentally different in form and content, since they are used by and for different actors and purposes. A gaming strategy is more about how, or the steps, to achieve a well-known goal, while a business strategy is more about positioning a company's products on the market or customer segment.

A security strategy that defines its future state and its alignment with business objectives in the coming years, and has quantifiable objectives to demonstrate its added value, will enable all the stakeholders to support its efforts. It should be noted that an information security (IS) strategy can be established on several levels. A global strategy can be supported by strategies in different areas, such as cybersecurity strategy, outsourcing strategy, cloud service strategy, and so on.

Creating a strategy is one of the first tasks of any security officer: setting the objectives of change and initiatives leading toward them. Nevertheless, for them to be supported, these objectives must be expressed in terms everyone can understand.

EXAMPLE

If mobility is a business goal, then the security strategy supporting it should include not only components for secure connections but also specific policies such as access restrictions to sensitive data. Presented in this way as the logical continuum of actions leading to a clearly defined objective based on appropriate risk analysis, the security strategy will be understood and accepted.

There are different views on the need to have a strategy. Some may argue that it is useless to develop a security strategy with distant objectives, because security only works in reactive mode. Recent studies and surveys by specialized firms, however, indicate that a security organization focused on strategy, governance, and risk has greater maturity than one focused solely on operations.

It is not uncommon for management to ask the CISO: "What is your strategy for such and such technology?" It is not the CISO's job to define a strategy for new technology; rather, the company or business unit that benefits from the technology must define the strategy together with the CISO or his or her team. Security can provide an analysis of associated risks and propose adjustments to the controls to ensure that the technology is deployed under good conditions. The security strategy must follow the business strategy, not the other way around.

EXAMPLE

A security team member or CISO cannot answer the question: "What is our strategy for cloud computing?" if there has been no prior discussion about business or information technology (IT) needs. Such a strategy depends on several factors: the type of data, the processes and applications concerned, the intended use, the storage location, the regulatory framework that applies to it, and so on. The company must first develop its change project with the potential use of an external cloud infrastructure. The security team can then propose controls based on a risk analysis, and then, the strategy can be defined jointly.

A security strategy is an essential tool for governance, although this is often neglected by the CISO in favor of technical security solutions decided locally. Without a strategy, these same solutions might be misunderstood and, more importantly, not achieve the true goal of protecting assets, which is what the business needs. Governing bodies need to know goals to make decisions. A security strategy presents a long-term framework, plan, or roadmap enabling operational solutions to be put in place. Therefore,

- A security strategy is a plan, validated by the company's management, presenting modifications to the current state of security to reach a goal (future state).
- It provides guidance for all the company's security initiatives and projects.

Strategy is the first mission of security governance. It must be developed before anything else. It anchors the security program, and all the governance building blocks are influenced by it. But a strategy is not fixed in time; it has to evolve with technological changes, business orientations, changes in the environment and the regulatory framework, the context and relations with external partners, new business models, and so on. A roadmap of projects related to strategic objectives will be maintained as a framework for the entire security program.

What should a strategy include?

4.2 Security Strategy Content

A security strategy may be expressed in more ways than one. There are many examples with a variety of form and content. However, the essential elements of a strategy are Mission, Context, Role and Responsibilities, Objectives, and Initiatives (Figure 4.1).

The *mission* is a short statement recalling security's main objectives, its main functions, and its contribution to business goals.

The *context* describes several elements necessary to understanding the strategy, in particular:
- The company's desire to protect its assets, and in particular the confidentiality, availability, and integrity of its data
- The security imperatives given the characteristics of the company, its sector of activity, the environment in which it operates, its risk appetite, and the legal and regulatory framework in which it operates
- The role of the strategy as a basic guideline for any future security initiatives and a reminder of principles that should guide any decision
- Remarks on the organization's current situation, major challenges, and future developments

Mission

Context

Roles and responsibilities

Strategic Objectives

Strategic Initiatives

Figure 4.1   Key elements of a security strategy.

The *Roles and Responsibilities* section is a reminder of the principles of governance, the roles and responsibilities of managing the security program, and the fact that security organization will have to be adapted to the objectives and initiatives of the organization.

Strategic Objectives or *Vision* for the coming period should be clearly mentioned. They are formulated in terms of maturity of processes and support for business objectives. Security must position itself as a key player in the development of the company and formulate a clear direction and its future positioning. This will allow all stakeholders to better understand the initiatives that will lead to it.

Strategic Security Initiatives, which will lead to an established vision, should be clearly enumerated with
  − A description of their contribution to business goals
  − Their key deliverables (expected results)
  − How their contribution is measured (with some key point indicators that monitor their evolution toward the objectives)

Despite its apparent simplicity, this is a relatively complicated exercise for any CISO. Indeed, they cannot elaborate a strategy by themselves, alone and in isolation. On the other hand, there is no commonly accepted model to define a strategy, which means different things to different people. CISOs are not often invited to discuss business strategies, which in turn, are often not communicated in a sufficiently explicit and measurable way. The danger of a "solitary" approach is the possibility of delivering a roadmap of security projects with no apparent links to business objectives. As such, it will not be understood as a strategy by most business managers, since it will not be aligned with their needs and will not meet their desire for technology changes to develop the business and provide better customer services.

The following is a methodical approach to achieve this goal.

What are the main steps in a strategy development project?

4.3 Approach to Defining a Strategy

A common mistake in developing a strategy is to list projects corresponding solely to elements that traditionally drive security programs: audit findings, vulnerabilities and threats, known risks, and regulatory constraints. A strategy must clearly take these elements into account, but to be convincing, it must explicitly mention and target business objectives for the reasons noted earlier. This alignment with business strategies is a challenge not only for security managers but for all technologists in general.

Many factors influence the development of a security strategy. They can be categorized as follows:

- Business operation strategies and needs
- External factors, including the legal and regulatory framework, the environment in which the company operates, and constraints linked to working with external partners
- Imperatives to close IS maturity gaps
- Risk mitigation

The process to develop a strategy can be summarized as shown in Figure 4.2.

Besides traditional business units, the IT department, corporate entities, Human Resources (HR), and others should be considered as partners in the context of developing a security strategy.

To be able to define objectives (security vision) and initiatives to achieve them, numerous factors must be taken into consideration within a methodical approach aimed at capturing the needs of the business units. The main steps, tools, and expected outcomes for each step will be presented next. We will not develop project management best practices in detail, as this is not our objective here; rather, we will simply mention the following important key factors for a strategy project to be a success.

A strategy *steering committee* must be set up with the primary role of providing necessary support to the project manager, making decisions about objectives and resources, and monitoring progress toward agreed objectives. It should be composed of individuals with relatively important decision-making authority, such as the chief risk officer (CRO), the chief information officer (CIO), one or more representatives from management, and one or more representatives from the main business units or sectors of activity.

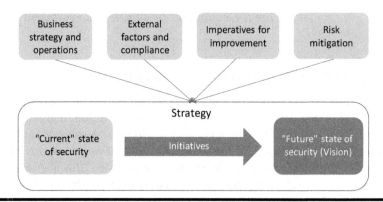

Figure 4.2 Security strategy development process.

The *team* that will participate in developing the security strategy consists of people selected from the business units. These experts will be responsible for conveying the strategic directions and evaluating security aspects in operations. They should be chosen based on their knowledge of the business unit's strategic vision, their knowledge of operations, and their demonstrated interest in IS.

The *project leader* will ideally be a CISO or their representative. They could also be an external consultant, but they must work under the close supervision of the security manager.

The strategy development project consists of four stages, the purpose of which is to provide all the elements necessary for its definition:

1. Establish what IS can do to better support business strategy (change)
2. Establish what IS can do to better support business operations (run)
3. Define IS Vision and Initiatives to improve overall IS effectiveness
4. Group the Initiatives and establish a project roadmap
5. Formulate a strategy
6. Communicate on IS strategy

4.3.1 Initiatives to Support Business Strategy

As a first step, it is very important to be able to sense a company's needs, change initiatives, IS expectations, and "pet projects."

- Understand business imperatives and their success factors.
- Understand strategic projects, and possibly infer other strategic directions not clearly communicated.
- Identify initiatives and goals where security can bring value.
- Identify security rules that are considered a hindrance to reaching business objectives.
- Determine how security can contribute to the achievement of business objectives.
- Define with the business lines which indicators will be used to measure the adequacy of IS with regard to business objectives.

EXAMPLE

HR services have a strategic objective to develop their Internet recruitment service. Security can contribute to this objective in different ways, including setting up personal data protection controls, integrating authentication components provided by third-party application providers, and so on. Support for such initiatives can also be beneficial to other business units with similar needs, such as defining an integration architecture of different authentication methods.

Figure 4.3   Security initiatives supporting business objectives (change).

The expected outcome from this phase will be

1. Knowledge of the business strategic objectives
2. A list of security initiatives that can contribute to the achievement of business strategic objectives
3. Indicators to measure the degree of adequacy of security with regard to strategic objectives (Figure 4.3)

Business strategies are often not defined or clearly stated, although they are expressed through initiatives, new projects, visions, or the results of strategy review sessions. It is therefore not surprising that a document called *enterprise strategy* or *business strategy* does not exist; rather, at best, there is a multitude of documents or presentations that mention it.

In what follows, we will consider the business strategy of a company as a whole or of one of its business units or divisions without going into the complexity of the business. The approach to the security strategy will be the same.

The Sherwood Applied Business Security Architecture (SABSA) framework advocates an enterprise approach, which is very laudable and certainly preferable: *"The concept of enterprise carries the meaning that the organization is perceived as a single entity rather than as a collection of cooperating units. In particular this concept embraces the notion of end-to-end business processes."* Nevertheless, the business-unit-by-business-unit approach has the merit of reinforcing the security position and does not detract from the "enterprise" perspective, which will be given later in the consolidation exercise.

The main steps to identifying business initiatives and listing the security initiatives to support them are the following:

1. Prepare: set the goals, timing, and deliverables.
2. Compile a questionnaire allowing strategic business initiatives to be identified along with security initiatives that can help.
3. Map strategic business initiatives. Hold meetings with business unit representatives to clarify their strategic initiatives.
4. Consolidate strategic business initiatives and draft underlying security initiatives.

Before starting to review the business strategy, carefully select the experts who will be on the steering committee and team (business unit representatives), define objectives, and convene the committee and team for a kick-off session where the objectives, method, and timing will be presented.

The session in which the project manager works with business unit representatives to gather strategic directions should be prepared very carefully. Business units often do not have well-defined strategies or roadmaps. This is why the project preparation session is very important, and the backing of management and the board is paramount in this regard. It is not uncommon for unit managers to maintain their view that security is a support that should be kept outside of business concerns and concentrate on technical protection. In this case, a presentation of the expected benefits could be very useful. Another danger could come from business unit managers who, having misunderstood the meaning of the security strategy project, delegate persons to work on it who do not have sufficient knowledge of business objectives or a position allowing them to transmit all the relevant information. This is why the role of a project leader who is well informed about the company's realities is extremely important.

Compile a questionnaire that should reflect the objective; that is, drafting a list of strategic business initiatives along with how security can add value to each of them. The questionnaire can be compiled in different ways depending on the context of the business, its characteristics, or knowledge we already have. However, for the sake of efficiency and to preserve the appeal of a consultative approach such as this, a simple and effective approach should be maintained. This is ultimately an exchange that should be seen as beneficial to all parties.

Here is an example of a questionnaire:

1. What is the mission of your unit?
2. Have you defined strategic objectives for the coming period? For each objective, list the expectations of information security that can help achieve it.
3. Have you started projects, or do you have a roadmap to achieve these objectives? If yes, list them and note for each one the expectations of information security.
4. What are the main challenges to achieving your objectives? For each of these challenges, how do you see the added value of security?
5. What are the opportunities in your activities for the next few years? What could be the added value of information security?
6. Are you aware of similar winning strategies adopted by your competitors? Are there any specific security components (tools, processes, organization) that could help?

7. Independently of your own goals, how should security controls or guidelines change to fit the context of your business (you have yet to define a strategy, but you know this will be essential)?
8. Do you foresee radical changes in your products and services that will require the adjustment of technical or security components?

The pre-established questionnaire will serve as a common thread during sessions with business unit representatives. Insist on the priority of a clear statement of business objectives. Proposals on how security can help business units realize their strategies will come later. If the business units have only vague objectives, the consequences for IS will be even more so.

It is important to reiterate that this is not a brainstorming session on business strategies. If the units are unable to formulate their change strategy, this simply means that there is no strategy, and their operations will continue to use the processes in place. Security contributions to current operations will be discussed in Phase 2: "Security Initiatives to Support Business Operations."

The results of the questionnaire can be presented in the form of a summary table containing the strategic objectives of the business units, their vision of security contributions, and the desired completion timeframe.

EXAMPLE

Financial institution

Strategic Objective	Business Initiatives to Support the Objective	Deadline	Security Contribution
1. Offer financial products including cryptocurrencies	1.1 Establish a cryptocurrency strategy. 1.2 Define and implement products including cryptocurrencies.	1 year	Integrate blockchain and key protection issues in security controls
2. Outsourcing customer relationship monitoring (CRM) operations in the cloud	2.1. Establish an outsourcing strategy. 2.2. Deploy the currently in-house infrastructure to the external provider.	6 months	Do risk assessment and establish necessary controls Deploy security controls needed for the cloud

The strategic initiatives and the contribution from security could be summarized as follows:

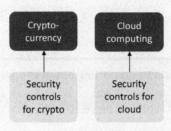

4.3.2 Initiatives to Support Business Operations

The second phase in the development of a security strategy consists of proposing security initiatives to bridge perceived gaps in process maturity to support operational business needs.

It is often said that security measures are not exactly adapted to business needs and even hinder day-to-day operations. Reviewing a company's security strategy is therefore an opportunity to better define the changes that security could make to improve this perception.

EXAMPLE

Many employees often express the need to use new means of communication and data sharing through external platforms. Their question "Why can't we use these means for professional data exchange?" will most likely receive this answer by the CISO: "Because our data is confidential and our policies don't allow it." In fact, instead of this answer, the CISO should ask the following question: "What data or documents would you be willing to share on external platforms?" and the users' response will then certainly not be "Everything!"

Policies must therefore be refined and controls put in place that allow or prevent this sharing according to the classification of the content. If a risk and cost–benefit analysis is made together with the interested business professionals, a general prohibition might be agreed! The difference is that in the latter case, the decision will be made by the business units themselves and not by IS staff.

In this phase, the project leader will tend to identify security processes that can be improved to better support current business operations.

Figure 4.4 Security initiatives supporting business operations (run).

The expected outcome from this phase will be

1. Business operational efficiency goals
2. Security maturity gaps from the point of view of business operations
3. Grouping initiatives to support business objectives (Figure 4.4)

The main phases in establishing security initiatives to support business operations are as follows:

1. Establish a maturity model of security services.
2. Make a gap analysis using the maturity model.
3. Consolidate improvement points into initiatives.

4.3.2.1 Establish a Maturity Model of Security Services

Opportunities to gain feedback from business lines on the effectiveness and usefulness of security controls are rare and must be productively used. The establishment of a maturity model of security services will allow a project leader to capture the opinion of business leaders on the perceived adequacy of security controls in place. This is why we should propose a questionnaire and maturity assessment tool to systematically register their opinions on the perceived adequacy of security measures.

Maturity assessment tools will be presented in more detail in Chapter 9 (Security Metrics). Determining the degree of user satisfaction with security solutions can be done using a variation of the ISO 15504 (Information Technology - Process Assessment) process maturity level scale (Figure 4.5).

1. Incomplete: Inexistent or poorly defined.
2. Performed: Used occasionally (ad hoc).
3. Established: Organization-wide standard (usable).
4. Predictable: Aligned to meet the organization's need.
5. Optimizing: Organization is focused on continuous improvement.

For every security service being evaluated, the following three evaluation criteria will be established:

- Current maturity
- Desired maturity
- Priority (1. Low, 2. Moderate, 3. High)

The first two allow us to measure the importance of the perceived gap, while the third helps prioritize it. These three criteria make it possible to calculate an indicator called *Importance* as follows (Figure 4.6):

$$\text{Importance} = (\text{Desired maturity} - \text{Current maturity}) \times \text{Priority}$$

The importance of desired change will be between 0 and 12. This allows us to set a threshold from which business needs will be considered. Topics of higher importance require as detailed an explanation as possible of the reasons for this situation.

EXAMPLE

Suppose we have submitted two subjects/security services to be evaluated by a business line (see following table):

1. Security policies and guidelines—relevance to your business
2. Accessibility of security policies and guidelines

According to the qualifiers given by business representatives, we understand that the security regulatory framework should be improved, but this is not really the priority. It is more important to improve the accessibility of these same documents for their daily operations.

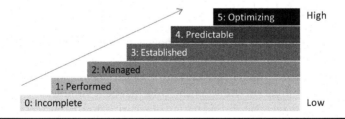

Figure 4.5   Maturity levels.

Subject	Detail	Current Maturity	Desired Maturity	Priority	Importance
Business related security service	Detailed explanation	1. Performed 2. Managed 3. Established 4. Predictible 5. Optimizing	1. Performed 2. Managed 3. Established 4. Predictible 5. Optimizing	1. Low (1 Y) 2. Medium (6 M) 3. High (now)	Calculated: 1 - 3 Low 4 - 6 Medium 7 - 9 High 10 - 12 Urgent

Figure 4.6   Maturity model of security services.

Subject	Detail	Current Maturity	Desired Maturity	Priority	Importance
Business related security service	Detailed explanation	1. Performed 2. Managed 3. Established 4. Predictible 5. Optimizing	1. Performed 2. Managed 3. Established 4. Predictible 5. Optimizing	1. Low (1 Y) 2. Medium (6 M) 3. High (now)	Calculated: 1 – 3 Low 4 – 6 Medium 7 – 9 High 10 – 12 Urgent
1 Security policies and guidelines - relevance to our business	Degree of adequacy of policies and guidelines for the needs of our business.	2	3	2	2
2 Accessibility of security policies and guidelines	Ease to find policies and guidelines for our needs	1	4	3	9

An explanation will be given for Point 2 to better understand the reason for this evaluation: for example, "New employees have difficulty finding security guidelines and examples on the intranet. The index or full text search should be improved."

The topics to be evaluated can be found in different sources, such as the company security control catalog (see Chapter 8, Program Management), standards such as the International Organization for Standardization (ISO) 2700x, National Institute of Standards and Technology (NIST), Control Objectives for Information and Related Technology (CobIT), SABSA framework (service management matrix), or maturity models such as I-OSM3 (Open Information Security Management Maturity Model, The Open Group 2011).

There follows a nonexhaustive list of topics and classifications that could be used to draft a "perceived maturity" questionnaire for security services.

Security governance (encompasses topics related to governance and security oversight)
  – Strategy (related to business strategies)
  – Adequacy of policies and guidelines
  – Accessibility and availability of policies and guidelines
  – Security organization (roles and responsibilities, CISO, team, involvement of business unit management, involvement of company management)
  – Security program management, prioritization, visibility
  – Risk management, consideration of security risks in business processes or projects (proactivity, adequacy of controls, etc.)
  – Asset management, classification, associated responsibilities (data owners) and security measures to protect infrastructure components

Security in relation to human resources (all topics related to people as actors in IS)
  – Support of the security team
  – Level of employee awareness, continued training, communication
  – Added value of security committees or representatives
  – Technical security skills needed in business lines

Security processes and their suitability to business needs
  – Effectiveness of security controls in business processes
  – Consideration of legal and regulatory compliance in security processes
  – Identity and access rights management
  – Continuity management
  – Physical security
  – Change management process, acquisition and developments
  – Outsourcing and supplier management
Technology
  – Internet and external communications
  – Office document protection system
  – Access to applications and IT resources
  – Adaptability of security solutions to new technologies

The abovementioned topics are not an exhaustive list of everything that can be addressed in a questionnaire for the business units. The goal here is not to formulate yet another method to evaluate security processes but rather, to propose a pragmatic approach that allows the quick identification of improvement points related to current operations. This exercise in itself should not present an obstacle to continuous improvement. Business representatives do not have a lot of time to spend discussing security. Results from initial meetings may help improve the questionnaire during periodic strategic reviews.

4.3.2.2 Gap Analysis Using the Maturity Model

A session to identify gaps in the perception of security maturity levels is a privileged moment in which to initiate constructive dialogue. The different topics and questions must be understood and discussed. It is therefore not recommended to send the questionnaire to different experts and hope that they will send back a maturity chart without any explanation or discussion. Business units should understand that the exercise is intended to provide relevant information to elaborate or review the security strategy. They should be willing to invest their time, hoping to have a return on that investment.

4.3.2.3 Consolidate Improvement Points into Initiatives

The first result of a gap analysis could be an important table of gaps by topic and business unit (Figure 4.7). As soon as the sessions with business leaders have made it possible to establish this mapping, the next step is to select the subjects that have the most significant gaps among the business units.

Topics are then grouped into initiatives. The following example shows improvement points consolidated into three initiatives.

EXAMPLE

1. *Review policies and guidelines* regarding the secure exchange of documents with external correspondents and the accessibility of confidential data on the move (e.g., encryption of personal data) and establish the corresponding operational controls.
2. *Establish security responsibilities in business units*: let the document owners manage access rights to office documents.
3. Plan a *certification of access rights* by business unit managers.

	BU 1	BU 2								BU m
Topic 1	4	12	6	4	12	4	12	6	4	12
Topic 2	2	4	2	6	2	5	4	9	6	2
	9	6	5	6	4	4	6	5	6	12
	6	12	8	4	12	6	12	2	12	9
	9	5	4	6	2	4	5	9	6	4
	4	12	12	4	12	4	12	6	4	12
	4	4	9	6	2	2	4	9	6	2
	12	6	5	6	12	12	6	12	6	12
	6	4	4	4	9	6	8	4	4	9
Topic n	8	5	2	6	2	9	5	8	6	5

Figure 4.7 Example of security services maturity gaps with estimated "Importance".

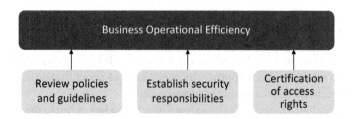

Figure 4.8 Security initiatives supporting business operations.

An exercise closing session with all the participants would be very beneficial to validate the results. In this way, participants could comment on the initiatives decided within their own units. Security initiatives supporting business operations can be summarized as follows (Figure 4.8).

4.3.3 Initiatives to Improve Information Security Effectiveness

Security, as a corporate or functional unit within or outside of IT, must also ensure the improvement of its own efficiency. IS vision and strategic initiatives can be established by observing risk evolution, maturity gaps, audit findings, strengths, weaknesses, opportunities, and threats (SWOT) analyses, technology evolution, organizational changes, regulations, resource availability, and so on.

The expected outcome from this phase will be

1. A vision for information security
2. Strategic initiatives to achieve this vision (Figure 4.9)

Contributing to business initiatives is an important goal. However, if security does not have the required capacity, an organization facilitating governance and management, and sufficient process maturity, it simply cannot aspire to become a reliable partner. A security committee under the leadership of the CISO should assess the state of security, set objectives, and choose initiatives that make it possible to reach them. There are different ways to set strategic objectives for IS:

SWOT analysis. An examination of the strengths, weaknesses, opportunities, and threats in different areas, such as the effectiveness of controls, technical solutions, organization and processes, finances and costs, human factors, the external environment, the legal and regulatory framework, and a comparison with similar industrial sectors, already gives us a good idea of potential improvement points.

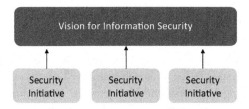

Figure 4.9 Security initiatives supporting the goals of improving maturity.

Maturity models. Maturity models can be used to show gaps between the maturity levels of current and desired processes. Many models exist and are often based on the standards. Specialized consulting firms or advisors will also be able to give an overview of benchmarks among companies in the same sector.

Audit findings. Audit recommendations are important drivers and justifications for new security initiatives. Boards of directors and management generally have great confidence in these recommendations.

Risk assessment. The risk assessment process helps identify the weaknesses of the controls in place and thus helps define objectives and more strategic initiatives.

New technologies. New technologies are increasingly in demand, and security must take this into account. Some justified requests will need quick adaptations (such as using different means of communication or consumerization) and others, which present a fundamental paradigm shift, will need more appropriate means (such as digitization, fintech, or blockchain).

An analysis of the security posture could lead to the same findings of maturity gaps already noted during interviews with the business units. In addition, gaps concerning the regulatory framework that is specific to security, the security of the infrastructures and applications, or certain technical controls can only be identified by security specialists.

EXAMPLE

Taking our example from the financial institution, suppose that the security team has identified the following two initiatives that should be implemented over the short term:

- Cybersecurity guidelines with specific organizational aspects
- Provisioning of access rights

In this case, the identity and access management initiatives previously identified and the provisioning of access rights will be integrated into an Identity and Access Management global initiative.

4.3.4 Grouping of Initiatives and Establishment of a Project Roadmap

The initiatives identified so far may overlap (e.g., between business and security objectives). So, the goal is to formulate an optimized or consolidated list of initiatives to support strategic business and IS objectives. These initiatives could also be broken down into projects and presented in the form of a roadmap.

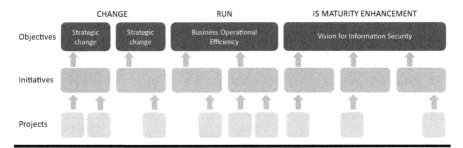

Figure 4.10   Set of initiatives and security projects.

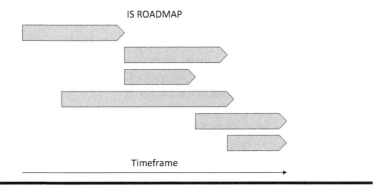

Figure 4.11   Roadmap of IS initiatives/projects.

The expected outcome from this phase will be

1. Security initiatives and projects supporting strategic objectives (Figure 4.10)
2. Initiative roadmap (planning in time) (Figure 4.11)

4.3.5 Formulation of a Strategy

Having established all the elements, we are finally able to formulate a security strategy. There are many examples of security strategy designs and presentations to draw from; however, it would be prudent to present our strategy by focusing on expressed business needs.

If we resume the strategy composition set out in Section 4.2 and take the example used throughout this chapter, we can summarize the strategy as follows. We will not formulate the mission, context, and roles and responsibilities, as they are specific to each organization. Strategic objectives and strategic security initiatives will be based on the example used throughout this chapter.

EXAMPLE

1. Mission
2. Context
3. Roles and Responsibilities
4. Strategic Objectives

IS ensures the protection of corporate assets and actively participates in business development. In particular, it helps achieve the following business objectives:

1. Introduce new financial products encompassing cryptocurrencies
2. Outsource some application infrastructures and storage to external cloud providers
3. Improve the operational efficiency of all the business units by adapting controls allowing business units greater autonomy in controlling access rights and adapting policies, procedures, and tools in the domain of data transfers and communication

The continuous improvement of company capabilities in line with risk appetite and cost optimization remains a strategic objective for IS. The new objectives are as follows:

1. Strengthen cyber-threat protection skills, in particular through stricter policies and guidelines that encompass a specific security organization
2. Automatize the management of access rights

5. Strategic Security Initiatives

Strategic security initiatives to support the objectives outlined previously for the coming period can be summarized as follows:

5.1. Establish security controls for cryptocurrencies

Goal: Offer security components to enable the introduction of financial products and services using cryptocurrencies

Success criteria: Entity's ability to offer products and services including cryptocurrencies easily and on demand

5.2. Assess the risk of using third-party cloud infrastructures and propose security measures

Goal: Establish a risk analysis and provide the company with a policy and guidelines having measurable key criteria that allow business units to decide quickly and intelligently whether and how much they want to outsource the management of application infrastructures and storage to third-party clouds.

Success criteria: Ability to deploy solutions in the external cloud with a defined and assured security baseline

5.3. Delegate security responsibility to the business units

Goal: Transfer certain controls to the business units to optimize resources and operational efficiency. In this context, the following responsibilities will take priority:

- Responsibility for assigning access rights, periodic verification, and update requests
- Management of security risk related to business unit processes

Success criteria: Reduction of the timeframe when providing access rights

5.4. Define Cybersecurity Policy

Goal: Formulate a cybersecurity policy for the company. Once the policy has been accepted by the board of directors, security will ensure that lower-level guidelines and documents are drafted to create a cyber-threat protection system.

Success criteria: All the business units as well as corporate departments, IT, and HR will be aware of cyber threats and the means of protection against cyberattacks. Effective controls will be put in place to ensure the adequate resilience of the operations according to service-level agreements (SLAs) to be defined.

5.5. Identity and Access Management

Goals: Manage identities and access rights to company resources in a more automated way by applying management principles based on roles or business rules. Provide business units with the opportunity to verify their employees' access rights themselves.

Success criteria: Heads of business units are able to carry out the annual certification of access rights. Reaction time and the allocation of access rights to a new employee should decrease by 10%, all else being unchanged (same number of requests for the same number of operators).

The strategic objectives supported by the security initiatives are shown as follows:

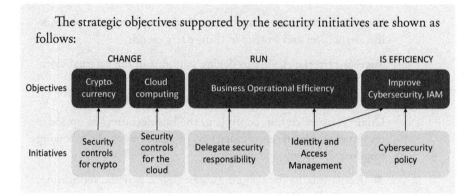

How should a security strategy be communicated?

4.4 Security Strategy Communication

When preparing a strategy document, avoid presenting security initiatives solely as protection against threats. This gives a sense of prohibition instead of reinforcement. We know that security controls are designed to reduce risk, but they also help create the conditions to deploy new solutions. Therefore, it is better to use positive terms and say that security measures help to achieve strategic goals instead of negative terms that point out their limitations. Emphasize what security measures make possible instead of enumerating what they prevent, reduce, or prohibit.

EXAMPLE

Security contributions can be expressed in two ways.

Negative Approach	Positive Approach
Reduce the risk of data leakage from PC loss or theft	Facilitate work on the move by ensuring the confidentiality of PC content
Prohibit unauthorized access to applications	Protect a company's confidential and important information by optimizing access rights
Reduce cyberattack risk against web servers (DOS—Denial Of Service)	Improve the resilience of infrastructures and ensure continuing service to web customers
Prohibit sending messages containing confidential data	Facilitate use of the means of communication while ensuring data confidentiality

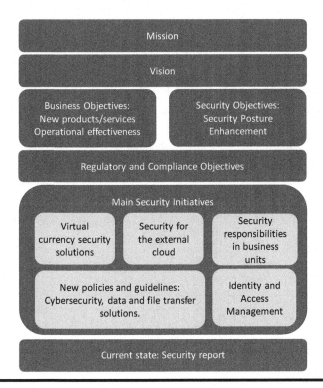

Figure 4.12   Simple presentation of a security strategy.

The "Strategy" document is a starting point for more detailed presentations or explanations. Strategic initiatives or objectives can be presented in a much more visual way at annual meetings or corporate events. The example in Figure 4.12 is the presentation of a security strategy on a page.

4.5 Conclusion

Establishing a formal company security strategy is of paramount importance in security governance. This step should not be underestimated, since it influences the security processes, organization, activities, and controls that will be put in place. The strategy document is important, but the process leading to it is even more important, because it strengthens the collaboration of all the stakeholders and legitimizes the results achieved.

To maintain a pragmatic orientation, it is often not necessary to proceed through all the listed steps. Some managers or board members may already have a very clear idea of what their security program needs to achieve and therefore, do not need to analyze and build consensus among the business units, especially since this exercise could inadvertently provide an opportunity for units to compete for security or IT resources.

The process and tools to formulate a security strategy presented in this chapter are just one example of what can be done in this area. The importance lies in adopting a formal approach to the establishment and revision of a security strategy. This will lead to better governance, put security issues on decision-makers' agendas, and strengthen prioritization with the collaboration of all the stakeholders around a common goal.

Chapter 5

Policies

Security policies and lower-level instructions consolidate the principles applied in operations to protect company assets. They should contain instructions for all the information system users in the course of their work. Policies and instructions also serve as a reference of conformity for auditors. They are therefore an important level of information security (IS) governance.

All the stakeholders call for clear security rules. Management needs a regulatory framework that reassures partners, promotes the deployment of a coherent security architecture, and dispels the doubts of engineers in charge of setting up technical controls. Security officers are unanimous in their belief that high-level policies and operational instructions are critical to the success of any security program. However, developing security regulations in the current context presents a challenge for security managers. Business diversity, geographical distribution, different legislations, outsourcing operations, interdependence with suppliers, customer diversity, and new technologies are only a few of the features of what can be called an *extended enterprise*.

This chapter provides answers to the following questions:

- What is an internal regulatory framework?
- What is the difference between a policy, a guideline, and a standard?
- How should regulatory framework documents be organized?
- What is included in a security policy, and how is it structured?
- How is a documentation framework set up?

What is an internal regulatory framework?

5.1 Internal Regulatory Framework Principles

An internal regulatory framework can be defined as a set of policies, guidelines, and lower-level instructions that impose rules on company operations. With respect to security, this framework encompasses all the policies, guidelines, and standards dealing with conduct, setting up and using controls to protect the confidentiality, availability, and integrity of the company's assets. Before explaining how to develop and maintain internal regulation, let us recall the following key points.

An internal regulatory framework is a governance tool. It translates, in terms more binding and directly applicable to the company's processes, a certain strategic desire to protect assets. It should reflect the needs of the business and support its operations. It must be elaborated with the business units for their needs and be validated and complete (without gaps or ambiguity). It must be understood, acknowledged, and supported by management. In the absence of regulations, operational units (including information technology [IT]) will make subjective interpretations of protection requirements and controls, which will weaken the architecture and the protection system as a whole.

EXAMPLE

Sometimes, in the absence of clear guidelines on certain topics, one might be tempted to advocate using standards such as ISO 27001/2, especially for the needs of security specialists responsible for implementing operational controls. Taking this shortcut is obviously not acceptable, since the standards do not advocate how to meet requirements. As noted previously, different solutions exist for each requirement depending on a company's context. Therefore, it is important for the internal regulatory framework to be complete. Standards can be used as a reference to ensure that all areas have been covered.

Regulatory framework documents must cover all security instructions and be easily accessible to every employee. They should be available on the intranet in a framework or structure that is easily understandable and facilitates consultation and research by different criteria. An internal regulatory framework needs to be reviewed and adapted regularly according to defined processes. One or more committees must be in charge of their validation, publication, and adaptation. The main features of a regulatory framework are that it should be implementable, realistic, consistent, comprehensive, enforceable, directive, documented, and accessible.

A policy (high-level document) must remain neutral in relation to the products or technical solutions used to implement it. It must be resistant to technological changes and stable over time. Security policies must clearly express the requirements based on a description of the company's risk-related security posture. In real terms, this means that principles recognized as useful at the highest level of management must be clearly expressed instead of remaining vague and leaving room for doubt.

EXAMPLE

It is better to use this wording:

"To protect our data and resources, we advocate the systematic application of the least privilege principle in all control processes—only persons who really need classified or confidential data to carry out their operational activities will be granted access to them"

instead of this wording:

"To protect our data and resources, we advocate the application of centralized and rule-based access rights management."

The board of directors and its management must validate policies, be responsible for them, and guarantee their application. All security controls or program improvement initiatives will be based on a policy or guidelines accepted or validated by governance bodies.

What is the difference between a policy, a guideline, and a standard?

5.2 Classification of Regulatory Framework Documents

Internal regulatory framework documents can be classified in different ways. Following is a classification that is found most often in companies.

5.2.1 Classification by Document Nature or Hierarchy

Policies, as top-level documents, encompass the requirements and objectives set by management and the board of directors. For them to be implemented, they should be accompanied by more explanatory documents, which may be called *guidelines*, *standards*, or *procedures*. Hierarchical classification allows them to be organized according to the level of document abstraction or scope. Such a representation is shown in Figure 5.1.

Policies may be preceded by a very special document called a *charter*. A security charter is a single document, valid for the entire company, that includes the highest-level statements of intent and expresses the will of the board and the management. This short document (one to two pages) gives a vision for security, presents

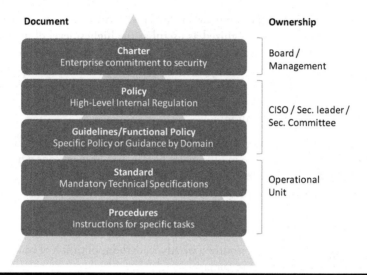

Figure 5.1   Hierarchy of documents in a regulatory framework.

global objectives, expresses risk appetite, sets guidelines for security organization, and gives a clear mandate for security program management. Considered the property of the board and management, it is signed by their representatives and engages their responsibility in its implementation.

Policies are documents at the highest level of the hierarchy. They reflect the wishes expressed in the charter and translate them into binding terms for all the stakeholders. Policies explain how to protect the fundamental assets of the company, guide everyone's security efforts, and ensure legal and regulatory compliance. In general, they consist of the following components:

- An explanation of the context
- The raison d'être of the policy
- General principles
- The scope and its recipients
- Governance imperatives of the security management system
- The internal regulatory framework
- The organization of security system management, the primary functions and responsibilities of all actors in the field of security, including user responsibilities, and a description of security postures in all areas

Policies are validated by the board and management but remain the property of the security committees and the CISO.

Guidelines, directives, or functional policies are documents that summarize security requirements for processes, business units, or specific areas. They may also contain more detailed explanations of certain policy concepts, such as the responsibilities of data owners, how technologies or products are used (Internet, mobile devices, cloud computing), the employee code of conduct, and so on. This level of document hierarchy in the internal regulatory framework does not refer to the names of specific technologies or products and is under the responsibility of the CISO and security committees in charge of supervision.

Standards translate the requirements of policies and guidelines into operational terms for system users. These are specific instructions in relation to top-level requirements such as baseline security specifications, system security configurations, instructions for using mobile devices, encryption systems or document protection, password rules, emergency procedures, and so on. These documents are developed by and the property of the heads of the operational units (business units for instructions specific to their operations) or IT for everything related to securing the systems.

Procedures or documents of the lowest level can be seen as "recipes." These are technical documents that specify in detail the operational procedures (e.g., procedures for hardening, encryption, password recovery, etc.). They are the responsibility and the property of persons in charge of the products or procedures in question.

EXAMPLE

To illustrate the differences between the levels of regulatory documents, we will use two examples: identity and access rights management and data protection.

IDENTITY AND ACCESS RIGHTS MANAGEMENT

Security Charter:

> "We advocate centralized management and the supervision of access rights ..."

At the policy or functional policy level:

> "Access rights are assigned based on business roles ... Business roles are established by business unit managers ... Roles are built on the principle of least privilege (sufficient to perform a specific task) ... Data Owners validate data access requests ... The organization, roles and responsibilities are as follows ..."

At the standard level (operations):

> "When authorization has been given by the employee's manager and HR, the operator triggers the privilege provision process on different platforms."

DATA PROTECTION

Security Charter:

"Our data must be protected according to their level of confidentiality ..."

At the policy or functional policy level:

"Data classification is as follows ... Data protection rules by class are as follows ... Any application processing data classified as highly confidential must use a strong authentication system ..."

At the standard level (operations):

"To develop applications using strong authentication the following standards should be used ..."

The hierarchical classification of internal regulation documents is mentioned most often in security literature. We can consider the number of documents to be inversely proportional to their hierarchical level, hence forming a pyramid.

5.2.2 Classification by Business Unit or Business Sector

Large companies with several separate or geographically distributed business units could opt for different regulatory frameworks for their units. R&D and sales in pharmaceutical industry may not have the same risk appetite. The former deal with confidential data and can thus adopt a series of protective measures which would not be acceptable by the latter.

The requirements of internal regulations can thus vary within the same company. This is called *segregation* or *differentiation* of the security regulatory framework. Despite its simplicity, segregating the regulatory framework runs into difficulties, since the same IT infrastructures are used. Take the example of the virtualization of application servers. If a company's IT architecture does not take data classification level into account as part of its physical architecture, it could happen that the same physical servers host the application servers of different classes of confidentiality. This could prevent the segregation of regulations on access rights or availability, or at least make it very difficult. When IT infrastructures are shared by business units with differing risk appetites, a single policy adapted to units with the lowest risk appetite will penalize the others.

We could theoretically have different internal regulations by business unit, activity sector, geographical distribution, and so on (Figure 5.2).

Figure 5.2   Segregated internal regulations.

EXAMPLE

With the availability of personal productivity applications and mobile devices such as smartphones, tablets, or laptops, internal regulations can authorize the use of such devices (bring your own device [BYOD]) depending on the risk appetite of each unit. These devices will probably be prohibited in a watch manufacturer's assembly department but authorized in the marketing and sales departments.

5.2.3 Classification by Domain

Many security domains, such as identity and access management (IAM), mobility, IT development, human risk, or new technologies, may require a set of internal regulatory documents ranging from policy to technical procedures. In such a case, a third dimension must be included, which is the regulation of a specific domain across all business units (Figure 5.3).

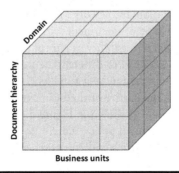

Figure 5.3   Three-dimensional regulatory framework.

EXAMPLES

IAM processes can vary from one organizational unit to another in the same company, particularly following major restructuring, mergers, or acquisitions. Consequently, the policies, guidelines, and standards linked to this activity could differ among the units.

Internal regulations on the use of mobile devices could also vary from one company unit to another depending on risk appetite, data characteristics, applications in use, and so on.

Geographical units could operate under different legislations and thus use guidelines adapted to their operational processes.

How should internal regulatory framework documents be organized?

5.3 Documentation Framework for Internal Regulations

Every company needs a documentation framework for its internal regulations ranging from policy to procedures. The design of this framework is very important, because it facilitates an understanding of the regulations and their acceptance by the employees, strengthens governance, and allows easy maintenance by those who are responsible. The matrix or three-dimensional document framework presented earlier is suitable for large companies with a diversity of business units and risk appetites. Smaller firms obviously do not need to develop such structures and could be satisfied with a document summarizing the rules for business operations and a set of standards for IT.

The mistake that we often see is an accumulation of documents of different hierarchical levels that sometimes overlap with very little room left for a more formally organized documentation framework. It is therefore important to clearly define the location of each type of document within a company or business unit, thereby facilitating document accessibility as part of the company's intranet.

In cases where there is no need to differentiate policies or guidelines between business units, classification by hierarchy is sufficient. Companies that need to segregate policies according to the nature of the business can use a simplified version of the three-dimensional model as shown in Figure 5.4.

The security charter and general policy remain unique for the entire company. Some differences in security policies, risk appetite, organization, or context may exist within this same policy for different business units, provided they are clearly presented. In the intersections between domains and units, documents of different levels will be found concerning a specific domain (e.g., mobility) for a specific unit

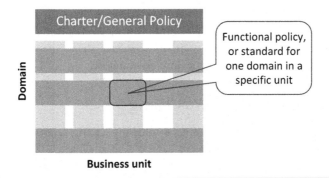

Figure 5.4   Two-dimensional regulatory framework.

(e.g., sales). If it is necessary to have a policy for a specific domain, we can use the term *functional policy*.

Functional policies are extremely useful when a very high-level set of rules is needed in a specific domain. Here are some features of the target domain that can be used when deciding whether to establish a functional policy specific to it or to adapt the general security policy:

■ Some singularities in the context (internal or external)
■ Specific nature of risks, threats, and vulnerabilities
■ Specific features of the legal and regulatory framework
■ Characteristic aspects in security organization (roles and responsibilities)
■ Domain-specific concepts and terminologies
■ Particularities of the controls to put in place

EXAMPLE

Cybersecurity, personal data protection, and IAM can be seen as specific areas or security domains that deserve their own functional policies.

What is included in a security policy, and how is it structured?

5.4 Content of a Security Charter and Policy

In what follows, we will see the content of a charter and a policy (or a functional policy) in more detail. There is no universally recognized model or framework considered the best for a security policy. Each organization can design its policy document according to its needs. There are, however, some general recommendations that can be given regarding a policy's content and form. They are intended to make it more readable, more comprehensive, and ultimately more useful to all the stakeholders in the organization. Some main outlines have already been stated. We will now see how they translate concretely into documents.

5.4.1 Contents of a Security Charter

The highest-level document expressing a company's main security orientation to protect its property may take different names, such as Charter, Code of Conduct, Statement of Intent, and so on. It communicates management's strong commitment to security and formulates the mandate given to it. A security charter describes a company's main objectives with regard to IS without specifying how to achieve them. It expresses management's commitment to its protection system by referring to the context of business conduct, compliance with the legal and regulatory framework, the requirements for ethical employee behavior, the values and culture of the company, the principles of security protection and individual responsibilities. The main chapters and a summary of their contents are as follows.

Introduction or context
- Presentation of the context and main issues for the company, its constraints, and the importance it gives to the protection of its values
- Reminder of the company's culture and the reasons why it supports security efforts
- Expression of willingness to have an adequate security system
- Corporate responsibility for the protection of assets including personal information (customers, employees, suppliers, etc.)

Scope and target audience
- Presentation of the charter's scope and to whom it is addressed
- Special mention of the importance of the documentation framework and its usefulness in managing the security program

High-level responsibilities
- Summary presentation of strategic roles and responsibilities: data owners, governing bodies, executive security management, employee responsibilities, and so on

Some principles to be mentioned
- Protecting company values
- Risk management
- Employee rights and responsibilities

Managerial objectives
- Security governance and organization objectives
- Security management objectives and involvement in the company's operations

5.4.2 Content of a Security Policy

A policy or functional policy states the broad orientations and guiding principles for security as a whole or for a specific domain. There are many examples of security policies. The following is a summary of the main chapters as an example without claiming to be exhaustive.

Introduction or context
- Internal and external context of the company, the issues and importance of the security policy with regard to achieving business objectives
- Purpose of the policy, area to be covered, and the reason for its existence
- Announcement of high-level requirements

Scope and target audience
- Scope of the present policy—to whom it is addressed and who should apply it
- Principles on which the policy is based (regulatory and normative frameworks)
- Purpose of the policy and the wishes of the initiators or owners of the policy

Positioning of the policy in the internal regulatory framework
- Reminder, if necessary, of the documentation framework of internal regulations and the (hierarchical) positioning of this policy

Principles
- Enumeration of the fundamental principles of the policy (what the policy seeks to achieve)

Policy statements
- High-level statements that lay down the objectives of the policy
- Explanation of each statement's rationale, its raison d'être, and how it should be applied (without mentioning how it should be done)

Organization, roles, and responsibilities
- Governance and management of the information security
- Main functions and responsibilities: board of directors, committees, management, security team and CISO, business units and their security representatives, IT and operations, data owners, and security specialists
- Responsibility of all the employees and their obligation to comply with the policy
- Responsible, accountable, consulted and informed (RACI) matrix summarizing the responsibilities of all functions involved

Orientations by specific areas
    Top-level guidance for some security areas or domains may be included in a general policy if there is no need to develop specific functional policies.

- Risk management concept
- Human security
- Definition of assets and requirements for their protection
- Physical security (safety)
- Data protection, data privacy
- IT security (acquisition, configuration, change management, use, outsourcing)
- Business continuity
- IAM
- Compliance
- Incident management
- Reporting system
- Additional explanations specific to a domain (e.g., categories of cyberattacks if it is a cybersecurity functional policy)

Disciplinary action in the case of noncompliance
Review process
Glossary
- Explanation of some specific terms for greater clarity

How is a documentation framework set up?

5.5 Process of Establishing a Regulatory Framework

Finally, how should we proceed to build or review an internal regulatory framework? What are the steps to develop policies, guidelines, or standards? Can we use templates, and most importantly, how can we make sure that the framework is complete?

There are multiple answers to these questions. Remember, however, that it is not desirable to build a documentation framework based on predefined examples or templates, since this weakens security governance. If management views a documentation framework as useless, then it is better to do nothing than to build one as an alibi. Senior executives need to be involved and validate policy content at different levels. The documents of a regulatory framework must also serve all the employees in the performance of their daily tasks. It must therefore be designed and accepted by all the stakeholders.

There follow some pragmatic steps suitable for both the construction and the revision of a regulatory framework.

1. Preparation
1.1 Understand the business context and strategy, especially with respect to risk appetites and security needs in different business units. Understand the existing framework and whether it is partially adapted or not.

1.2 Understand which assets need to be protected. If necessary, map the data, flows, and applications in collaboration with the business units. Classify, if not already done, these assets according to the standards of the company or according to an ad hoc classification (e.g., public, limited, confidential).

1.3 Review the catalog of security risks, risk assessments, and associated controls. Establish, if possible, a maturity map of the controls associated with the main risks.

1.3 Decide whether to segregate general policies between the different units. If the company is engaged in different businesses with different risk appetites, the units should be considered as companies with differentiated approaches to developing their regulatory frameworks.

1.4 Define the architecture of the regulatory framework (based on the three dimensions explained previously or some other). Decide how the regulatory framework will be accessed.

1.5 Identify who will participate in the development of the regulatory framework; ideally, they will be representatives of management, the business units, and IT. Ensure that management and the board feel that they own what will become the charter and general corporate security policy.

2. Policy elaboration

2.1 Discuss and decide on the organization and functions of security governance and management (see more in Chapter 6, Organization).

2.2 With the team in charge of implementing security controls and those in charge of business unit operations, identify important points requiring clarification in the regulatory framework. This bottom-up approach is crucial, as this will ultimately give legitimacy to the future policy. This can be done through a questionnaire or security process maturity model developed as part of the strategy (see the previous chapter).

2.3 Establish the charter and general security policy in collaboration with members of the team. Use the layout proposed in previous chapters.

2.4 Have the business units and IT validate the charter and the policy. This is very important, because the charter and the policy should be fully supported by operations. Stick to the SMART rule (specific, measurable, agreeable, realistic and time-bound).

2.5 Ensure that policies are validated by the board and management.

3. Developing functional policies or guidelines

3.1 Set up a team of people involved in the operational management of specific security domains requiring a particular functional policy (e.g. cybersecurity, IAM, continuity, mobility, or data protection). Ensure that this policy is supported by a leader or person responsible for its future application.

3.2 Proceed with developing the functional policies as for a general policy (2.1–2.5).

4. Establishing standards

When establishing internal standards, ISO 27001 (and its Annex A) can be used as a checklist to verify the completeness and coverage of the regulatory framework.

Table 5.1 presents a proposal for document positioning in an internal regulatory framework dealing with the requirements of ISO 27001. Standards, of course, must follow the recommendations of policies, guidelines, or functional policies and provide other necessary instructions to operations. If a requirement is not specifically mentioned in Table 5.1, it will be dealt with by a higher-level document. For example, "A.11 Physical and Environmental Security" and all the lower-level requirements will be covered in the Physical Security Functional Policy document.

The following is a checklist of whether all precautions were taken during the development of the regulatory framework.

1. Do our internal regulation documents have a good level of granularity?

   Business characteristics define the correct level of granularity. For an enterprise with all operational functions controlled internally, high granularity (few details) may be sufficient.
2. Have we covered all the subjects?

   If not, identify the gaps, communicate them, and plan the corrections. This primarily concerns future topics such as regulations on new technologies or threats. Internal project planning or a project roadmap to elaborate new regulatory documents is very useful for audits and all the stakeholders. We can also take advantage of change projects to include the development of a functional policy or missing procedures.
3. Can we optimize the regulatory framework and eventually remove, lighten, or reorganize certain documents?

   Before developing a new functional policy, see whether it would be better to include it in an existing policy or directive and then bring it up to date. For example, policies on the protection of personal data could be integrated into existing data protection policies.
4. Are our internal regulations up to date and accessible to everyone? Have we established review processes and responsibilities for all the regulatory framework documents?

Last, remember that a documentation framework that has no perceived value for the business units, IT, and corporate and HR functions has no reason to exist. The best way to ensure its adequacy is to submit it systematically and as often as possible to key stakeholders during awareness sessions, when launching new change projects, or during coordination sessions between security and the business units.

Table 5.1   Positioning Documents in an Internal Regulatory Framework Dealing with the Requirements of the ISO 27001 Standard

ISO 27001 Reference Control Objective (Annex A)	Position in a Framework
A.5 Information security policies	Internal regulatory framework
A.6 Organization of information security	Policy
A.6.2 Mobile devices and teleworking	Guideline / Functional policy
A.7 Human resource security	Guideline / Functional policy
A.8 Asset management	Guideline / Functional policy
A.8.2 Information classification	Policy
A.8.3 Media handling	Standard / Procedure
A.9 Access control	Guideline / Functional policy
A.9.2.1 User registration and de-registration	Standard / Procedure
A.9.2.2 User access provisioning	Standard / Procedure
A.9.2.3 Management of privileged access rights	Standard / Procedure
A.9.2.4 Management of secret authentication information of users	Standard / Procedure
A.9.2.5 Review of user access rights	Standard / Procedure
A.9.2.6 Removal or adjustment of access rights	Standard / Procedure
A.9.3 User responsibilities	Policy
A.9.4 System and application access control	Standard / Procedure
A.10 Cryptography	Standard / Procedure
A.11 Physical and environmental security	Standard / Procedure
A.12 Operations security	Standard / Procedure
A.13 Communications securrity	Standard / Procedure

(Continued)

Table 5.1 (CONTINUED)   Positioning Documents in an Internal Regulatory Framework Dealing with the Requirements of the ISO 27001 Standard

ISO 27001 Reference Control Objective (Annex A)	Position in a Framework
A.14 System acquisition, development and maintenance	Standard / Procedure
A.15 Supplier relationships	Guideline / Functional policy
A.16 Information security incident management	Standard / Procedure
A.17 Information security aspects of business continuity management	Guideline / Functional policy
A.18 Compliance	Policy / Guideline

5.6 Conclusion

We have presented in this chapter the importance and different characteristics of the internal regulatory framework and a methodical approach to establishing or revising it. It is obviously not a question of recipes that must be followed at all costs and literally, but rather, the principles on which we can rely, the needs of each organization being different. However, it is important to bear in mind the objective of establishing this framework: the collection of all instructions to facilitate the application of protection strategies. The company can adopt different forms or documentary frameworks for its lower-level policies and documents, but they must be comprehensive and consistent and meet the needs of all stakeholders.

Chapter 6

Organization

The term *security organization* includes different functions, organizational units, roles, and responsibilities within the framework of an information security management system (ISMS). It is broadly defined in the general policy based on requirements mentioned in the charter. If security organization is defective, a company might not explicitly cover certain responsibilities, leading to shortcomings in the program and weakening the company's posture and the protection of its assets.

Providing a company with security organization adapted to its needs is one of the main responsibilities of management and the board of directors. Appointing a security officer is not enough. The company's issues and context must be thoroughly understood to propose adequate security organization.

This chapter gives answers to these key questions:

- What are the main roles and responsibilities in an ISMS?
- How will the role of the chief information security officer (CISO) and their team evolve?
- What are the main security organizational structures?
- What skills will be needed in the future?

What are the main roles and responsibilities in an ISMS?

6.1 Roles and Responsibilities in Information Security (IS)

As already mentioned, there is no clear boundary between governance and security management. Taking another look at our diagram of the continuum between strategy and operations (see Figure 1.3, Chapter 1), we can say that governance tasks are distributed generally among the following functions:

- Board of directors
- Security committees
- Business unit management (including the chief information officer [CIO])

while operational management tasks are divided between the following functions:

- The CISO and their team
- Security operations management (Figure 6.1)

The board of directors is the supreme body of corporate governance and as such, of IS governance. It is accountable for risks and actions taken to mitigate them, validates strategies, makes sure that resources are used responsibly, and is the privileged recipient of performance reports and audits. Monitoring performance is part of its responsibilities vis-à-vis the stakeholders. For the board of directors, compliance with the legal and regulatory frameworks should result from healthy management and not be a goal in itself.

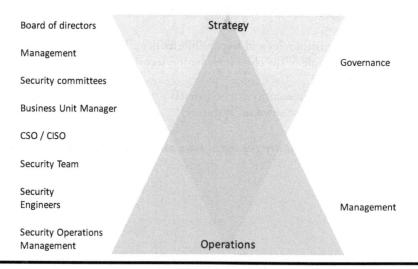

Figure 6.1   Distribution of responsibilities within governance and management.

Security committees can be formed on demand with various responsibilities: to establish or validate strategies and policies, prioritize initiatives, decide on issues requiring a strategic decision, or represent the board and management in all security program decision-making processes. These committees can take different forms and usually consist of representatives of the business units, corporate and human resources (HR) functions, information technology (IT) management, and the CISO.

Business unit managers generally have an important role to play in coordinating and supporting security initiatives as part of a defined strategy. Since the strategy was developed with the business units for their needs, unit managers actively take part in disseminating and supporting a security culture within their respective units. This goal is aided by the CISO's role in coordinating and strategically aligning security with the needs of the business units and management.

The CISO and their team play a vital role in the company's security organization, because they centralize the majority of management and security operational activities. The importance and responsibilities of the CISO and their team have been increasingly recognized in recent years. They have greater visibility, take on more strategic responsibilities, are more governance and risk oriented, and report more and more outside of IT and to C-level executives.

EXAMPLE

In the current context requiring tighter control of costs while ensuring IS compliance with regulatory requirements or technological developments, CISOs are increasingly invited to participate in strategic decisions and report to bodies outside IT.

Technological changes, new business models, and process digitalization present companies with new challenges. New responsibilities are increasingly proposed to the CISO not only in security risk mitigation related to new technologies but also in the domain of governance. These include

- Reporting and security communication to the governing body, committees, and business units
- Proposing the security strategy
- Developing the regulatory framework
- Implementing security controls and program management
- Security risk management (identification, assessment, and treatment)
- Developing an awareness program for all the stakeholders
- Monitoring (threats, vulnerabilities, compliance, and control efficiency)

Operations managers and security specialists are part of the teams in charge of operating the security controls, tools, and other technical solutions. They are primarily in charge of

- Infrastructure security (network, servers, workstations, and endpoints)
- Equipment management (firewalls and intrusion prevention/detection systems [IPS/IDS])
- Security information and event management (SIEM)
- Security Operation Center (SOC)
- Incident management
- Identity and access management

The ISO 27014 standard specifies two main bodies in IS governance: the governing body and executive management. They act jointly within governance processes, as mentioned in Chapter 1. The governing body has essentially a decision-making role. It may consist of members of management, the board, or business unit managers. A security committee can also play this role. The tasks of executive management can be assumed by the IS manager and the CISO and their team.

EXAMPLE

Let us take the example of "Monitor" (achieving strategic objectives) in the ISO 27014 standard. This process requires several inputs, some of which should be the responsibility of the governing body, including:

- Assess the effectiveness of information security management activities.
- Ensure conformance with internal and external requirements.
- Consider the changing business, legal and regulatory environment and their potential impact on information risk.

However, it is often found in practice that the CISO and their team take charge of these tasks, which are intended to help in decision-making, because management considers them most qualified. The effectiveness of the ISMS is evaluated by the security specialists themselves, the degree of compliance is appraised by the CISO, and the need for change is presented without formal risk analysis or assessment of the return on investment. This obviously does not encourage the governing body to assume its security responsibilities.

Collaboration between the governing body and IS management can also be schematized by an iterative process aimed at continuously improved alignment between controls in place and the needs of the company (Figure 6.2). The governing body sets security objectives derived from company objectives. These objectives then have a decisive influence on the IS program, which is under the responsibility of the CISO. Controls will be deployed to meet protection needs. The CISO will monitor the effectiveness of the controls and report back to the governing body, which can then adjust high-level objectives, and so on.

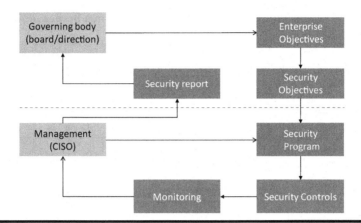

Figure 6.2 Distribution of roles and responsibilities between governance and management.

The CISO is therefore responsible for implementation of the program, controls, and operations. Strategy, risk appetite, and security policies remain the responsibility of the governing body. Translating the strategy into IS objectives and then into an action plan and controls is the responsibility of the CISO.

We can also summarize the main responsibilities in the governance and management of IS by a responsible, accountable, consulted and informed (RACI) matrix applied to the three-level control framework (TLCF) model (Table 6.1).

Another representation of the responsibilities that should be assumed by the governance functions identified earlier is given in Table 6.2. If we take the objective "Strategic Alignment," the role of the board of directors is to "Set directions for a demonstrable alignment," whereas the role of the CISO is to "Develop security strategy, oversee the security program and initiatives." The role of the board in performance measurement is to "Set directions for reporting of security effectiveness."

Finally, regardless of how governance and management bodies are set up, the extent of their prerogatives must always be borne in mind. In small companies, several functions will be performed by the same person, whereas in larger organizations, there might be entire teams.

How will the role of security officer evolve?

6.2 New Demands on the CISO and Their Team

Technical controls are essential and form the basis of any security program (also called instance of security program). However, the reactive approach in building this system does not guarantee optimal protection, especially not today with the

Table 6.1 Responsibilities of the Different Governance Bodies in the TLCF Blocks

R: Responsible A: Accountable C: Consulted I: Informed	Board	Management	CISO and Team	IT	HR	Business Unit
Strategy	A	I	R	C	C	C
Regulatory framework	I	A	R	C	C	C
Charter	A	I	R	C	C	C
Policies	I	A	R	C	C	C
Guidelines	I	A	R	C	C	C
Standards	I	I	A	R	R	R
Risk management	A	I	R	C	C	C
Program management	I	A	R	C	C	C
Reporting and Oversight	A	I	R	C	C	C
Asset management	I	A	C	R	R	R
Compliance management	A	I	R	C	C	C
Metrics and KPI	A	I	R	C	C	C

development of new business models, activities extending outside the company perimeter, and new means of communication. A new approach is needed in organizing the activities of the CISO and their team, particularly in developing strategies, integrating business units when a security program is set up, improving the adaptation of controls to business unit needs, and a proactive approach to risk. The reasons for this are multiple.

Technology cannot adapt quickly to new threats coming not only from cyberspace but also from inside the company, caused by new communication technologies and IT consumerization, extending activities, and integrating the services of third parties. Company boundaries are no longer rigid, and the trend of extending activities creates new challenges for security managers. To adapt to this evolution, CISOs must improve their planning and justify their initiatives by adopting a program based on company realities.

Table 6.2 Distribution of Responsibilities among Different IS Governance Bodies

Management Level	Strategic Alignment	Risk Management	Value Delivery	Performance Measurement	Resource Management	Integration
Board of directors/trustees	Set direction for a demonstrable alignment	Set direction for a risk management policy that applies to all activities and regulatory compliance.	Set direction for reporting of security activity costs and value of information protected.	Set direction for reporting of security effectiveness.	Set direction for a policy of knowledge management and resource utilization.	Set direction for a policy of assuring process integration.
Senior executives	Institute processes to integrate security with business objectives.	Ensure that roles and responsibilities include risk management in all activities. Monitor regulatory compliance.	Require business case studies of security initiatives and value of information protected.	Require monitoring and metrics for reporting security activities.	Ensure processes for knowledge capture and efficiency metrics.	Provide oversight of all management process functions and plans for integration.
Steering committee	Review and assist security strategy and integration efforts, ensure that business unit managers and process owners support integration.	Identify emerging risks, promote business unit security practices, and identify compliance issues.	Review and advise adequacy of security initiatives to serve business functions and value delivered in terms of enabled services.	Review and advise the extent to which security initiatives meet business objectives.	Review processes for knowledge capture and dissemi-nation	Identify critical business processes and management assurance providers. Direct assurance integration efforts.

(Continued)

Table 6.2 (CONTINUED)   Distribution of Responsibilities among Different IS Governance Bodies

Management Level	Strategic Alignment	Risk Management	Value Delivery	Performance Measurement	Resource Management	Integration
Chief information security officer	Develop security strategy, oversee the security program and initiatives, and liaise with business unit managers and process owners for ongoing alignment.	Ensure risk and business impact assessments, develop risk mitigation strategies, and enforce policy and regulatory compliance.	Monitor utilization and effective-ness of security resources and reputation and the delivery of trust.	Develop and implement monitoring and metrics collection and analysis and reporting approaches. Direct and monitor security activities.	Develop methods for knowledge capture and dissemi-nation. Develop metrics for effectiveness and efficiency.	Liaise with other management process functions. Ensure that gaps and overlaps are identified and addressed.

Source: Information Security Governance: Guidance for Boards of Directors and Executive Management, 2nd edition, IT Governance Institute, 2006

This new context requires a review of the organization of security teams. The activities of operational security teams need to be more integrated into business operations and with broader skills than just technical. These changes will bring greater acknowledgement of CISOs and their teams and acceptance of them as a partner in business development discussions. The security team will no longer be composed exclusively of specialists in protection technologies. Its positioning in the overall organization will depend on company characteristics and real needs. In the most complex situations, it will not only ensure technology operations and deployment but also deal with risks and architectures while ensuring effective coordination with business units and governance.

The demands on security are increasing. The current context, technological evolutions in the digital economy, and the interdependence of economic partners play an important role in the growing demands being made of security officers and their teams. Boards of directors and management require CISOs to provide optimal protection and deliver tangible value to the business units, but in a context of stagnant budgets. The CISO's position is also changing from technical manager within IT to a more executive role reporting directly to the highest levels in the company or C-level.

Although this evolution of the CISO's responsibilities is certainly encouraging, it is not always accompanied by the necessary revision of underlying organizations. Boards and management often ask the CISO and their teams to take on more responsibility without the necessary investments and adaptation of resources. The relative immaturity of corporate security governance certainly has something to do with it. This results in CISOs and security teams that are often overwhelmed by new tasks. They continue to struggle against increasingly sophisticated threats and fail to meet expectations regarding a greater focus on strategy, governance, and proactive risk management.

Traditionally focused on operations, the CISO and their team must now extend their activities and become more involved in managing initiatives for better governance, compliance, and alignment with business goals. Their scope of security responsibilities is expanding and now ranges from strategy to operations. This "big gap" in the continuum between strategies, needs, and business requirements and the necessary reinforcement of operational protections in the current context of cyber threats and employee IT consumerization will intensify in the future (Figure 6.3).

It is obvious that with no change in resources, security teams are unable to ensure smoothly running operations and meet strategic needs while managing risks proactively. In this context, there are two possibilities:

1. Adapt security organization by adding resources to ensure greater support for governance, strategy, and risks, or
2. Outsource or delegate security operations by changing the requirement specifications of existing teams.

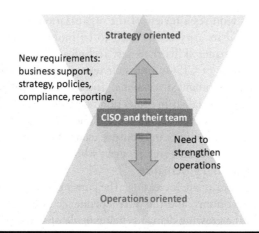

Figure 6.3   Evolution of the responsibilities of the CISO.

Many companies offer security operation outsourcing services as security as a service (SaaS or SecaaS). Nevertheless, this outsourcing of security operations is only possible under certain conditions. For it to be economically expedient, the maturity level must be high, satisfying the following conditions:

■ Security operations are well established and optimized
■ The controls are effective
■ Services are based on service-level agreements (SLAs)
■ Defined standards are respected in all operations
■ The infrastructure is adapted, and access rights are secured
■ There is a regular monitoring (follow-up) process. A reporting system is defined and based on stable metrics
■ Jurisdiction over security operations remains internal. Changes are initiated solely by the internal operations manager
■ Risk scenarios are established and monitored
■ Metrics developed in the outsourcing framework can also be used to report to the governing body
■ Outsourced operations must be auditable, especially regarding compliance with the standards, continuity, agreed controls or means to protect sensitive data
■ Outsourcing does not diminish the level of protection
■ The organization of other activities is not weakened by outsourcing. Released resources can change profile and handle other tasks

So, there are two major poles of responsibility for the CISO. Security organization will depend on their position on the operations–strategy or governance risk and compliance (GRC) axis as presented in Figure 6.3. Some key features of these two orientations are presented in the following paragraphs.

6.2.1 Security Organization Oriented toward Strategy and Business Needs

In a security organization geared to the GRC pole, the focus is on strategic alignment, risk management, compliance, and support for business objectives. The maturity level is generally high for reporting, return on investment metrics, training, and awareness. Security representatives have their place in business forums and committees and are regularly consulted on issues related to the evolving security risks of new technologies. In such a configuration, the CISO often reports outside of IT, and their team is in charge of policies, compliance, and risks. Security operations are either outsourced or assumed by an IT team integrated into engineering, operations, or the infrastructure.

6.2.2 Security Organization Oriented toward Operations

In an operations-oriented organization, the CISO and security teams often reside within IT, with the CISO reporting directly to the CIO or a lower level. They have very little opportunity to interact with the business units, are not involved in strategy debates, and most often focus on the operational and technical aspects of security. Their main mission is to take care of the deployment, optimization, and monitoring of security tools and technologies. The CISO in charge of these teams has the same profile and great technical expertise.

The advantages of such organization are found in the high level of technicality, mastery of security tools, and ability to choose the best solutions and integrate different technologies. The disadvantage is that having very little contact with business needs, the CISO and their teams remain locked in their comfort zone and feel no urge to take strategic change initiatives. This propensity leads to the danger of security continuing to be viewed as a service that "says no" and has difficulty finding a modus vivendi with employees who are keen on new modes of communication (consumerization). Business units often have to look to external suppliers for easier solutions for their communication or exchange needs with suppliers or customers.

EXAMPLE

Operational security teams will probably not be asked for their opinion on the means of integrating blockchain solutions for the business units unless they have obtained a specific mandate from their superiors. Supporting changes is not part of their remit, especially in the context of IT that is oriented toward production optimization, functional results, and reducing costs.

How will the responsibilities of the security teams evolve?

6.3 Roles and Responsibilities of the Security Teams

The traditional activities of security teams can be divided into two main groups: security engineering and security operations. Without going into too much detail, these two groups include the following activities.

Security engineering:

- Application security
- Threat and vulnerability management
- Security in projects and new technologies

Security operations:

- Infrastructure security (configuration, network, end point)
- Managing security components
- Monitoring, device management and SOC
- Incident management and investigations
- Identity and access management

Security teams today generally take on all these activities, providing great added value to IT departments. Many books and standards provide more details on the objectives and best practices of operational-level security management.

The new demands on the CISO and their team can also be divided into two groups. The first concerns a *business relationship* orientation and encompasses activities aimed at strengthening the links and coordination between the governing body, the business units, and security operations. It involves integrating strategies into operations and ensuring better two-way communication between governance and business units, on the one hand, and teams implementing controls, on the other. The second group can be called *proactive risk management* and encompasses all the activities that provide better risk analysis and treatment in a changing context by taking into account new technologies, new business models and working methods, the empowerment of users or consumerization, activity outsourcing, cloud computing, mobile technologies, and so on.

The primary new demands encompassed in a business relationship can be summarized as follows.

Business communication, security account management, and marketing: Business managers are often reluctant to discuss security risks with technical profiles, since they consider this is not their area of expertise. The fact that IT will patch a server exposed on the Internet presenting an easy hacking target does not provide consumers of IT resources with valued information. However, if they are told that the services offered by this server might not be available due to an intrusion, this might lead them to pay more attention to security arguments. In addition, the business units have specific security needs that the CISO team can satisfy: context-specific training or awareness, risk identification and security controls related to their specific operations, guidelines and standards, and so on. These services are very valuable, but they require specific security resources such as account management or customer relationship management. Security marketing is also an activity that facilitates governance: communicating the added value of security with the right tools and at the right level. Telling success stories of benefits gained through security allows it to be integrated into decision-making processes with better positioning. "Security inside" or "Designed with security in mind" could become a quality label for services offered to clients and partners.

Strategy and business alignment: In the previous chapter, we discussed the importance of developing a security strategy and aligning it with business needs. Indeed, the regular monitoring of business directions and needs could facilitate security alignment. Establishing a means of exchanging information through an account manager or business unit representative as a security advocate, or vice versa, could only be beneficial.

Business reporting and metrics: Good governance needs security reports based on reliable key performance indicators expressing trends in an easily understandable language. It is no longer enough to present raw metrics produced by protection systems, such as the number of patches applied. Trends should be monitored on how security helps the business achieve its objectives. This will be discussed in more detail in the chapters on reporting and metrics.

Awareness and support: Awareness-raising has always been one of the main tasks of the CISO and their team. However, it is no longer enough to recall guidelines. Needs are changing in this area as well, and business units now require support sessions focused on topics that concern them first and foremost. Standardized awareness sessions focused solely on end users might not resonate sufficiently with key executives and other decision-makers. Sensitization (awareness) efforts must focus more on the reality of the job combined with support for day-to-day activities.

Compliance and program management: Security has always deployed controls to satisfy a particular regulation, audit report, customer request, and so on. Program management must include the regulatory requirements along with counterbalancing them with initiatives that can bring value to the business. Good governance takes care of the security program and puts all requirements in perspective, be they internal or external, audit findings, new threats, or requests from partners. Maintaining a clear mapping with requirements and roadmaps allows businesses to understand how security projects are linked and how they contribute to common objectives.

Security is no longer an obstacle to development but rather, a success factor. New demands on the security teams primarily result in their greater involvement in managing changes, especially in anticipating and mitigating new risks (proactive risk management).

Policy management: Managing the regulatory framework as a fundamental component of governance remains in the hands of the security team. It is up to the CISO team to maintain policies and help the business units, including IT, uphold their standards in line with the needs of the company. Changing requests for exceptions often indicates inadequate policies and guidelines.

Third-party and externalization risk management: Many companies outsource their activities or rely on external service providers in the value production chain. Security teams are asked to protect shared data and resources as if they were internal. This is a very difficult situation for security experts, because it is almost impossible to secure such operations after the fact. The security team must therefore be involved in the selection process and participate in a proactive risk analysis. It can help in the selection of partners, application of the recommended protection standards, audits, and due diligence.

Proactive risk assessment: Risk assessment services related to new projects and business initiatives are highly appreciated. This is one of the rare occasions when the security team can demonstrate its contribution to the change process.

EXAMPLE

Using cloud services coupled with an application provided by a third-party supplier is an attractive solution for business units. However, if this initiative is conducted without support from security team, it is a safe bet that audits or risk analysis just before the start of production will shed light on new vulnerabilities. Risk analysis carried out beforehand by the security team could expose the risks and propose potential solutions.

Security architecture: Establishing and strengthening security architecture that combines technologies and policy-based processes will be one of the most sought-after capabilities in security teams in coming years. Starting from the company's policy and objectives or business initiatives, a security architect will establish the standards and concepts for the teams in charge of setting up technical controls. The security architect has a dual role. They can not only identify and communicate risks to governing bodies but also provide solutions that best fit the corporate context. Once a decision is made, the architect works out the concept and standards, and participates in elaborating the solution. Architects and engineers also contribute to projects and ensure that concepts and standards are respected. They represent security in forums and participate in the work of the company architect group.

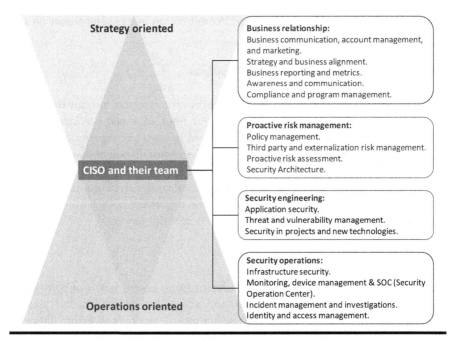

Figure 6.4   Set of responsibilities of the CISO and their team.

After all that has been said, traditional operations-oriented activities and new activities that are closer to the strategy, risk, and governance pole are shown schematically in Figure 6.4.

New tasks—OK, but what new areas have to be covered?

6.4 New Areas of Responsibility for the CISO and Their Team

In addition to qualitative changes that can be seen in security services, especially a certain vertical evolution of the CISO and their team, new areas related to security are looming on the horizon that could very likely influence security service specifications. These include cybersecurity, human risks and investigations, fraud management, and services in the field of personal data protection (data privacy).

Cybersecurity

Security and IT teams are naturally responsible for implementing cyber-threat protection measures. Protections that must be put in place often go beyond the confines of the enterprise. The CISO must therefore participate actively in discussion forums, collaborate in state (government) coordination bodies, and report on the events observed.

Human Risk Management and Investigations

Numerous statistics, surveys, and recent events in various sectors indicate that major threats do not come from isolated hackers but from advanced persistent threats (APTs) with internal complicity or doors opened in negligent security devices (for example, opening attached files in emails resulting in installation of malicious code) and also from malicious employees. The management of human risks includes setting up new controls enabling the detection of precursor signals of unusual activities. Human risks should be addressed in specific HR departments, but investigative or screening technological skills are often sought in security services.

Fraud Management

Fraud attempts can be manifested in different forms. New means of communication, the availability of personal data, and new technologies obviously present opportunities for malicious people. These are mostly attempts to extort financial assets, confidential information, or benefits of any kind by exploiting business operations. The intentional transgression of internal rules (which may be called an offense) cannot be considered fraud until the realization of the benefit has been proved. As with human risks, fraud management should be provided outside the security services. Nevertheless, security specialists will be in increasing demand in this area, if only for investigative or forensic issues. They will also have to put specific indicators or controls in place to detect fraud attempts.

Data Privacy

Protective measures for confidential or personal data, whether required by regulations or by the business itself, affect information security. Some examples of this impact were given in Chapter 3. As far as security organization is concerned, new responsibilities required by regulations primarily involve the data processor, the data controller, the data owner, and the data protection officer (DPO).

What are the main security organizational structures?

6.5 Security Organizational Structures

The security organizational structure reflects the role that a company wants to give its security team. This structure also determines its ability to achieve set objectives. The positioning of the different functions influences the strategy of recruiting security specialists and the place that will be held by the security officer himself or herself.

There is no optimal or unique security organization applicable to all companies. Any attempt to present an ideal model is therefore impossible. The sector, size, and characteristics of the company will determine the positioning and responsibilities of the team in charge of security. Each configuration of security organization has its own logic, so it is important to understand the features and strengths of each one. The evolution of the security team to the highest strategic level should not be a goal in itself but should result from the will of the company in line with its context.

Security organization can usually be classified into one of these four archetypes:

1. Operations-oriented security
2. IT security
3. Enterprise security
4. Distributed security

6.5.1 Operations-Oriented Security

Operations-oriented security is characterized by a focus on technologies and operational controls (Figure 6.5). This structure is usually integrated into IT operations.

In such an organization, the security officer and their team are responsible for securing the IT infrastructure, choosing the most appropriate technologies, and keeping costs under control. Their main objective is to limit the number of incidents (such as malfunctioning and unavailable security equipment) and combat new threats and vulnerabilities. The security officer usually does not

Figure 6.5 Operations-oriented security.

have the title of CISO. They are consulted on technical aspects of security, participate in IT projects to protect IT resources and data, but have no contacts outside of IT. They are sometimes invited to comment on the technical aspects of business initiatives.

6.5.2 IT Security

IT security is an organization that deals with functional policies and security standards at the IT level, the integration of technical solutions into projects, and application security. The charter and the general security policy are not part of its prerogatives. Two teams can be found: one part of IT engineering responsible for security solutions, concepts, and technologies; and the other in charge of operations such as the one presented earlier. Such an organization generally has a high concentration of skills in all security technology areas (Figure 6.6).

The highest-level security components, such as corporate directories, strong authentication technologies and systems, application security concepts and standards, and so on, are part of its responsibilities. Security engineers are systematically asked to participate in IT projects as support. Security risks are managed within the context of IT risks. Compliance aspects are treated in IT-specific projects in the same way as all other development or change projects.

The security manager may hold the title of CISO, even if it is not a real C-level. They report directly to the CIO and may be in charge of engineering or security operations teams. In some configurations, they are part of the IT management committee and participate in decisions on technological developments. The CISO has very few contacts outside of IT, except when asked about security-related technologies. They may have a functional relationship with the enterprise's risk manager as a security risk expert. They advise the CIO and other IT managers but are not part of the company's strategic committees.

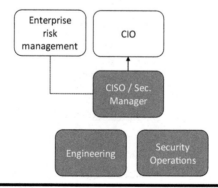

Figure 6.6 IT security.

6.5.3 Enterprise Security

If a company is willing to raise security to a strategic level and include it in resolving business needs as a partner in the same way as IT, then we call this organization *enterprise security*. IS functions, including those focused on risk and governance, help create business opportunities. Security is intended to give support to the business units, actively take care of their needs and technologies, act as a consultant on security risks related to new opportunities, and proactively contribute to the resolution of problems related to compliance, such as the protection of personal data (data privacy).

Such a security organization actively deals with policies, proactive risk management in the context of business opportunities, architectures, compliance, awareness programs at all levels, reporting and metrics for governance needs, strategies, and active communication with the business units (Figure 6.7).

Security teams in such an organization report to the CISO or CSO, who occupies a real C-level outside of IT. The CISO reports to the CEO or chief risk officer (CRO) and has authority and visibility at the company level. They are on strategy committees and manage a budget covering the security program for the whole organization.

Such an organization can bring together other areas of security, such as physical security, human security, and business continuity, as mentioned in the previous chapter. It can also take charge of large-scale projects such as compliance or direct security teams in different geographic regions within large companies.

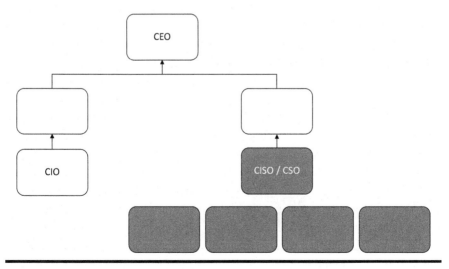

Figure 6.7   Enterprise security.

6.5.4 *Distributed Security*

In very large organizations, for matters related to cost, operational efficiency, and keeping expertise closer to operations, it is often preferable to establish a security organization with distributed competence centers. This organization covers the features of enterprise security as mentioned earlier, but the security teams remain in various business units with a matrix organization and reporting lines between the CISO/CSO and local officials (Figure 6.8).

This form of organization can be the most natural and realistic in the current context. Strong governance through committees or governing bodies can compensate for some loss of direct CISO authority among the security teams. This configuration, however, requires not only a high level of maturity in governance but also a security culture formalized within the internal regulatory framework.

What skills will be needed in the future?

6.6 Security Profiles

Security organizations are set to change in the coming years under the influence of new technologies, new business models, and more stringent regulations. It is therefore useful to review some of the skills that will certainly be needed in different security organizations.

Each security organization requires multiple skills. First, the structural model of security organization needs to be defined and then, the skills that might be lacking and how to redefine each employee's role. A good balance

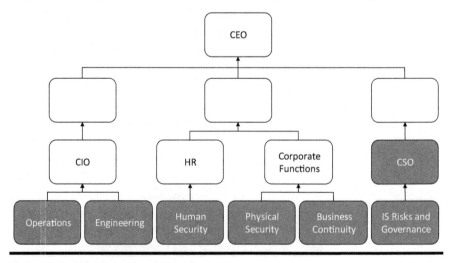

Figure 6.8 Distributed security.

needs to be found between technical skills, expertise in risk management, anticipation capacity in the areas of threats and vulnerabilities, interest in business prospects, communication skills, and so on. If the maturity of security organization needs to evolve toward greater alignment with the business units and strategy, then a culture of customer service must be instilled in the security teams.

Revising or setting up adequate security organization is not easy. It is therefore important to include all the stakeholders in the discussions and approach this task as a company project or initiative. There follow some profiles that appear essential today, bearing in mind that several functions can be held by the same person.

Security Administrator

This profile has great technical skills and focuses on the qualities of operations. They have specific training in protection technologies and/or past practice in the field of system infrastructures. Their main objective is to ensure the protection of the perimeter and infrastructures by setting up technical barriers.

Security Engineer

The security engineer looks for the best technical, and possibly organizational, solutions based on the specifications presented to them. They focus on the quality of the standards and the efficiency and flexibility of the solutions put in place. Their role overlaps with that of the security architect regarding technical solutions. They often do not have a very broad business understanding. Such a profile is in great demand as a consultant for business and IT sectors when choosing among different options to secure data and the infrastructure. Most often, they specialize in certain security technologies or domains such as application security, system and database security, access management, corporate directory, and so on. They are actively involved in IT projects as an advisor for security solutions.

Security Coordinator

The security coordinator acts as a facilitator between different teams as part of a distributed security organization (see earlier). Their main role is to explain the requirements and points of view between IS risks and governance, and operations or engineering. They are often part of IT, but due to their responsibilities, they have many contacts with all the other teams and in particular the CISO. They mainly focus on policies and standards and their interpretation and application in the business processes. Such a profile has training and experience in all areas of security and great communication skills.

Human Security Analyst

To properly assess and address HR risks, many companies use specially trained analysts to perform screenings and behavioral research and analysis. They focus on fraud models and other legal indicators to identify risk behavior.

CISO with Extended Responsibilities

Closer rapprochement is being seen in companies between information security, physical security, human security, and business continuity because of similar and often overlapping protection objectives. The CISO could thus evolve toward the position of CSO responsible for these four domains with dedicated teams. This is often motivated by a company's desire to establish a centralized management system for all areas involved in protecting the integrity, availability, and confidentiality of their assets, along with better monitoring and reporting. This obviously implies a CSO position outside of IT and at the same level as the other C-level executives with direct reporting to the CEO or board of directors. They have a special relationship with the CRO (Chief Risk Officer).

Security Delegate

The security delegate is a person who acts as business spokesperson while maintaining strong expertise in the areas of risk and IS. Their main role is to bring business and IS together and dispel the image of IS as a brake to business development. They communicate security concerns and prospects to the business units and, conversely, present the objectives of the business to the security teams, thus facilitating a rapprochement of the two visions (Figure 6.9).

They have a privileged relationship with the business manager and the CISO. They are part of project teams or committees on both the business side and the security side; they take care of awareness or support sessions specific to the business and ensure the follow-up of requests. This role is traditionally performed by the CISO, but as we will see later, this depends on their position in security organization, the maturity of the security services, and of course, the size of the company. Security delegates can have different titles, such as security account manager, business security leader, business information security officer (BISO), security coordinator, and so on.

Third-Party Security Coordinator

Business operations are less and less confined within a company's infrastructure. Security coordination with providers and implementers of outsourced services is becoming a major concern. The role of the coordinator in this context is to ensure compliance with security rules and adapt them if necessary. They are also in charge of assessing risks and proposing measures for their mitigation.

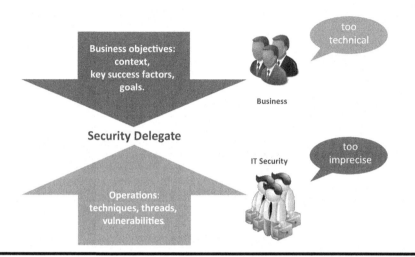

Figure 6.9   Role of security delegate.

To be able to take on the new requirements and those mentioned previously, especially with the evolution of security services toward more strategic positions, the new functions in the following list could emerge in many companies.

Security Architect

The role of security architect is to ensure the development of security architecture as mentioned earlier. They must be familiar with business operations but also have thorough knowledge of technological capabilities. Their main role is to assess risks in the context of operations. Business unit managers are not sufficiently familiar with the controls in place and as such, are not able to correctly assess the residual risk. The security architect must be able to propose security solutions encompassing policies, standards, and technical solutions based on the functional needs expressed by the business and the requirements of the desired maturity level. The extent of their remit depends greatly on their position. In all cases, they should be part of the company's architecture committee.

Data Protection Officer

The DPO will naturally be found among the ranks of security specialists most familiar with the data protection controls put in place. Their main responsibilities are to understand how data is processed and to be able to establish whether the protections in place meet regulatory requirements. This position must be independent of hierarchical structures and have autonomy, such as reporting directly to the board of directors or to regulatory authorities. It can also be outsourced.

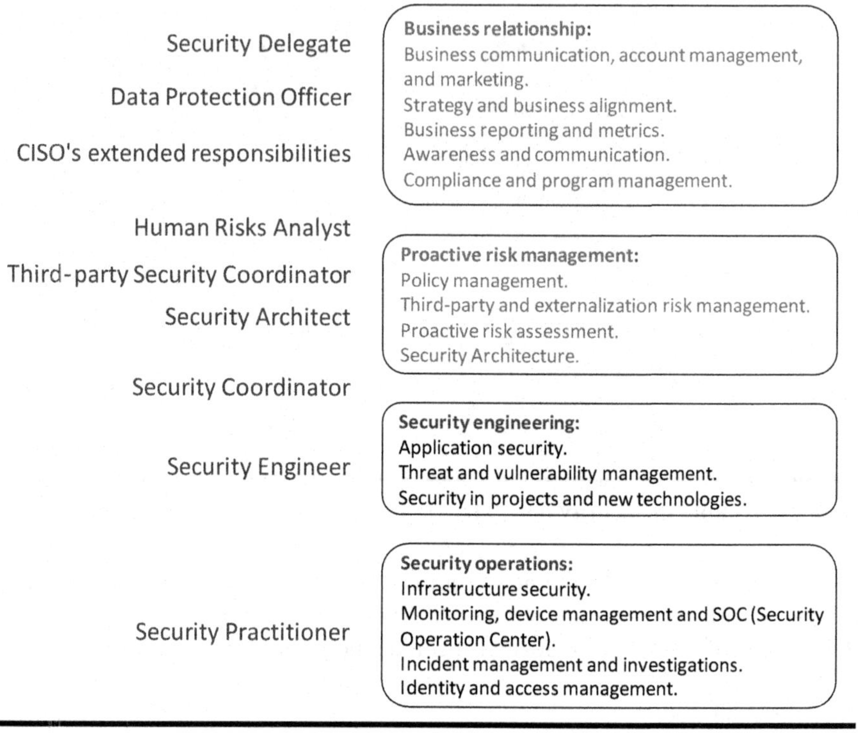

Security Delegate

Data Protection Officer

CISO's extended responsibilities

Business relationship:
Business communication, account management, and marketing.
Strategy and business alignment.
Business reporting and metrics.
Awareness and communication.
Compliance and program management.

Human Risks Analyst

Third-party Security Coordinator

Security Architect

Proactive risk management:
Policy management.
Third-party and externalization risk management.
Proactive risk assessment.
Security Architecture.

Security Coordinator

Security Engineer

Security engineering:
Application security.
Threat and vulnerability management.
Security in projects and new technologies.

Security Practitioner

Security operations:
Infrastructure security.
Monitoring, device management and SOC (Security Operation Center).
Incident management and investigations.
Identity and access management.

Figure 6.10   New skills and security functions.

The correspondence between various profiles discussed herein and the set of functions in security teams can be schematized as on Figure 6.10.

6.7 Conclusion

Security organizations are set to change in the coming years under the influence of new technologies, new business models, and more stringent regulations. New skills will also be sought among those responsible for security operations and program management. Each company's strategy and context will define the most appropriate security organization.

The possible organizations presented in this chapter provide some insight into setting up or adapting security organization so that it facilitates governance and offers support to the business units in achieving their objectives. A deeper examination of the subject to better understand current trends can lead to some major reorganizations of security functions within large structures in coming years. However, it should never be forgotten that security organization must remain at the service of the company's objectives. Decision-makers and boards of directors, who play an important role in governance, need to consider security organization as a major player in achieving their strategy.

Chapter 7

Risk Management

Risks are an inherent part of business, and every business executive is preoccupied with their mitigation. The impact of certain risks can have dramatic consequences, posing a major threat to a company. Security risk management is of paramount importance due to the very nature of the protection provided by a security program. Risk analysis and mitigation are the raison d'être of any security program. Opinions are sometimes divided between those who consider that security risks cannot be measured with precision and those who claim, on the contrary, that it can be done with very elaborate methods. This chapter presents a pragmatic approach to managing security risks as an essential element of security program governance and management.

This chapter provides answers to the following questions:

- How does risk management contribute to security governance?
- What is the security risk management process?
- Why is a risk management concept important?
- How can risks be identified, analyzed, evaluated, and treated?
- How can risks be presented and monitored?

What is information security risk?

7.1 Information Security Risks

According to ISO 31000 (ISO 31000:2018, Risk management - Guidelines), security risk may be defined as the "effect of uncertainty on objectives."

> An effect is a deviation from the expected. It can be positive, negative, or both, and can address, create, or result in opportunities and threats.
> Objectives can have different aspects and categories, and can be applied at different levels.
> Risk is usually expressed in terms of risk sources (3.4), potential events (3.5), their consequences (3.6), and their likelihood (3.7).

Security risks are part of a company's operational risks. Other categories of risk include financial, legal, human, compliance, reputational, etc. The multitude of security risk scenarios and potential impacts makes it almost impossible to provide a comprehensive inventory of all security risk scenarios. Therefore, depending on its context and specificities, each company will have to design its own risk management system adapted to its needs.

By analyzing and addressing its security risks, a company can optimize its operational costs. If it believes that security risk management is not really mandatory and it suffices to implement standard technical protections, a company not only exposes itself to sanctions provided by the legal and regulatory framework, but also weakens its overall security posture, is unable to optimize security-related expenses, and exposes itself to potentially significant damage.

Unfortunately, an insurance policy cannot be taken out against the consequences of security risks. If, under certain conditions, indemnity can be offered against the effects of nonavailability or blackmail in the context of cybersecurity risks, this is not generally possible for all scenarios. An insurance policy covers a certain risk by paying a fee, but this implies that the risk, its consequences, and the amount of the fee can be defined. No insurance policy offers this service due to the variety of conditions and consequences related to security risks.

Risk management should cover as many scenarios as possible. If a risk has not been identified, this does not mean that it does not exist. On the contrary, this risk will be implicitly accepted, which can have dramatic consequences. An inherent risk can be accepted without any measures, but this must be done consciously.

The board of directors is ultimately responsible for the risks taken by a company. The chief information security officer (CISO) and their team are usually responsible for security risk management, but it is the board of directors that ultimately approves the risk report and mitigation plans. The resulting decisions belong to them.

The spectrum of security risks is constantly changing, and many new risk scenarios have not yet been identified. New business models and technological change bring new threats for which companies are not always prepared.

How does security risk management contribute to governance?

7.2 Risks and Governance

The goal of security risk management is to analyze and present the state of risk, making it possible to prioritize and improve mitigation measures. Through risk management, CISOs and information security professionals have the opportunity to influence decisions and increase the visibility of the added value of their efforts. Unfortunately, to reduce costs, many executives agree to simplify risk management under the pretext that nothing changes over time, the risks have been known for a long time, and in any case, security will not be improved by adding these unproductive tasks. So, they are reluctant to involve operations experts, deepen their knowledge of business risks, or carry out a systematic identification or analysis. Managers themselves are often not sufficiently stimulated to finance the implementation of formal risk management processes because of the doubts they have about their return on investment. This attitude turns a blind eye to the real dangers incurred by the company.

EXAMPLE

The nature and intensity of risks in the field of information security are changing. The studies and surveys of specialized firms show different trends from year to year, which are often linked to changes in technology and changes in business models. For example, security risks related to internal threats or business partners have certainly increased in recent years. Advanced Persistent Threat (APT) or threats targeting a particular enterprise by non-detectable intrusions by the protection systems replaced the threats of traditional hackers. Firms that rely heavily on robotics or the use of automation solutions for operations are certainly more vulnerable to cyber threats. The examples are numerous.

Risk managers are therefore given more and more responsibility in the current context. Boards, management, business unit managers, auditors, external partners, and customers all want to be reassured about the existence of a formal risk management process that is proved and helps the company protect its assets.

If there is anything that can influence decisions, it is the establishment of a risk policy containing the context, evaluation criteria, and a clear and comprehensible report on the evolution of risk. These aspects could ultimately make the difference between a comprehensive risk approach that brings value and an approach that has no support and will have little effect.

For risk management to add value to the business and facilitate information security governance, a formal process should be established based on the following principles:

1. *Have a security risk management policy and concept*: Define the framework and concept of risk management and establish the context, criteria, and risk appetites. Define the risk management process, with roles and responsibilities.
2. *Identify risks*: Have an inventory of categorized risks containing all the necessary information about each risk. All risk scenarios should be covered by identified risks.
3. *Analyze risks*: Understand existing controls and determine risk levels.
4. *Evaluate risks*: Compare risk levels with company criteria and set priorities. Establish (decide) the desired risk levels.
5. *Treat unaccepted risks*: Identify risk treatment options and carry out a risk treatment plan.
6. *Have a system for risk monitoring, reporting, and communication*: Establish reports and risk communication plans for all stakeholders.

A more detailed explanation of each principle and the means to achieve them will be given further on. When establishing a formal risk management process, we will rely on the recommendations of the standards, especially ISO 31000 and 27005.

Many standards, good practices, methods, frameworks, and tools for information technology (IT) and security risk management can be consulted that propose a methodological framework with specific guidelines. The goal here is not to present or compare them. This information is widely available, and readers are invited to familiarize themselves. Let us mention some of the better known:

▪ *ISO 31000*: Risk management—Guidelines, 2018. Provides principles and guidelines on risk management.
▪ *ISO 31010*: Risk management—Risk assessment techniques, 2009.
▪ *ISO 27005*: 2018 Information technology—Security techniques—Information security risk management. Provides guidelines for information security risk management.
▪ *RISK IT*: Information Systems Audit and Control Association (ISACA), 2009. It is a complement to Control Objectives for Information and Related Technology (CobIT) for IT risk management.
▪ *OCTAVE (Operationally Critical Threat, Asset, and Vulnerability Evaluation)*: Software Engineering Institute (SEI), Carnegie Mellon University, 2001. Oriented analysis of computer security risks, specifically vulnerabilities and threats.

- *EBIOS (Expression des Besoins et Identification des Objectifs de Sécurité)*: National Agency for the Security of Information Systems (ANSSI), 2010. Information system security risk management.
- Enterprise Risk Management: Integrating with Strategy and Performance, COSO (Committee of Sponsoring Organizations of the Treadway Commission), 2004, update 2017.

We will now present a pragmatic way to implement a formal risk management process.

How should we manage risks?

7.3 Risk Management Process

Let us note from the outset that the standards or good practices, as stated earlier, are very useful when identifying the requirements of a risk management process. However, it must be borne in mind that the process serves a company first and foremost to set up measures against its most important risks. The process must remain simple, understandable, and acceptable to all stakeholders. A risk management process can indeed become very complex. If large companies can afford to adopt a strict methodology, the majority cannot due to the cost it generates. On the other hand, every company can accept the major principles, making their information risk management process as complete as possible within their context.

The ISO 31000 standard presents a set of principles, concepts, and a process for implementing risk management. The general concepts make it adaptable to the risk management needs of every organization. It also states that risk management must take into account several factors, such as company objectives, context, structure, activities, processes, functions, projects, products and services, and specific assets and practices.

The ISO 27005 standard deals specifically with the management of information security risks and as such, is an extension of ISO 27001/2 and principles in ISO 31000. Its annexes contain recommendations for implementing the process, in particular:

- *Annex A*: Defining the scope and boundaries of the information security risk management process.
- *Annex B*: Identification and valuation of assets and impact assessment.
- *Annex C*: Examples of typical threats.
- *Annex D*: Vulnerabilities and methods for vulnerability assessment.
- *Annex E*: Information security risk assessment approaches.
- *Annex F*: Constraints for risk modification.

Figure 7.1   Major components of the ISO 31000 risk management framework.

The titles of the annexes are sufficiently explicit and do not require additional comment. They are extremely useful for all the steps that will be presented in the following.

ISO 31000 standard gives generic recommendations on risk management. (©ISO Adapted from ISO/IEC 31000:2018 with permission of the American National Standard Institute (ANSI) on behalf of the International Organization for Standardization. All rights reserved.)

Chapter 4 (Principles) sets out the requirements that each organization must meet for its risk management process to be effective.

Chapter 5 (Framework) presents the components of the framework essential for risk management and its integration into significant activities and functions (Figure 7.1). These components can be summarized as follows:

■ Leadership and commitment: top management should demonstrate leadership and commitment, accountability for risk management, and oversight.
■ Integration: integration of risk management under existing structures and context of the organization.
■ Design: understanding the context, articulating risk management commitment, defining roles and responsibilities, allocating resources, establishing communication.
■ Implementation: of the risk management framework.
■ Evaluation: periodically evaluate the effectiveness of the risk management framework.
■ Improvement: monitor and adapt risk management framework.

Chapter 6 (Process) describes the risk management process through activities presented in Figure 7.2. These activities will be referenced more in detail in what follows.

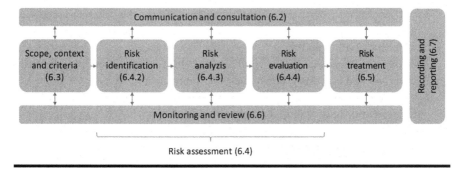

Figure 7.2   Risk management process according to ISO 31000.

Why is a risk management policy important?

7.4 Establishing a Risk Management Policy

A risk policy describes why risk management is necessary and how it will be handled by the company. It serves primarily the following two objectives:

1. Establish the company's risk management framework and process.
2. Define the risk management context.

EXAMPLE

In ISO 31000, the first of these objectives is contained in the Framework, and the second is the first step in the risk management process. Context setting has four key elements according to this standard: external context, internal context, risk management context, and risk criteria. With regard to information security, the ISO 27005 standard notes that the context must mention the criteria of risk evaluation, impact, and acceptance.

A company's general security policy often does not fully explain the context and risk management process. Therefore, a specific information security risk management policy should be defined as a complement to the general policy. This policy may have different names, such as *security risk management concept, framework*, or *guidelines*.

The elaboration of the policy can be inspired by the standards or good practice guidelines. For simplicity, a risk management policy should contain at least the following elements:

Context: Consideration of the company's objectives and the contexts (internal and external) in which it carries out its activities. For information security, the importance of information and its preservation should be mentioned.

Definition of risk (security risk): What is meant by risk, the different categories of risk, and in particular, the fact that a security risk results from a threat exploiting a vulnerability.

Objectives and principles: A clear statement of the company's risk management objectives and especially, how to achieve them.

Scope: Definition of the policy's scope, whether functional or geographical. Its duration and validity should also be mentioned.

Legal aspect: The legal and regulatory bases that the policy will cover.

Framework: Clarification of how risk management activities should flow and an explanation of the process and who is responsible.

Risk categorization: Better risk allocation for monitoring, aggregation/consolidation, and reporting purposes.

Risk appetite: An expression in quantitative or qualitative terms of the level of risk that a company is prepared to take. Risk attitude expresses its willingness to confront, or not, certain risks and, if so, how. It gives a precise definition of the qualitative and quantitative criteria.

EXAMPLE

Qualitative criteria include statements such as: "the company will only engage in new activities if its risk management process allows the new risks to be maintained at a level defined as acceptable by the board of directors."

Quantitative criteria mean statements such as: "the company will only engage in new activities if its risk management process allows it to maintain risk below the 'medium' level defined by probability and impact thresholds".

If a company is able to calculate all the losses due to the realization of certain risks (operational losses), then it can set a threshold whereupon risk will no longer be acceptable:

If the ratio losses/gross income >x%, then the risk will no longer be acceptable.

Roles and responsibilities in risk management: The role and responsibility of each organizational unit should be defined: in particular, the board of directors, heads of the business units (functional, geographical, and corporate), control and audit bodies, teams in charge of operational risk management, various decision-making committees, the CISO, and information security team.

Risk management process: Defining the process enables a company to better govern risk management activities. The responsibilities, objectives, and expected results of each activity should be described. Communication consists of a reporting system, and its objectives, content, presentation methods, recipients, and publication frequencies must be mentioned.

Documentation and risk attributes: Risk documentation has to do with how risks are presented (e.g. inventory, risk map) and the information that is associated with each risk (see later).

Assessment method and risk map: The aim is to define how risks are assessed, in particular the calculation of likelihood or occurrences in a given period, impact categories, and the calculation of risk values.

EXAMPLE

If a company chooses to assign a risk value according to the following formula:

$$\text{Value of risk} = \text{Likelihood} \times \text{Impact}$$

with likelihood degrees defined as 1—Rare, 2—Unlikely, 3—Possible, 4—Likely, and 5—Almost certain, and impacts as 1—Low, 2—Minor, 3—Moderate, 4—Major, and 5—Extreme, then the risks could be classified by gravity according to their value:

1 – 3	Low risk
4 – 6	Moderate risk
8 – 12	High risk
15 – 25	Extremely high risk

and visualized in the following matrix:

Likelihood		Low (1)	Minor (2)	Moderate (3)	Major (4)	Extreme (5)
Almost certain	5	5	10	15	20	25
Likely	4	4	8	12	16	20
Possible	3	3	6	9	12	15
Unlikely	2	2	4	6	8	10
Rare	1	1	2	3	4	5

Impact

Considerations for special cases: A company must specify how it wishes certain risks or events to be treated: for example, risks with a potentially very high impact but with very low probability, high risks, risks considered as major (top risks), etc.

Specific instructions regarding the risk management process: Some very explicit standards can be set in the policy to help managers and risk officers decide how to treat specific risks cases.

> **EXAMPLE**
>
> A company can decree when to accept, avoid, reduce, or transfer risk.
>
> Requiring incidents to be categorized in certain ways facilitates their company-wide consolidation. By establishing standards and a taxonomy in the management of incidents (leakage, loss, error, fault, fraud, etc.), a company will be better able to evaluate the corrective measures in place, react to changes in trends, and communicate.
>
> Criteria for the presentation of assessment matrices and criteria for likelihood and impact calculations can also be established (see Risk Assessment section).

How can risks be identified, analyzed, evaluated, and treated?

7.5 Risk Identification

Risk identification aims at the following objectives:

- Identify threats and vulnerabilities, areas of potential impacts and their nature, and causes and circumstances of risk events.
- Establish an inventory or list of risks that may have an impact on the company achieving its objectives.
- Establish whether there is a correlation (dependency) between risks.

Risk identification should take place not only during periodic risk reviews but also for each new project, change request integration of new partners or suppliers, strategic changes, etc. Knowing which assets to protect is essential in this step (see the Chapter 11 on Asset Management).

First, all the events and circumstances that might generate risk must be identified. Two fundamental approaches exist: top-down and bottom-up.

In the top-down approach, we start from an analysis of known threats and vulnerabilities or those presented in the standards or proposed by risk identification methods. We ask ourselves whether they could be considered risks to our assets in our context. Many methods and tools offer very comprehensive questionnaires to facilitate the risk identification process. However, identifying all possible risk scenarios is not very useful. With knowledge of the company, we can quickly focus on those that will be relevant in our context.

EXAMPLE

Annex C of ISO 27005 contains examples of threats, and Annex D has vulnerabilities that can be used to identify risks. Risks can be identified by combining threats and vulnerabilities (a risk is a threat that exploits a vulnerability). For example, combining the threat "Unauthorized use of equipment" and the vulnerability "Wrong allocation of access rights" identifies the risk "Access to unauthorized data by malicious people."

The bottom-up approach identifies risks by examining risk scenarios based on experiences and operations. Threats and vulnerabilities observed by security operations specialists, business unit operations managers, and employees result in the formulation of risk scenarios.

Risk Classification

A formal taxonomy or classification allows a company to group risks of a similar nature and analyze them better, and facilitates reporting. This can be done using the recommendations of the standards presented earlier. Classifications for industrial sectors, such as Basel III for the financial industry, SEI (Software Engineering Institute) for software development, National Institute of Standards and Technology (NIST) 800-30 for information security risks, or Risk IT from ISACA for IT risks, are also available. Other ways to identify risk categories include the expertise of specialized firms, classification according to the company's objectives that could be impacted, taxonomies already available in other sectors of the company, etc. However, for pragmatic reasons, it is sometimes more judicious to take these proposals as a starting point for building one's own taxonomy and making sure a large category has not been missed.

EXAMPLE

There are countless examples of the classification of security risks. Following is a first-level classification:

1. Theft or fraud (internal, external)
2. Data leakage by negligence (includes the loss of data supports or mobile devices)
3. Noncompliance of the security system
4. Unavailability of infrastructures and/or services
5. Confidentiality and data protection
6. Human risks

7. Business continuity and service availability
8. Processes and organization
9. Operational errors

The risk "Access to unauthorized data by malicious person," as identified in the previous example, could be classified in 1. Theft or fraud (internal, external).

In this classification, cybersecurity risks are classified in several categories. If a company wants to classify risks by domain, it can easily use categories such as cybersecurity, access rights, etc. In this case, the risk mentioned earlier should be subdivided into two: "Access to unauthorized data by malicious person from the outside"—in cybersecurity and "Access to unauthorized data by malicious person internally"—in access rights.

Risk Inventory

The purpose of establishing a security risk inventory is to define and list all the risks that will be analyzed in subsequent stages. It is of paramount importance for the rest of the process, as it serves as a basis for risk communication, analysis, and reporting.

Various methods are available to identify security risks, including the norms and standards presented earlier. Several sources should be combined using both the top-down and the bottom-up approach. In the following, we simply recall several pragmatic approaches that can be applied to identify risks and build a comprehensive risk inventory.

Combine threats and vulnerabilities: As mentioned in the earlier example, we can identify risks by combining threats and vulnerabilities of assets. This is a top-down approach.
Use internal expertise: Different scenarios can be identified by bringing together people from different areas of expertise and instigating a discussion on potential security risks. This is a combination of the top-down and bottom-up approaches.
Use the expertise of the audit and specialized firms: Auditors and security consulting firms can help make an initial list of risks or risk scenarios. Numerous professional associations also publish good practices in this field for their members. This can help identify the majority of risks.
Use studies on trends in the field of security: These studies are published by specialized firms and provide good insight into security risks. Many events that have had an impact on corporate objectives or results might be identified as risks.

Separation and Aggregation of Risks

One of the biggest problems in the process of identifying risks and consolidating an inventory is the mixing of different risk levels and overlapping risks.

Risk level can be defined as the degree of detail when using threat and vulnerability scenarios to describe a risk. A very large amount of risk is difficult to manage. It is recommended to aggregate risk scenarios at the highest level, as long as indicators can be proposed to assess their likelihood and impact. In fact, the lower the level, the easier it is to find good indicators. The interest has to be weighed between having many risks that are easy to measure and a few high-level risks that are comprehensible at the governance level but are difficult to measure.

Risk overlap means that several risks are similar in terms of threats, vulnerabilities, and potential impact. This situation complicates the analysis and treatment of risks and does not provide additional information on needed protection, since the same controls act on different risks with different degrees of efficiency.

EXAMPLE

The risk "1. Data leakage by negligence" encompasses many scenarios and could be subdivided into lower-level risks as follows:

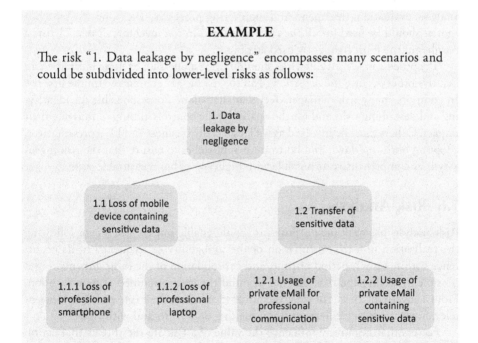

This is the result of a top-down analysis in the process of identifying risks. The risk "1. Data leakage by negligence" is of a very high level and could be considered a category rather than a risk. The two risks, 1.1 and 1.2, of the lower level are well separated and will have different key risk indicators (KRIs). Risks 1.1.1 and 1.1.2 are probably two scenarios of the same risk, and their analysis will not bring anything new concerning the controls that should be deployed. Risks 1.2.1 and 1.2.2 overlap but are interesting because of the specific metrics that can be associated with them (business data leak incidents). In this case, it will be better to keep one of the two scenarios.

Therefore, we can reduce (optimize) the number of risks contained in the inventory and keep the following three risks, which will all be classified under the category "Data leakage by negligence":

Loss of mobile device containing sensitive data	Transfer of sensitive data	Usage of private eMail containing sensitive data

Description of Risks

Each identified risk is described by a number of attributes that will be used in the analysis, evaluation, treatment, and monitoring processes. The same attribute categories should be used for all the risks contained in the inventory. Table 7.1 lists a number of the most frequently used attributes.

The process of identifying risks should not be a one-shot exercise but rather, an iterative process, since the detection of all the risks is not guaranteed on the first try. In addition, many risk managers feel that they alone are responsible for identifying and describing risks and for the quality of the controls aiming to mitigate their impact. Others must be involved as well, especially business and IT representatives, adopting both top-down and bottom-up approaches to ensure that the risk inventory is as comprehensive as possible with higher-level but measurable risks.

7.6 Risk Analysis

Risk analysis has multiple purposes. It should enable impact assessment following the realization of a risk, estimation of the probability or frequency of its occurrence within a given period of time, and consolidation of the indicators making it possible to qualify the risk, bearing in mind the controls aimed at its mitigation. From a governance point of view, the purpose of risk analysis is to provide sufficient relevant elements to facilitate decision-making on how to deal with risk.

Factors that negatively influence the value of a risk are the threats that act on the vulnerabilities that ultimately expose company assets. Risk-reducing factors include all the controls the company implements to protect assets, counter threats, and reduce vulnerabilities. Risk value is a point of equilibrium between the two extreme values (Figure 7.3).

Risk is analyzed to inform the board and management of the possibility of loss and the need to install appropriate protections. What makes the task particularly difficult for the risk manager is the need to explain how the value of a risk is

Table 7.1 Risk Attributes

Attribute	Content
Classification	Risk category according to the chosen taxonomy
Name	Short sentence that refers to the event or situation
Description	Unambiguous description of the risk
Target	Asset, physical location, objective or process that could be affected by the risk
Consequence	Description of the potential effect in case of risk realization
Inherent risk	Evaluation of the risk without existing controls
Likelihood	Estimate of the probability of risk occurring in a given period
Impact level	Estimate of the impact
Value	Calculated value according to the risk assessment method
Controls	
Existing control	List of existing controls aimed to mitigate the risk
Efficiency of control	For each control the efficiency of the control for the particular risk
Residual risk	Evaluation of the risk with existing controls
Likelihood	Estimate of the probability of risk occurring in a given period
Impact level	Estimate of the impact in case of the realization of the risk
Value	Calculated value according to the risk assessment method
KRI	List of Key Risk Indicators used to measure the likelihood and impact level
Actions	Actions to mitigate the risk if it is considered unacceptable according to risk appetite
Planned risk	Evaluation of the risk with existing controls and all the actions completed

(*Continued*)

Table 7.1 (CONTINUED)   Risk Attributes

Attribute	Content
Likelihood	Estimate of the probability of risk occurring in a given period
Impact level	Estimate of the impact in case of the realization of the risk
Value	Calculated value according to the risk assessment method
Risk owner	Individual or team accountable for risk management
Deadline	Planned date at which the risk will be reduced to the desired level

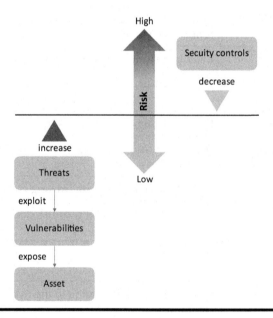

Figure 7.3   Risk value.

calculated from the many factors that influence it. Management is accustomed to dealing with absolute numbers: increase or decrease in turnover, profit/loss ratios, etc. They also expect to have clear indicators on the evolution of security risks and especially want to understand how they are calculated. The problem is not about understanding that a security risk exists but about being able to demonstrate how its value is calculated. The task becomes complicated when the level of risk remains stable over time despite investments. We know that this stems from the negative evolution of threats or vulnerabilities during a period of time, but how can it be explained with factual KRIs?

Skepticism vis-à-vis an improbable risk management added value, and especially risk analysis, should be countered using a simple and understandable risk measurement method. Risk analysis cannot remain subjective due to the major decisions it will inevitably influence. It is therefore essential to rely on a few factual indicators, although the mere fact of involving many experts may provide sufficient guarantees of objectivity. Even incomplete, a simple security risk assessment model provides a common language and sparks discussion with a large number of contributors, which will eventually produce information that can be used in the decision-making process.

Likelihood of Risk Occurrence

The likelihood of an event can be expressed by the potential number of its occurrences during a period of time. For example, if one type of incident occurs every week, then it can be said that there is a high probability that it will happen soon.

EXAMPLE

Assessment of the likelihood of a risk based on the frequency of occurrence of related incidents.

Likelihood	Frequency of observable events
Almost certain	weekly
Likely	monthly
Possible	yearly
Unlikely	1 – 5 years
Rare	> 5 years

The main difficulty in assessing the likelihood of a security risk occurrence (or an incident related to a risk) lies precisely in the absence of occurrences. We know it can happen but cannot deduce its likelihood based on previous occurrences. For example, even if our web server has not been attacked by a Denial Of Service (DOS), we know that this risk exists, but we do not know its likelihood. And yet, it is essential to provide at least an estimate. What is the likelihood of an advanced persistent threat (APT) intrusion or an internal fraud?

Assessing the likelihood of an occurrence in the field of information security means essentially relying on external data, statistics from suppliers or consulting firms, specialized reports, or contacts with similar industrial sectors. We therefore propose a scale assessing the probability of security risk events, presented in Table 7.2.

Table 7.2 Criteria to Estimate the Probability of Security Risks

Likelihood		Frequency of Observable Event Inside or Outside
Almost certain	5	Annual or monthly occurrence
Likely	4	Has occurred in the past in less than a year and will occur
Possible	3	Has occurred at least once in our or other organizations
Unlikely	2	Has never occurred in the organization
Rare	1	Is possible but has not occurred to date

			Impact				
	Regulatory		Minor non conformity	Remediation deadlines	Repetitive non compliance	Significant fine	Out of business
	Human		Minor injuries	First aid required	Hospitalization	Multiple serious injuries	Death
	Financial		< 1% of budet	1% - 3% of budget	3% - 6% of budget	6% - 10% of budget	> 10% of budget
	Reputational		Customer dissatisfaction	Some customer complaints	Spotlight and local echo	Major complaints and media coverage	Deterioration of the image in the long term
			Insignificant 1	Minor 2	Moderate 3	Major 4	Extreme 5
Annual or monthly occurrence (< year)	Almost certain	5	Repeatable minor incidents	10	15	20	Announced disaster
Has occurred in the past in less than a year and will occure	Likely	4	4	8	12	(1)	20
Has occurred at least once in our or other organizations	Possible	3	(2)	(10)	9	(1)	15
Has never occurred in the organization	Unlikely	2	(4)	(3)	(2)	(2)	10
Is possible but has not occurred to date	Rare	1	Negligible	2	(3)	4	Almost impossible disaster

(Likelihood)

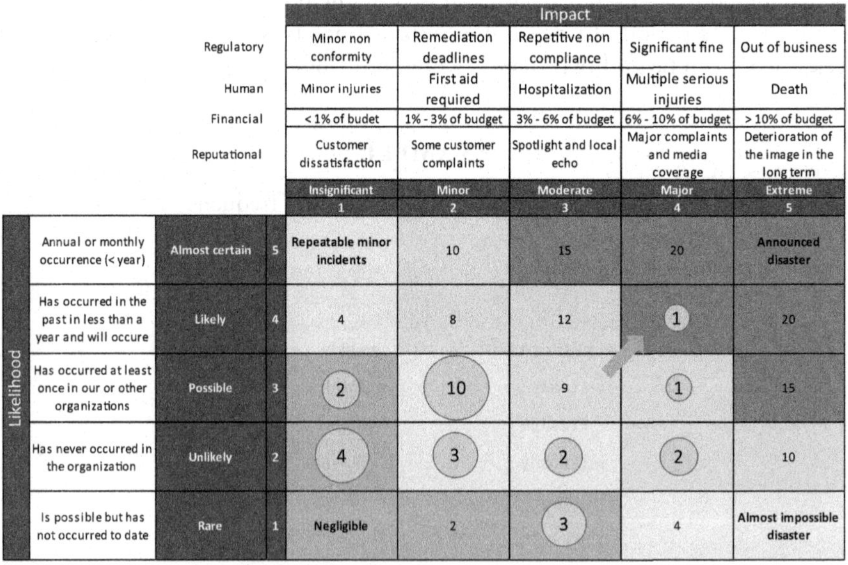

Figure 7.4 Example of a security risk matrix with different impact scales.

We can obviously use any scale, but it is important to get as close as possible to the company's standards for other types of risks. We can even go as far as using the same scales as for other company operational risks, mentioning that the events are observed both internally and externally.

Risk Impact

Risks have different types of impact. We could limit ourselves to financial impacts or consider other types, such as reputational, human, legal, or regulatory. As with probabilities, an estimate of the impact could be on a scale of 1 to 5. A risk matrix with four scales of different risk impacts is presented in Figure 7.4. Risk value is calculated using the formula Value = Likelihood × Impact.

Effectiveness of Controls

A risk may be observed before or after the application of mitigation controls. An inherent risk is a risk that has not been mitigated by the controls in place. Residual risk is the state of the same risk after the application of controls. The controls act either on decreasing the likelihood of threats occurring (e.g. an intrusion detection system) or on vulnerabilities (e.g. encryption). It is also possible to introduce the notion of desired risk, which is the level of risk sought after the deployment of complementary controls.

A control system that is 100 percent effective would reduce a risk to 0. In contrast, a totally ineffective control system will have no effect on inherent risk. Therefore, if we can determine the effectiveness of controls in a range between 0 and 1, the risk calculation formula could be as follows:

$$\text{Value of residual risk} = \text{Value of inherent risk} \times (1 - \text{effectiveness of controls})$$

To facilitate the understanding of the risk analysis, additional explanations may be given in its attributes to justify or explain its evaluation.

Quantitative Methods of Risk Analysis

Many books are specialized in quantitative methods of risk analysis. We do not intend to present them here, as this is not our goal. Nevertheless, let us mention the factor analysis of information risk (FAIR) approach [Measuring and Managing Information Risk: A FAIR Approach, Jack Freund, Jack Jones, Elsevier 2015]. The fundamental question in every risk analysis is how to accurately and factually calculate the measure of risk.

The general idea behind the FAIR method is to propose a way to break down a risk into factors (FAIR ontology) and then measure these factors to quantify the risk. The FAIR ontology "*represents a model of how risk works by describing the factors that make up risk and their relationships to one another. These relationships can then be described mathematically, which allows us to calculate risk from measurements and estimates of those factors*".

If we assume that risk is analyzed to inform decision-makers about the future potential of loss, then risk can be decomposed into factors, as in Figure 7.5.

According to the same source, the factors are defined as follows:

Loss event frequency: The probable frequency, within a given time-frame, that loss will materialize from a threat agent's action.
Threat event frequency: The probable frequency, within a given time-frame, that threat will act in a manner that may result in loss.
Contact frequency: The probable frequency, within a given time-frame, that threat agents will come into contact with assets.

Figure 7.5 FAIR ontology.

Probability of action: The probability that a threat agent will act on an asset once contact has occurred.

Vulnerability: The probability that a threat agent's actions will result in loss.

Threat capability: The capability of a threat agent.

Difficulty: The level of difficulty that a threat agent must overcome.

Loss magnitude: The probable magnitude of primary and secondary loss resulting from an event.

Primary loss magnitude: Primary stakeholder loss that materializes directly as a result of the event.

Secondary risk: Primary stakeholder loss-exposure that exists due to the potential for secondary stakeholder reactions to the primary event.

Secondary loss event frequency: The percentage of primary events that have secondary effects.

Secondary loss magnitude: Loss associated with secondary stakeholder reactions.

By applying a process of assessing each risk factor (proposed in the book cited) and then going up the hierarchy of factors, it is possible to formulate a risk value with precision.

7.7 Risk Assessment

Risks are assessed to determine the acceptability of a residual risk by applying the criteria and thresholds defined by risk appetite based on KRIs. During risk assessment, all risk impacts should be considered, even those beyond the borders of the entity responsible for the assessment. Sometimes, this requires complementary investigations.

From a governance perspective, risk assessment should provide the information needed to make decisions about actions to be taken and the criteria used to prioritize, continue investigations, or address risks. To ensure that the value of risk and potential impacts is properly interpreted by committees, boards, or management, it is essential that risk managers provide all the necessary information and criteria used in assessing the risk.

EXAMPLE

In its general policy or concept of managing security risks, a company has defined a method to assess and present risks according to likelihood and impact. It has also defined thresholds allowing risks to be classified according to four categories: Low, Medium, High, and Very high. High or very high risks will be given priority.

The company's risk management policy stipulates: "All high and very high risks should be reported immediately to the Chief Risk Officer and included in the semi-annual reports to the board of directors. For high risks, a remediation action plan must be submitted within three months. Very high risks will not be accepted under any circumstances and immediate action is required with a detailed plan on the appropriate treatment. The CISO is responsible for making proposals for actions and their follow-up. If a very high risk cannot be reduced, the decision to maintain risky activities rests with the board of directors."

The risk assessment options are presented as follows according to the risk value or gravity.

Risk value	Gravity	Description	Actions
15 – 25	Very high risk	Unacceptable risk. Must be followed and reviewed regularly. Reporting at the board level and management	Immediate action needed: transfer, avoid, or reduce. Followed and reported by CISO.
8 – 12	High risk	Potentially inacceptable level. Must be constantly monitored and reported to the Risk Committee.	Action plan is mandatory under the responsibility of the CISO and / or responsible of geographical unit.
4 – 6	Moderate risk	Requires attention and needs to be reviewed annually. Reporting at the CISO level and security committee.	Regular follow-up actions as well as the assignment of a risk responsibility.
1 – 3	Low risk	Does not require any special actions but must be reviewed annually.	No action is planned outside the controls in place.

For a high risk, the company will have to set up an action plan under the responsibility of the CISO or a regional manager.

It might happen that the conditions needed to make a decision have not been met, and the risk has to undergo further analysis. This could happen above all to risks initially considered as high. In this case, those responsible for deciding how to assess risks might ask for further details on its likelihood and/or impact.

7.8 Risk Treatment

After identifying, evaluating, and prioritizing, risk treatment considers all the options to address risks that are deemed unacceptable. The treatment plan must take into consideration the cost/benefit of controls, their ability to reduce the likelihood or impacts, monitoring and reporting requirements, deadlines, and responsibilities.

From a governance perspective, this step should respond to concerns such as criteria used to compare different risk treatment options, planning, availability of resources, cost/benefit analysis, potential for long-term risk reduction, monitoring the treatment, etc.

EXAMPLE

Management often asks the risk manager the following question: "Despite all our security investments, why does the risk level remain the same?"

The overall level of security risks in a company often remains stable over time and even deteriorates in certain cases, despite investments and constant efforts to improve controls. This state of affairs is explained by the security program's lagging behind the evolution of threats, vulnerabilities, and the internal and external context. If this were not the case, every company would sooner or later reduce the level of their risks.

To be able to explain why the state of risk is not as expected, a thorough follow-up must be conducted of the treatment plan's performance and indicators concerning threats, vulnerabilities, and context.

Risk treatment is an area in which architects, engineers, and security specialists can demonstrate all their know-how. If the chosen option requires mitigating or reducing the risk, they will be able to design controls to reduce the probability of the occurrence of threats or vulnerabilities. These controls might be technical or organizational, dealing with policy or guidelines, awareness, monitoring, etc.

The different risk treatment options can be classified into four main categories: acceptance, avoidance, transfer, or reduction.

Acceptance of Risk

The acceptance of a risk is often motivated by the level of risk reduction cost, which can often exceed the expected benefits or even the impact of the risk itself. In this case, a company can decide to cover the potential damage in the case of risk realization. It is even conceivable to take out an insurance policy for very specific and well-defined risks (such as financial loss following cyberattacks). Therefore, no risk reduction measures will be planned, but the evolution of risk will doubtless be highly monitored so as to be able to act should there be an increase in the probability of occurrence.

Avoidance of Risk

Not all risks can be avoided. A risk that can be avoided is a risk related exclusively to a process or service that can be postponed or discontinued. In this case, if risk reduction costs are too high, the company may decide to suspend the activity and thus avoid the risk that ensues.

EXAMPLE

The outsourcing of an IT development or a service can be dropped should the supplier have insufficient measures to protect confidential data.

Transfer of Risk

Transferring information security risks is extremely difficult due to the very nature of risks related to confidentiality, integrity, and availability. An insurance policy can cover damages related to natural events but cannot cover the damages of loss of image due to deficiencies in data protection, for example. Outsourcing transfers the risks related to this activity, but the ultimate responsibility toward the customer remains with the parent company. In general, operational risks with significant impact and low probability (e.g. incidents with financial impacts) are potentially transferable to specialized insurance companies.

Reduction of Risks

Risk reduction remains one of the key activities of the information security team. Preventive controls will reduce the probability of a risk occurring (e.g. antivirus), while protection controls (e.g. encryption) reduce potential impacts. If the residual risk level remains unacceptable, an action plan should reduce it to the desired level, provided that the threats and vulnerabilities stay the same.

How can risks be presented and monitored?

7.9 Reporting, Communication, and Risk Monitoring

To complete the risk management process, it is important to be able to monitor the evolution of risk and the action plan, to communicate with a factual approach, and to produce reports for the stakeholders and the committee responsible for risk assessment and prioritization. The following subsections cover several ways to present the state of risk that can be used for reporting, as well as communications and monitoring.

Evolution of the Context, Threats, and Vulnerabilities

To better understand the state of risks, we must have insight into the evolution of factors that can influence them. Table 7.3 proposes a way to present the evolution of the most representative internal and external factors that can negatively influence security risks. The column "Negative Influence on Risk" provides an indication of the negative level of the factors. The column "Trend" expresses the evolution observed during a time-period. The "Comments" column contains all the additional information needed to understand the level and trends.

Risk Mapping

The term *risk mapping* generally implies a representation of all the risks with their attributes as previously proposed. It is a means of representing all the risks with their main characteristics in a compact form. Risk management tools offer various presentations of these maps, which are often configurable for each company's needs. The most common form is a table in which each line is devoted to a risk and the columns generally take up the attributes, as shown in Table 7.1. Risk status (inherent, residual, or expected) is often represented by three columns: Likelihood, Impact, and Level.

State of High and Very High Risks

High and very high risks are often given special attention by senior management, since they are a priority for the company. Various strategies can be adopted to present these risks, but what needs to be shown above all is their evolution and the achievement level of the actions planned for their treatment. An example of such

Table 7.3   Factors That Negatively Influence Risks

Factors	Degree of Negative Influence	Trend	Comment
Cyber threats	High	↗	General evolution of cyber threats.
Vulnerabilities	Medium	⟶	General state and evolution of the vulnerabilities. Incidents.
Weak awareness	Low	↗	Level of awareness of employees. Examples.
Human risks	Low	↘	Commentary on the general evolution of human risks and main challenges (e.g. turnover).
Resilience	Medium	→	Recovery ability after incidents or attacks.
Lack of resources	Medium	↗	Comment on the availability of resources to achieve risk mitigation goals.

a presentation is given in Table 7.4. The Trend column presents the general evolution of risk.

Heat-Map

To be able to present the positioning of all the residual risks, we often use a variation of a heat-map. The example presented in Figure 7.6 shows the distribution of risks with an indication of the number of risks with the same value. This presentation is useful if it is accompanied by a reference to risk descriptions and their trends.

Different names exist for the risk cases appearing in the four corners of the heat-map. These cases should be rare, but their treatment should be better explained in the risk management policy or concept, especially those with potentially extreme impacts.

Table 7.4 Example of High-Risk Monitoring

Risk	Residual Level	Trend	Key Indicators	Actions	Status	Planned Level
External fraud	H	↗	• Number of attempts • Damage suffered • Reaction time	• Awareness • Revision of guidelines • Means of detection • External coordination	According to plan 60%	M
Third-party intrusion	H	→	• Penetration test results • External statistics	• Awareness • Elimination of vulnerabilities • Prevention improvement	According to plan 50%	M
Web server attack	H	→	• Result of penetration tests • Level of server updates	• Upgrade configurations	Late 20%	M
DDoS (Distributed Denial of service)	E	↗	• Observations in similar industry	• Migrate to DNS provider protection	Urgent	M

			Impact						
			Insignificant	Minor	Moderate	Major	Extreme
			1	2	3	4	5
Likelihhod	Almost certain	5	Repeatable minor incidents	10	15	20	Announced disaster
	Likely	4	4	8	12	(1)	20
	Possible	3	(2)	(10)	9	(1)	15
	Unlikely	2	(4)	(3)	(2)	(2)	10
	Rare	1	Negligible	2	(3)	4	Almost impossible disaster

Figure 7.6   Example of a heat-map.

7.10 Conclusion

Risk management is currently a mature discipline. Many specialized works have been devoted to it and should be consulted, especially for in-depth knowledge of quantitative methods. However, with regard to security risk management, some precautions must be taken so that the process adds value to the governance of the program: identify and rationalize the number of risks to be analyzed; pay attention to the KRIs that will justify and explain the level of the risks; if possible, adopt the same standards used for other company operational risks; and present the state of risk coherently. The security risk management process is an indispensable tool for governance and must be understood and accepted by everyone. It is one of the major drivers of any security program and as such, is a fundamental process.

Chapter 8

Program Management

Information security (IS) governance must be based on a sound process. It is no longer sufficient for a chief information security officer (CISO) to present protective measures and justify them with increasing threats. Today more than ever, the process leading to the implementation of controls must be understood and accepted by all the stakeholders. Results alone are not enough. Security controls have traditionally been set up to address threats, reduce the risk of an incident, or ensure compliance with regulations. Such an approach, which can be described as opportunistic or bottom-up, is no longer sustainable, since managers do not have control over costs or longer-term planning.

Setting up a security program management process or information security management system (ISMS) is therefore of paramount importance to any decision-maker. Introducing a management system based on an iterative process involving the governing body and business units ensures the quality of the decisions and especially the support of all the stakeholders.

This chapter provides answers to the following questions:

- What is a security program?
- How is a program established?
- What are the program's components?
- What are the essential tools in managing the program?
- How does the program review cycle work in practice?

What is a security program?

8.1 Security Program

There are several interpretations or proposals for defining the term *security program*. In what follows, a security program consists of all the measures deployed by a company to protect its assets, above all strategic, tactical, and operational controls according to the three-level model, and more generally, all the activities, regulatory framework, and processes related to IS.

Security program management includes steering and supervising the controls in place, operational activities, change projects, planning, and coordination. The management of a security program corresponds to the definition of an ISMS as proposed in the standard ISO 27001. Therefore, the two appellations are interchangeable and generally designate the same thing.

A security program meets the requirements of the strategy and the internal and external regulatory framework. It is carried out according to a defined organization and includes risk treatments and projects aimed at improving maturity as decided by the governing body. Running a security program is the main responsibility of a CISO. They must first ensure the proper working operations of all the controls and then carry out the strategic security initiatives as defined earlier.

Program management according to a formalized process is of utmost importance. Demonstrating that security reduces risk is important, but building trust in the process itself is even more important. Confidence in the results, indeed, depends on trust in the process. So, treating one risk is fine, but demonstrating that all the risks have been identified, and their treatment is planned, is even better. Therefore, managing the program in the form of an iterative process of continuous improvement and involving decision-making bodies is essential for effective governance. This ability to ensure that nothing has been left to chance instills confidence in senior officials. This also reassures auditors, regulators, and all the stakeholders.

The design of a security program establishes a virtuous circle of problem-solving, risk reduction, and prioritization leading to continuous improvement and preventing the recurrence of the same irregularities. Senior managers and board members expect the ISMS or security program in place to protect the company according to the strategy and policies.

Security program activities are guided by a documented process. For a program to be accepted by all the stakeholders, it must be based on the recommendations of the standards or audit findings and must also include improvement points decided within a process integrating the following objectives: risk mitigation, alignment with business needs, integration of new technologies, response to audit findings, improvement of maturity, etc. Security teams today still set up security controls that have not always been justified or formally accepted as part of a decision process. Controls, often technical solutions, are installed in response to visible threats outside of defined planning or architecture. This is where a security project roadmap gains importance as a supervision and management tool.

How is a security program established?

8.2 Program Review Cycle

Constructing an iterative security program review cycle is the only way to activate management decisions about security that legitimize the actions that will be taken. The program review cycle forms the core of an ISMS.

Establishing a review cycle or virtuous circle can obviously start from the concept of continuous improvement "Plan-Do-Check-Act" originally proposed by Walter Shewhart and made popular by Edward Deming and in particular in ISO 9001, which is devoted to quality and continuous improvement. We propose a simplified cycle composed of three processes: Decide, Do, and Monitor, and three deliverables: Plan, Metrics, and Feedback (Figure 8.1).

The main components of the cycle can be described as follows:

Decide: The Decide process comprises all of the decision-making steps regarding program objectives for a given period. The purpose is to establish or validate a roadmap of initiatives or improvement projects based on the elements provided by the Monitor process.

The main actors are the governing body and the CISO. The governing body can take different forms, such as a prioritization committee, a security committee, or some other. They must have the authority to decide, prioritize initiatives, and allocate resources.

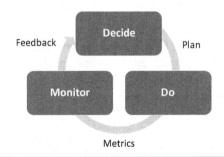

Figure 8.1 **Security program review cycle.**

Plan: The result of the Decide process is an ISMS business plan for the next period. The Plan consists mainly of two types of projects:
- projects that maintain or strengthen controls and risk treatment (Maintain)
- projects that offer new services (Change) such as those required by the strategy (see later)

Do: The Do process carries out the ISMS plan based on the objectives established in the Decide process. This includes not only projects or initiatives as set out in the strategy, for example, but also objectives to improve current processes and controls, financial objectives, or any other objective related to the security program.

The main actors in the realization of the plan are the CISO, the security team, information technology (IT) operations, and management, as well as all employees engaged in security controls.

Metrics: The results of this process will be evaluated using metrics and key performance indicators (KPIs) and will facilitate the observations made in the Monitor process. Metrics are used for reporting purposes.

Monitor: This process includes oversight, evaluating program results, and compiling reports that will be used in the Decide process. It groups together all the elements necessary for decision-making. Using metrics to evaluate and report to the decision-makers is primarily the responsibility of the CISO and their team.

Feedback: Consists of reports used for decision-making:
- Report on the achievement of strategic initiatives
- Risk report (and treatment plan)
- Maturity report (and improvement plan)
- Report on the progress of the roadmap or projects

EXAMPLE

The governing body has decided to transfer some security responsibilities to the business units (see the example in Chapter 4, Strategy). A plan was elaborated under the aegis of the CISO; then, implementation began, resulting in the modification of certain controls, in particular those related to managing identities and access rights, and the authorizations of certain exceptions. The metrics used to measure the degree of achievement will be those typically used to monitor project progress. It will also be possible to measure the operational efficiency in such a change, in particular the reduction of the load on teams responsible for managing access rights. These KPIs will be part of the reports produced as part of the Monitor process. At the next review of the program, the governing body will thus be able to decide whether to continue with this strategy.

At this point, it should be noted that new security projects can only be initiated if they are justified by the need to treat a risk, improve the security posture or process maturity, respond to audit findings, or implement strategic initiatives. An ISMS is not just a set of operational controls. It is above all a systematic approach of continuous improvement to ensure the best protection of a company's assets. The ISO 27001 standard, containing good practices necessary to develop an ISMS and its review cycle, can be used. The following key principles advocated by the standard should be taken into account when developing the security program:

- Security organization context (strategy and strategic alignment)
- Management support and organization within the framework of the ISMS
- Importance of the policies and regulatory framework
- Risk management: identification, assessment, and treatment
- Planning and goal setting based on risk analysis
- Provision of resources
- Awareness and communication
- Establishment and management of controls
- Performance evaluation
- Continuous improvement and management of nonconformities

The security program review cycle as outlined earlier encompasses the ISO 27001 recommendations contained in the Requirements for an Information Security Management System. The control objectives contained in its Annex A—Reference control objectives and controls—relate more specifically to controls that are part of an ISMS and are embodied in the catalog of controls that will be discussed later.

With reference to the three-level control framework (TLCF) model, the building blocks provide all the elements needed to establish an ISMS (Figure 8.2).

Figure 8.2   Program management use input from other building blocs.

How other building blocks contribute to the management of the program are discussed below.

Strategy: Strategic objectives and initiatives are fundamental components of decision-making in the Decide process. The priorities established for the program must take these objectives into account.

Policies: The regulatory framework sets the requirements for a security program. Its documents contain the rules that must be respected and instructions on how to implement controls.

Organization: Program management includes defining the roles and responsibilities of the governing body, committees, the CISO and their team, IT, and all the other stakeholders. Responsibilities must be defined in the three processes Decide, Do, and Monitor.

Risk management: The management process highlights the principal dangers to the company's assets. This makes it possible to plan the reinforcement of controls within the program.

Reporting and oversight: The activities of this block, producing all the reports required in the Decide process, are also part of the Monitor process.

Asset management: Asset management controls take part indirectly in the management of the program through their contribution to the risk management process. Knowledge of the assets to be protected, the related responsibilities, and their classification is an indispensable source for any decision-making within the security program.

Compliance: The Compliance block provides all the gap analyses and recommendations for remediation to fill the gaps. It deals with both the external and the internal regulatory framework. Audit findings are also part of this block.

Metrics and KPI: Provides all the metrics needed for reporting as part of the Monitor process.

Let us take a closer look at the tools that are needed to make a pragmatic ISMS review cycle.

What are the essential tools in managing the program?

8.3 Essential Tools of a Security Program

Finally, what comprises a security program, and what are its main tools? It was noted in Chapter 2 that the set of controls can be categorized in different ways, especially in three levels of responsibility as proposed by the TLCF model. The security standards have adopted different ways to present the universe of security controls with accompanying categorizations. There are other elements in a security program, including all the governance and management activities, which may also be considered controls. Therefore, a security program consists of all the security controls. The management of the security program or ISMS entails setting up and constantly improving a universe of controls adapted to the company's needs.

Every company already has an IS program. What we need to know is whether it is adapted to the company's needs and context, and if not, how to improve it. The first thing to do is consult the standards to ensure that their requirements have been taken into account one way or another. The ISO 27001/2 standard is probably the best source to verify the completeness of a program.

If we take a closer look at the recommendations of the standards regarding the security program review cycle, they all stress the following four essential components:

1. Planning improvements
2. Identifying controls
3. Indicators or metrics to evaluate results
4. Reporting for planning purposes

We can therefore consider the plan (1) and a catalog (or inventory) of controls (2) to be a security program's main tools. Further details will be given later. Metrics (3) and reports (4) will be discussed in detail in the chapters devoted to them and will not be developed here.

Plan

The plan is embodied in a project roadmap. The role of this roadmap is to facilitate an understanding of priorities and provide support for decisions concerning the improvement of controls and implementation of changes. An easily understandable roadmap that will be reviewed as part of the security program review cycle is one of the main tools of governance. Projects that are part of the plan can be categorized by the type of improvement they bring to the controls:

1. Projects aimed at maintaining existing controls and their level of effectiveness ("maintain" projects)
2. Projects aimed at introducing new controls ("change" projects)

"Maintain" security projects generally do not introduce changes in the architecture or technologies used. They aim to maintain the level of protection or bring about improvements needed to better respond to evolving threats or vulnerabilities. On the other hand, "change" projects introduce new controls or major changes. These may include controls to meet new needs, the introduction of new technologies, architectural changes, or new areas of protection. The origins of these two types of projects are as follows (Table 8.1):

> *Examples of maintain projects*: Change of the encryption system, extending data leak prevention to scan "private" messages, upgrade of the baseline protection of Windows servers, cybersecurity policy review, etc.
>
> *Examples of change projects*: Develop strategy and policy for external cloud computing, introduction of a new smart card system, setting up security organization to support the outsourcing of IT developments, developing a new service within the Security Operation Center, etc.

The roadmap for security projects is an important element of communication. It can be presented in different ways, but the following information needs to be easily available (Figure 8.3):

Origin of the request/need: The origin of the project makes it possible to contextualize the need and facilitate prioritization.

Description: A short description facilitates an understanding of the project's objectives.

Planning and dependence: Graphical representation makes it easy to understand dependence on other projects and deadlines.

Outcome: The results or deliverables of the project should be summarized as a reminder.

Table 8.1   Types of Security Projects and their Drivers

Type	Origin
Maintain	Audit findings Risk treatment Compliance gaps Incidents Evolution of threats or vulnerabilities Penetration test results or resilience tests
Change	New technologies New business strategy support New business models Fundamental changes in security stance Changes in computer systems Maturity gaps

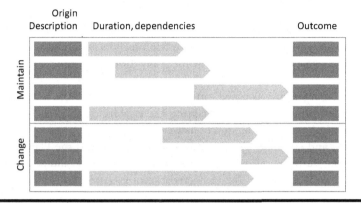

Figure 8.3   Roadmap of projects as part of a security program plan.

EXAMPLE

Origin: Strategic initiative.

Description: Introduction of smart cards for internal physical and logical access.

Dependence: Adaptation of the authentication system at the application level. Adapting controls to physical access points.

Outcome: Easy employee access to applications and premises.

Saves time for employees and saves 10 percent of help desk time used for password resets.

Reduces the risk of internal and external fraud by introducing strong authentication.

Alignment with best practices and regulations regarding the protection of confidential data.

An example of the presentation of a roadmap is given in Figure 8.3.

Control Catalog

Good governance requires knowledge of the security protections in place, the activities and daily concerns of security specialists, as well as the objectives and plans for improvement. The question is how to present all the controls established in the context of an ISMS so that they can be used for governance and by all those involved in elaborating or revising the security program.

We will use the term *catalog* or *inventory of controls* to designate a tool providing information about all the security controls deployed. Before proposing a systematic approach to designing such a catalog, let us first recall its main purpose and desired features. The catalog of controls can be for many different purposes:

Program management: As noted earlier, the management of the security program or ISMS primarily involves adapting the established controls (maintain) or the evolution or introduction of new controls (change). The knowledge of the impact and especially on which controls the projects of the Plan will act and for what purpose, ensures better management, planning, and implementation of the right resources. The characteristics of each control are noted with its maturity or level of effectiveness, leading to better management of priorities.

Governance and management oversight: To know the impact of its decisions, the governing body must have an overview of existing controls. Decisions on the treatment of risks will involve the controls associated with them. However, if the security officer cannot make a concise presentation of the controls associated with risks and desired improvements, knowledgeable decisions cannot be made.

Audit: Recurring audit requests are a reality in many companies. They come not only from regulators or internal auditors but also from customers or suppliers wanting better visibility of their partners' security postures. These time-consuming audits involving employees in the various areas of security and IT can be simplified using a catalog of security controls. Indeed, the first task of the auditors is to discover existing controls, who is responsible for them, especially whether they have been tested, and their level of maturity or effectiveness. Different auditors make similar requests to the same internal employees, which is very time-consuming. A catalog containing key information on controls would facilitate the auditors' work and help reduce the indirect costs of each audit.

Internal organization: Establishing a catalog of controls contributes to a better understanding of roles and responsibilities in the field of operational security management. Responsibility is defined for each control, resulting in more clarity in the security organization and management process.

A control catalog therefore consists of a list of security controls (or means of protection), each having a certain number of attributes, such as

■ Description
■ Name of the person or department responsible
■ Test frequency
■ Date of the last test
■ Current maturity
■ Desired (target) maturity
■ Explanation (justification) of the target maturity

The controls presented in the catalog should not include product names or deployed technologies. This is important to preserve sustainability. A catalog can obviously be elaborated using the standards, such as ISO 27001/2 or NIST, and especially how they classify the controls. The method proposed in ISO 27001 is interesting, because it makes it possible to develop a relatively short catalog of controls. When a standard is used, the company catalog specifies the attributes of the control set up for each recommendation or control objective in the standard.

EXAMPLE

Control catalog format established according to ISO 27002 (extract). The controls are presented on two levels (control and control guidance).

Domain	Responsible	Test frequency	Test date	Current Maturity	Desired Maturity
Control objective					
Control					
Control guidance					
...					
13 Communications security					
13.1 Network security management				3	3
13.1.1 Network controls	Network	M		2	2
Logging					
System authentication					
Connection restriction					
13.1.2 Security of network services	Business Unit	M		1	3
Encryption					
13.1.3 Segregation in networks	Network	M		1	3
13.2 Information transfer				3	3
13.2.1 Information transfer policies	Sec. Team	Y		2	3
13.2.2 Agreements on information transfer	Sec. Team	Y		2	3
13.2.3 Electronic messaging	Sec. Team	Y		2	3
13.2.4 Confidentiality agreements	Sec. Team	Y		2	3
...					

Controls are tested and measured for maturity (for details, see the Chapter 9: Security Metrics). Control guidance gives details of the practices that are part of the controls (e.g. logging is a practice in the context of network controls). The maturity levels of the control objectives are averages of the control maturities.

When developing the catalog, care must be taken that its size remains relatively small to facilitate its use and maintenance. Controls can obviously be expressed with a great amount of detail. The finer the granularity of the controls, the more complete the catalog, but it will be more difficult to maintain and use for governance purposes. The goal is not to detail everything that is done in the field of IS but rather, to present a coherent grouping of controls with the same objectives.

One criterion for selecting the level of detail needed would be referencing controls for the purpose of risk analysis and treatment. The more detailed the risks or risk scenarios, the more detailed the reference controls need to be.

EXAMPLE

If the risk or risk scenario is labeled "Unauthorized device connections to the network ...," then we will need the "Connection restriction" control at the control catalog level to be able to associate it with the risk and evaluate its effectiveness. However, if the risk encompasses multiple scenarios and is labeled "Inappropriate Network Usage," then "Network Control" control (Level 1) could encompass all the means deployed to mitigate various IT network risk scenarios.

A pragmatic approach to developing a control catalog might be to present only one level of controls but to group them together in organizational security domains. This approach tries to present all the controls by area of responsibility, which could facilitate an understanding of the ISMS.

EXAMPLE

Domain	Responsible	Test frequency	Test date	Current Maturity	Desired Maturity
1. Risk management					
Concept, policies, and process	CISO	A		2	3
...					
2. Communication and awareness					
Awareness sessions	CISO	A		2	3
...					
3. Identity and Access Management					
Policy and process	IAM team	A		3	4
Certification of access rights	IAM team	A		2	4
...					
4. Continuity					
BCM	BCM	A		3	4
Disaster Recovery	IT	A		2	4
...					
5. Baseline IT security					
Configuration management	IT Ops	M		2	3
...					
6. Incident management					
Policy, process	IT	A		2	3
...					
7. Network security					
Network security controls	Network	M		3	4
...					
etc.					

Whatever the form of the catalog of controls, its primary use as a tool of governance and IS management should be kept in mind. It reinforces responsibilities, allows the evolution of maturities to be monitored, is a reference for risk analysis, and facilitates the work of the auditors.

How does the program review cycle work in practice?

8.4 Review Cycle of an ISMS

An ISMS needs to establish an iterative process in the management of priorities, as we have just seen. The program review cycle is used primarily when annual plans or IS business plans are developed. What follows is an example of using the program review cycle in the context of developing an annual business plan for an IS program (Figure 8.4).

We must first have a set of reports that tell us about the status of the security program. This set of reports, which can be called *state of security*, consists of the following items produced in the Monitor process and as part of the Feedback:

1. *Report on risks* and, above all, a specification of the treatments required as a result of risk analysis.
2. *Report on the maturity of controls.* This report presents the gaps between desired and current maturities and highlights necessary and urgent improvements.
3. *Report on the status of projects* and especially the degree of completion planned for the period.

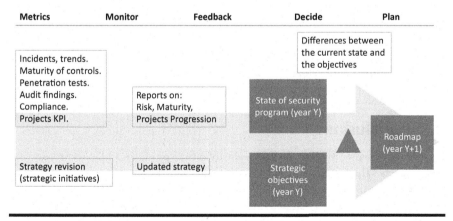

Figure 8.4   Diagram of developing an IS plan.

The risk report will tell us what treatments need to be planned to mitigate significant risks. The report on control maturity will enable us to prioritize improvements in controls in relation to the treatments required for risk mitigation. Finally, the project status report will help us decide whether to continue or reprioritize certain projects based on the new context, strategic changes, and other imperatives for the next period. Due to limited resources, it is not uncommon to reprioritize certain projects, but this must be done by the governing body or planning committee, who are familiar with the project portfolio.

The responsibility for drawing up these reports lies with the CISO and their team. They are produced using the metrics or KPIs resulting from the Do process, in particular the following:

- Incidents and trends
- Evaluation of control maturities
- Audit findings
- Compliance gap from the legal and regulatory framework
- Project (part of the plan) progress indicators

A *security strategy* is not set in stone and may change or be adapted to the business context or its evolution. A review of the strategy must be made upstream in the Monitor process. Project status reports must be supplemented by strategic orientations for the next period or a revised strategy. The responsibility for revising the strategy lies with a committee specifically constituted for this task but with the approval of the board of directors or a delegated committee as governing body.

The gap between objectives set for the current year and what has actually been achieved is determined in the Decide process. A new plan (or new objectives) will be elaborated based on this gap and new needs laid out in the strategy. The responsibility for drawing up the plan could lie with the governing body or a committee. Sponsorship for this new plan must be ensured so that it will be accepted by all the stakeholders.

The diagram in Figure 8.4 summarizes how the program review cycle and its elements are used to develop an annual plan for the IS program.

8.5 Conclusion

Security governance requires that the security officer produces a plan to protect corporate assets. The process of producing the plan is as important as the final result, because internal and external stakeholders need to know that mitigating risk and implementing the security strategy result from a process involving decision-makers. It enables them to trace security efforts from the identification of objectives to their achievement through a formalized process involving decision-making steps.

Most companies have adopted a systematic approach to guide security activities. This process deserves greater formalization involving forums or decision-making committees to manage priorities. The few steps and tools presented in this chapter can inspire security managers and governing bodies to put similar approaches in place to improve security program management process.

Chapter 9

Security Metrics

The lack of standards in the measurement of security is not a coincidence. Information security (IS) has no dimensions or characteristics of its own. The "size" of a company's security can be measured through its financial impact—its cost—but this is not enough without measuring other aspects: profit, flexibility, added business value, asset protection, etc. Several factors are behind this, including the diversity of security activities (from the strategic to the operational level), the impossibility of delineating its scope (technical, human, application, physical, etc.), and problems with the measurement units or objects being measured. Incidents, risk level, leakage, threat, loss, etc. mean different things to different people.

However, measuring security is essential for good governance. Senior management, which is ultimately accountable for security, requests reports that contain stable key point indicators (KPIs) of the adequacy of security. Companies need a pragmatic approach to monitoring the effectiveness of security countermeasures to enable them to adjust their program and decide on security investments, which need to be justified (explained) by some kind of quantitative measurements of the benefits. Metrics are also requested by the regulatory framework.

This chapter presents the main tools or practices to develop security metrics for governance and management purposes. They will be used in reporting, dashboards, or targeted studies for governance bodies to help them make decisions based on hard facts. Some specific metrics will be presented in the examples.

This chapter also provides answers to the following questions:

Why is it difficult to measure security?
What kind of measures can be used?
What are basic financial metrics?
Can we use some modeling to estimate ROSI or better assess the impact of change?

How can we answer the question "How is our security"?

Is there a more pragmatic approach to measure security?

How are security goals set and progress towards them measured?

How can operational effectiveness be measured?

How can we know the real cost of security?

How can we compare ourselves with others?

9.1 Why Is It Difficult to Measure Security?

It is generally acknowledged that management and boards of directors are not being given relevant or desired information allowing them to assess the overall level of security protection, the return on security investments, or cost–benefit ratios. Security is seen as a means to achieve business objectives, but ever-increasing investments foster a sense of frustration and misunderstanding among senior managers.

Having no answer to the question "What should be measured to know our state of security?" many believe that security is ultimately an insurance policy whose annual premium protects a company against a bad surprise. Obviously this is not the case. In addition, the company is tempted to reduce the premium while hoping that the disaster will never occur or, if it occurs, that the coverage will be sufficient. Many chief executive officers or officials are tempted to take this shortcut. Unfortunately, ISMS cannot be compared to insurance. Insurance protects many insured against a limited number of accidents with well-defined coverage, while a company's security protects a single insured against innumerable accidents with no evaluation of their probability, their impact, or how to indemnify them.

> ### EXAMPLE
>
> Financial loss due to the unavailability of services (from a cyberattack or natural hazard) can be insured against, but a company cannot be insured against loss of customer confidence, loss of confidential data, or theft of an industrial secret.

In the field of security, there are no universally accepted indicators to measure the adequacy of the controls in place. Incident observations (or their absence) or examining statistics generated by technical security devices (e.g. the number of viruses or attempted intrusions stopped) do not allow an opinion to be formed on the adequacy of security. How many incidents and of what type are allowed under "adequate security"? And what if none are observed? This makes it difficult to measure the effectiveness of security investments with any precision.

Companies do not share their data or statistics on vulnerability and incidents because of the negative image this information conveys. Some cases are reported in the media, but details are not provided that would have allowed conclusions to be drawn on the costs involved or the vulnerabilities exploited. There are also no common definitions or terminologies for an anonymous exchange of statistics. The terms *incident, attack, loss, investment*, etc. mean different things to different people. It is therefore difficult to compare available data, because there are no method or measurement calibration standards.

Easily available indicators often do not answer the questions asked by senior executives. Security devices generate numerous traces of activity, such as patches applied, vulnerabilities detected, alerts, intrusion attempts, volume of emails processed by antivirus tools, authentication errors, signs of system access, privilege changes, etc. Log management solutions are able to correlate these traces, generate reports, and thus ensure compliance with legal and normative requirements. However, high-level metrics require additional efforts to link and aggregate these different indicators. They must provide information on the expected results or improvements that benefit the company.

EXAMPLE

To find out whether investing in a new identity and access management (IAM) system was justified, there is no point in counting the number of privilege changes made over a period of time; rather, we should check whether we have decreased delays, optimized the use of available resources, or decreased the number of errors.

OK, but what can we do? What kind of different measurements can be used?

Despite the difficulty of accurately measuring security, several methods can be used to obtain pragmatic indicators or measurements and will be presented here. Let us first mention that metrics can be divided into two large blocks: quantitative metrics (expressed by commonly accepted units of measure) and qualitative metrics (expressed by subjective appreciation).

EXAMPLE

As part of the risk management concept, financial loss category thresholds can be set according to a percentage of the budget, as was the case in Chapter 7 (Risk Management). This implies that we are able to calculate the actual loss of a risk incident; for example, the consequence of a cyberattack. These are quantitative metrics. However, its likelihood cannot be calculated based on the number of incidents over a period of time, because this information is not available to us. We can then express it by a qualitative metric (Rare, Unlikely, Possible, Likely, or Almost certain) based on a subjective estimate.

Different strategies to measure IS can be classified into the following categories:

Financial metrics are concerned with the financial impact of investments in security controls.

Modeling allows investment decisions to be made based on a model that is used instead of real values.

Assessment (measurement) of the state of security consists of evaluating the state of security as a whole or in a specific domain (e.g. cybersecurity, continuity, or application security) using various qualitative evaluation tools.

Assumption-based metrics consists of guiding the measurement process according to what we want to demonstrate (or are not able to demonstrate).

Posture or maturity evaluation compared with the standards or regulatory framework is a qualitative metric on the level of maturity compared with the standards or benchmarks of good practices. Audits can be classified in this category.

Operational metrics measures the operational effectiveness of security activities.

Metrics of progress toward a goal is the establishment of metrics or KPIs to measure the degree of progress toward a set objective.

Cost analysis of costs in different security categories often provides highly relevant indicators for governance.

Benchmarking allows measurements among similar companies.

These categories will be developed in what follows.

9.2 Financial Metrics

Financial metrics in the field of IS help assess investment opportunities in protection solutions. To put it simply, security investments are considered justified if they cost less than potential losses (inherent risk). In the opposite case, they are totally unjustified. Note that this reasoning does not take into account the probability of an event occurring.

Annualized loss expectancy (ALE) is an evaluation of potential annual losses as the result of risks impacts. This assessment may concern all risks or only certain scenarios. As always with risks, there is a problem with measuring probability (see the preceding example). Recall once again that the calculation of ALE alone is meaningless unless it is accompanied by an assessment of the probability of occurrence of the risk.

The ALE measurement is often cited in relation to *total cost of ownership* (*TCO*), the idea being to compare the trends or evolution of the two values. TCO can be calculated relatively easily for security. It includes all costs, hardware, software, and human resources within the security or ISMS program (see also the later section on

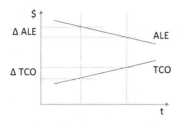

Figure 9.1   Expected trends of ALE and TCO.

cost analysis). TCO answers the question "How much does security cost?" TCO is well understood by senior officials, who are accustomed to comparing benefits and the evolution of expenses, including those related to security.

The gain from security investments alone—*economic value added* (*EVA*)—is difficult to calculate for the reasons mentioned previously, but it can be calculated indirectly by observing changes in ALE and TCO. Both trends are presented in Figure 9.1. The added value of security investments could then be expressed as

$$EVA = \Delta ALE \, / \, \Delta TCO$$

EVA should always be <1 for security investments to be cost-effective. Indeed, if EVA > 1 according to this formula, then security investments (TCO) are not enough to compensate for potential losses. If EVA = 1, then security costs just barely compensate for the evolution of potential losses.

EVA as expressed here can be considered the same as return on security investments (ROSI). Several tools or methods exist to calculate ROSI based on loss and investment analyses for specific security processes or controls.

The main difficulty with these methods is that the estimate of a loss must be associated with its probability of occurrence for all the business units and all the controls deployed, which may be very inaccurate. An accurate calculation method requires statistics over several years with precise figures on incidents, their typology, and estimates of losses incurred. And this is for estimates of direct losses. Indirect losses (such as loss of customers or reputation) are even more difficult to estimate. It clearly becomes impossible for businesses to effectively manage such a large amount of data in a constantly changing production environment while keeping pace with new technologies.

Trying to calculate return on security investment (ROSI) for all the security investments is very difficult, if not impossible for the reasons just mentioned. On the other hand, this is relatively easy to calculate for elements or isolated technical protection devices such as firewalls, intrusion detection systems, antiviruses, etc. Delineating the scope and identifying the purpose of the measurements are key in this process.

Before discussing the delineation of measurement domains and the evaluation of the ROSI, it is essential to understand the benefit provided by security controls. To make an analogy, the benefit of the braking system on a vehicle is obvious. We can then quantify the cost of a failure and estimate the ROSI, which will probably be very high. Without answers to these questions on the added value, we cannot design the metrics and calculate the ROSI.

EXAMPLE

To calculate the profit or added value of strong authentication, we can take the increase in the system's added value compared with authentication based on simple user ID and password. This added value can then be calculated by the reduction of the risk of fraud or the reduction of negative economic impact. Metrics to assess threats or vulnerabilities, for example, include the increase in the number of people who can easily access applications or the number of exposed applications. For financial impact, we can use cost of data breach surveys from specialized institutes and make an estimate or extrapolation in the particular context of the company.

But, is it really necessary to calculate ROSI accurately? It is more important to be able to assess its magnitude on the basis of a risk analysis. We will now focus on calculating ROSI based on the probability of incident occurrences and an estimation of their impact. To estimate the total cost of an incident, it is obviously necessary to know its impact and estimate the total cost of rectifying the damage. To estimate the impact, we can use publications on losses or arbitrarily set a cost. The same can be done to estimate probability based on different reports or specialized studies.

9.2.1 Calculation of ROSI Based on Risk Analyses

The benefit obtained from countermeasures is the difference between the inherent risk (without security controls) and the residual risk (after setting up countermeasures). If we consider that countermeasures modify the probability (P) of occurrences (e.g. the probability of the occurrence of an attack decreases because of measures such as antivirus or intrusion detection), risk impacts (or ALE) can then be calculated as follows:

$$\text{Impact of the inherent risk} = \text{Cost of incident} \times P\left(\text{inherent risk}\right)$$

$$\text{Impact of the residual risk} = \text{Cost of incident} \times P\left(\text{residual risk}\right)$$

The benefit can then be expressed as

$$\text{Benefit}\left(\text{EVA}\right) = \text{Impact of inherent risk} - \text{Impact of residual risk}$$

and the ROSI as

$$\text{ROSI} = \text{Benefit} - \text{Cost of countermeasures}$$

Discussions with management will thus be about calculating the probabilities of occurrence; in other words, how risks are analyzed. It should be possible to show how the security measures taken modify the probabilities of occurrence and/or the level of impact.

9.2.2 Protection Capacity Index

If we know the impact of inherent risk (IR) weighted by its probability of occurrence and the impact of residual risk (RR) weighted by its probability, then we can use an index called *protection capacity* (PC), expressed as

$$PC = \left(IR - RR\right) / IR$$

Protection capacity is ideal if the index tends to 1. This will happen if the impact of the residual risk is very small (or tends to 0) or if the difference between the inherent risk and the residual risk is very large. The idea behind this indicator is to attach a value to the means of protection in place or the degree of risk mitigation. If we know the operational costs or the cost of controls to reduce the risk, we will be able to follow the evolution of our protection capacity with the evolution of investments. The RI - RR difference presents the risk reduction capacity.

This leads to several reflections. First of all, only the operational costs directly related to the impacts of the analyzed risks should be taken into consideration. In other words, we need to look only at controls that reduce the analyzed risk. Ideally, the PC will be calculated by risk. Subsequently, it may be possible to aggregate the indices of several risks into one that has an average protection capacity.

By combining the indicators on the operational costs of controls and the indices of protection capacity by risk, we will be able to present a risk map highlighting the relationship: operational costs - protective capacity (Figure 9.2). This will also point out risks having high operational costs for which our protection capacity is low (bottom right field).

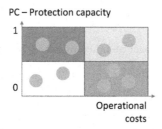

PC – Protection capacity

Operational costs

Figure 9.2   Risk distribution according to their protection capacity and operational costs.

EXAMPLE

A Distributed Denial Of Service (DDoS) cybersecurity risk or an attack aimed at making a web server unavailable by saturating it with queries will be mitigated by relatively expensive controls, which will probably be justified as long as the probability of occurrence or the impact is drastically reduced. In this case, protection capacity will be close to 1 despite the high operational costs. The risk will be located in the upper right corner in Figure 9.2.

The impact of the inherent risk of computer data loss is very high, but backups have reduced this likelihood, so the residual risk is very small. Therefore, protection capacity is close to 1 (very high), and operational costs are relatively low. The risk will therefore be located in the upper left corner in Figure 9.2.

Can we use some modeling to estimate ROSI or better assess the impact of change?

9.3 Modeling

Many disciplines use models to represent reality so as to simulate or observe the behavior of a system, make "what if" analyses, or extrapolate the effects of decisions.

All change projects involving new investments are characterized by a setup phase that increases costs, followed by an operational phase in which real costs (as operational costs per unit of value produced) decrease. Cost evolution modeling makes it possible to visualize not only the ROI of the envisaged solution but also the timeframe until the breakeven (BE) point, taking into account the initial investments (Figure 9.3). During the start-up of a new solution, setup costs are added to operational costs. Since the costs of the new solution will decrease once it is in operation, after amortizing the costs of carrying out the project, a BE point will be reached after a certain period of time. We will talk here about the *timeframe* of the ROI.

This approach makes it possible to plan expenses in relation to expected benefits. For such modeling to be possible, it is important to project the evolution of the operational costs of the current solution (status quo), the project costs, and the

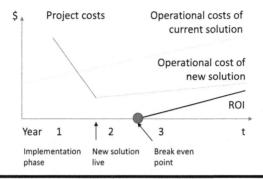

Figure 9.3   Modeling operational costs.

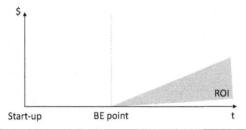

Figure 9.4   Confidence interval for ROI.

operational costs of the new solution. ROI will therefore be calculated as the difference in operational costs between the current solution (status quo) and the new solution.

Another advantage of a model like this is its simulation capabilities. We can observe changes in the BE point and the evolution of ROI by changing parameters such as the cost of the project and the evolution of operational expenses. In the absence of accurate measurements, this will highlight trends and also a ROI confidence interval (Figure 9.4).

There are numerous IS change projects requiring profitability modeling, such as setting up a team responsible for operations and security monitoring, introducing a new intrusion detection system, introducing new means of authentication, etc. All these cases involve determining the evolution of real costs or the cost–benefit ratios of the new solution compared with the old one.

EXAMPLE

A new role-based access rights management system will

- Improve efficiency in granting privileges
- Automatically propagate privileges to target platforms
- Validate privileges at regular frequencies
- Offer more flexibility for new needs

A simple calculation of ROI can be made based on the following data: project cost, annual operational cost of the new solution, and annual operational cost of the current solution for the same volume of processed access rights (same result). Operational costs will be obtained by adding labor costs, infrastructure costs, and indirect costs (e.g. errors). Since it is difficult to accurately estimate the operational benefit of a new solution, some assumptions and simulations can be made to arrive at an ROI confidence interval as shown in Figure 9.4.

Can we answer the question "How is our security?"

9.4 Measuring the State of Security

Security program posture, capacity, and maturity are synonyms for means that allow the state of security to be presented in a concise and standardized way. The need to answer the question "How is our security?" has spurred security managers to develop different measuring and presentation tools. Governance requires simple, standardized ways to visualize the state of security. To make an analogy, analyzing risks allows us to understand our "enemies" (threats), while security posture allows us to understand our "weapons" (quality of the controls).

As already mentioned, being compliant with a standard does not mean having adequate security. The different standards or good practices can, however, be used under certain conditions to assess security posture. The standards present the processes that are required but do not propose evaluation criteria or gradations of conformity. There are also no recommendations on how to satisfy the requirements.

EXAMPLE

Control objective A.8.3 Media handling in ISO 27002 recommends controls to "*prevent unauthorized disclosure, modification, removal or destruction of information stored on media*". The standard presents objectives and good practices but does not give indications on how it should be implemented. This process can have different levels of maturity in companies ranging from "non-existent" to "optimized" through all intermediate levels.

Some standards provide criteria for evaluating the security level. ISO 15408—Evaluation criteria for IT security (Common Criteria) enables the security certification of a computer system or product. A system that meets the requirements of a certain level also meets the requirements of a lower level. A similar approach to measuring resilience is proposed in the Software Engineering Institute "Measures for Managing Operational Resilance", Allen, Curtis, SEI, 2011. Resilience is assessed as being at a certain level if it meets the requirements of that level, including the requirements of the previous levels.

9.4.1 Maturity Models

Maturity models generally evaluate processes according to a scale of values. Standards such as International Organization for Standardization (ISO) 27001 or National Institute of Standards and Technology (NIST) may be used to establish a list of processes or control objectives for which maturity will be assessed. The maturity model then proposes evaluation criteria for each process on a scale of values. Many examples of value scales exist, such as the one proposed by ISO/International Electrotechnical Commission (IEC) 15504 Information technology—Process assessment (Figure 9.5).

Evaluation criteria for assigning a maturity value to a process or control objective must be designed to avoid the risk of arbitrary choice. They must be sufficiently explicit and, above all, unambiguous. The quality of a maturity model therefore depends on the quality of the evaluation criteria that are proposed for each process or objective being evaluated. An example of evaluation criteria for Control objective 5 Information security policies of the ISO 27001 standard is given in Table 9.1.

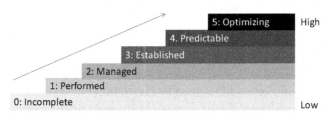

Figure 9.5   Different process maturity levels according to ISO 15504.

Table 9.1   Example of Maturity Evaluation Criteria

Evaluation Objective	Evaluation Criteria 0: Incomplete, 1: Performed, 2: Managed, 3: Established, 4: Predictable, 5: Optimizing	Maturity Level
Information security policies	0: There is no security policy 1: Some formal instructions exist and are applied 2: Security policy exists formally and covers the entire IS 3: The security policy exists, and its application is controlled 4: The security policy is applied and updated 5: The security policy is regularly adapted to the risks and needs of the business units	2

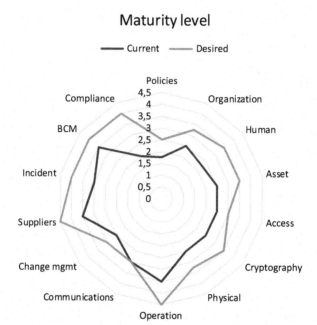

Figure 9.6   Example of representing the maturity of controls.

The tool that supports a maturity model makes it possible to evaluate objectives at multiple levels of detail and then calculate averages at the highest level. The example in Figure 9.6 shows the result of evaluating first-level control objectives according to a maturity model inspired by ISO 27001.

Several methods or tools exist to measure the maturity of a security program such as "Open Information Security Management Maturity Model (O-ISM3)" from The Open Group, or "A New Approach for Assessing the Maturity of Information Security" from ISACA. Large consulting firms also offer their own maturity measurement models. The "CERT Resilience Management Model (CERT-RMM)", Software Engineering Institute, 2016 allows for evaluating the resilience or ability to ensure business continuity encompassing security, business continuity, and IT operations.

A maturity model can be used as a multilevel communication tool in a company, since it makes it possible to justify and support the initiatives contained in the security program. This "why" information is essential, especially for teams in charge of compliance (e.g. the IT department).

The scope of maturity evaluation can be limited to the company unit level or security domains. For example, the maturity of security management processes in a subsidiary can be assessed. Let us also note that the exercise of evaluating with a maturity model, much like the risk assessment exercise, is an opportunity to discuss and compare views on security issues by involving business leaders, risk managers, auditors, or other specialists.

9.4.2 Security Index

Indexes are used in different domains to aggregate the indicators or values of their components. They are primarily used to present trends (stock market indexes, real estate indexes, price evolution indexes, etc.). As aggregates, they conceal the underlying details. Thus, a stock market index can remain stable despite the opposite evolution of two stock prices that are part of it. A security index will be able to summarize various indicators: risks, operational effectiveness, costs, etc. However, an index only makes sense if it aggregates indicators or measurements of the same type. A security risk index could be constructed according to the following formula:

$$\text{Risk index} = \frac{\text{High risk weight}}{\text{Weight of all risks}}$$

where risk weight $= \sum (\text{probability} \times \text{impact})$ of risk. Of course, other security indexes can be created, such as a maturity index aggregating the maturity levels of different requirements, a resilience capacity or recovery index after cyberattacks, etc.

It should be noted here that regardless of the security index created, it will only make sense if the metrics or indicators that compose it are established quantitatively or qualitatively based on stable evaluation criteria. In addition, it can indicate a trend but can by no means suggest points of improvement, which must be sought within its components. For example, if a security index such as the one proposed here shows a negative evolution compared with the previous period, we have to look for the new high risks and understand the reasons for their appearance.

Is there a more pragmatic approach to measuring security?

9.5 Assumption-Based Metrics

The proverb "You can't improve what you can't measure" may be complemented by "You can't measure if you don't know what you're looking for." Setting measurement objectives facilitates the choice of metrics. A measurement goal that is simple and detailed makes it easier to define the associated metrics. The more complex the measurement goals, the less useful metrics will be, and the harder they will be to find. The best would be an objective defined as an initial assumption. In such a case, the metrics will aim to confirm or refute the assumption. For example, if we consider that the level of awareness is not adequate in a company department, we can set up a questionnaire or a survey to "measure" it precisely.

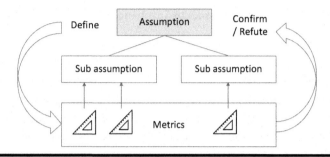

Figure 9.7   Metrics associated with assumptions.

To facilitate metric definition, a strategy would be to subdivide the initial assumption into subassumptions and then define the metrics in relation to these subassumptions so as to be able to confirm or refute them (Figure 9.7).

Different assumption-based measuring methods exist, such as the "McKinsey Diagnostic Method", Goal–Question–Metric (GQM) (The Goal Question Metric Aproach, Basili, Caldiera, Rombach, University Of Maryland, 1994).

EXAMPLE

To ensure that all critical processes are taken into account as part of disaster recovery procedures following major incidents, it was decided to check whether service-level agreements (SLAs) were defined and tested.

Assumption/Objective	Subassumption	Metrics
There is a clear SLA on the time to recovery for critical processes	All critical processes are formally identified	Number of critical processes identified/ total number of critical processes
	There is an SLA for time to recovery for all identified critical processes	Number of critical processes without an adequate SLA
	Recovery tests include all critical processes	Number of critical processes tested during a period

How are security goals set and progress toward them measured?

9.6 Measuring Progress toward Security Goals

The balanced scorecard (BSC) is a popular tool for tracking performance and advancing toward goals that support the business strategy [The Balanced Scorecard: Translating Strategy into Action, Robert S. Kaplan, David P. Norton, Harvard Business Review Press, 1996]. As a well-known management tool, it provides a formal basis to establish and communicate results. It can be used to monitor security performance, thereby helping to position security as an equal partner with other business units. As a tool for monitoring security objectives, it can also facilitate management's appropriation of security issues.

Financial performance alone does not provide all the information needed to assess the contribution of a unit to the consolidated results of the company. The BSC approach advocates benchmarking according to the objectives set in the following four perspectives: Operations, Client Relationship, Evolution (Learning and Growth), and Finance. The four perspectives must contribute to supporting the company's strategy and vision (Figure 9.8). A core question is associated with each perspective to guide the user in choosing the objectives and performance indicators that will be applied.

BSC best practices in the field of security mention in particular the importance of aligning objectives with those of the business. The security strategy as defined earlier should serve as a high-level reference when developing measurement objectives and the indicators that will be associated with them. Strategic objectives can be complemented by more detailed objectives in each of the BSC perspectives. Following are some recommendations for the development of BSCs for security governance.

Operations Perspective: "How can we improve our security processes?"
   We will measure to improve the performances of our security processes to better support the business and align with the company's strategy. We will measure process efficiency and associated costs.

Figure 9.8   Four perspectives in the balanced scorecard.

Client Perspective: "How should security be perceived by our customers?"

We will focus our goals and metrics on security processes impacting internal or external customers or on activities that support customer-centric business processes. Security operations must be perceived by our customers as contributors to their own success.

Evolution Perspective: "How can we improve our capacity to react to threats and contribute to business opportunities?"

We will measure our level of preparation and training to support the changes imposed by the evolution of business. In this context, the maturity objectives stated earlier may prove useful.

Finances Perspective: "How can security contribute to improving the financial performance of the company?"

We will measure returns on security investments or financial objectives. Since it is difficult to measure ROSI directly (as mentioned before), we can focus on objectives that improve the effectiveness of controls contributing to the financial performance of business processes.

An example of the BSC for security governance is presented in Chapter 10 (Reporting and Oversight).

Many works deal with the issue of developing security BSCs. They contain instructions and critical analyses of BSCs as well as a review of DOs and DON'Ts. The greatest attention must be given to the choice of objectives and their associated metrics. There are no standard measurements that can be proposed. Objectives can be identified using the strategy, risk analysis, maturity studies, or audit findings. The objectives should not be multiplied, and the number of metrics per objective should be limited to three or four. The BSC method can also be used for a part of security organization or a specific area of security.

How can operational effectiveness be measured?

9.7 Measuring Operational Performance

Security operations can be assimilated into the controls set up within the framework of a security program. For example, a Security Operation Center (SOC) monitors threat status by means of intrusion detection technologies, data loss prevention solutions, consoles, or incident tracking. Operational performance can be measured and presented through figures, ratios, and trends. Operational efficiency metrics can be used as complementary indicators for risk management and maturity analyses. Table 9.2 shows some examples of indicators and trends in the area of operational efficiency.

Table 9.2   Examples of Operational Efficiency Measures

Measurement Objective	Metric	Trend ↗ Better ↘ Worse
Awareness	Percentage od employees trained on high risks	↗
Efficiency in resolving audit findings	Average delays in resolving audit findings	↘
Configuration management	Number of patched systems/number of systems to be patched	↘
Incident handling	Mean time to resolve incident	↗
	Number of specific analyses conducted	→
	Average effort for specific analyses	↘
Unavailability rate of security components	Security component downtime	↗
Identity and access management	Average delay in processing requests to change access rights	→
	Error rate	→
Security support in change projects	Number of noncompliances detected/ number of projects	↗
Alert processing	Average time to detect and respond	↗
Application security	Mean time to fix vulnerability	↘

How can we know the real cost of security?

9.8 Security Cost Analysis

The cost of security or TCO, as discussed above, can be an important indicator for governance, especially if it is related to other factors, such as the evolution of the company's overall expenses, the number of employees, the evolution of risks, factors generating cost, etc. An accurate answer to the question often asked of boards of directors, "How much does security cost?" requires taking all the different real costs into consideration. Quoting a figure is not enough; it must be explained and linked to many other elements so that it is really clear.

Security expenses must be analyzed according to the principles of cost accounting. To do this, each security expense should be logged in one of the following categories:

- Labor, overhead, installations, depreciation (direct costs)
- Internal services used (Indirect costs)
- IS service concerned (according to IS services offered)
- Key of the distribution of charges to other departments in the company

Cost accounting methods already in practice for other units of the company can be used. In this way, security costs (expenses) can be analyzed using the same standards and presented in the same familiar format to the management and the board of directors. The costs or expenses can be distributed in different ways, taking into account the objectives of the analyses that may be made later. For example, if we want to know the proportion of the costs of external services (consulting) out of overall costs, they will have to be logged in a special expense account. We can then highlight the following relations or analyses:

- Distribution of costs in different categories (direct, indirect)
- Detail and evolution of the costs of each category
- Change in expenses compared with other indicators such as changes in turn-over, number of employees, evolution of threats, etc.
- Distribution of expenses related to business or geographic units
- Evolution of expenses over several years
- Breakdown of expenses by service areas provided (IS, continuity, SOC, physical security, IAM, etc.)

Cost accounting techniques will not be discussed here, because many specialized works are dedicated to them. Cost accounting is a discipline that allows full or partial cost calculations and is the basis of and main tool in business management. To be able to present meaningful reports, it is essential to collect the data according to the presentation that we want to make. Different examples of presenting analytical costs will be given in Chapter 10 (Reporting and Oversight).

How can we compare ourselves with others?

9.9 Benchmarking

The term *benchmarking* refers to comparing companies or their respective processes that offer the same services to gain insight into potential improvement. A set of quantified comparison indicators is produced, which facilitates decision-making and the definition of objectives. Comparing companies in the same sector is a widespread technique that is appreciated by company executives. It makes it possible to measure and compare the results of different strategies. Nevertheless, apart from comparing public financial results, it is difficult to compare companies in operational areas, particularly IS processes, because data on incidents or the means of protection are not publicly available.

Nonetheless, there are several methods enabling benchmarking analyses in the field of security. Studies or surveys conducted by different specialized firms on specific topics such as cybersecurity or the maturity of certain processes contain relevant information allowing an appreciation of what others are doing. They also have knowledge bases on the practices of their customers. These data are confidential, but they can offer anonymized benchmarking services.

Thematic seminars or conferences are also a place to exchange and compare practices in different companies. Surveys are often conducted at these meetings, and the results are made available to the participants. Some companies agree to share information about security processes with each other, especially if they are in the same sector. This enables not only a comparison and clarification of strategic approaches but also an exchange of experiences in solving problems.

Business associations of companies in the same sector often conduct studies of the practices of their members and share this information. Chief information security officer (CISO) forums or associations provide opportunities to conduct mini-surveys, providing information on what others are doing. External auditors also provide a source of information on practices in other companies. They cannot transmit confidential data, but they may recall certain trends observed elsewhere in their comments related to audit findings. In connection with a finding, they might mention how the company compares with an average observed elsewhere. The company can also mandate an expert to carry out a study on the positioning of a security service compared with similar offers at other companies.

9.10 Conclusion

Having reliable metrics and indicators is a sine qua non for good governance. Security is no exception to this rule. Regulatory frameworks also require companies to have reliable indicators in the decision-making process.

Developing security indicators is not easy; it requires effort on the part of managers and those in charge of the development, aggregation, and maintenance of the indicators, which must serve a previously set objective. The opposite approach of trying to exploit available indicators should be avoided above all. Metrics are used to provide factual elements in the process of oversight and reporting, as we will see in the next chapter. For this reason, it is safer to try to answer the questions that managers ask in a language they understand using well-known tools or methods such as financial metrics, modeling, maturity or posture, objective- or assumption-based metrics, measuring progress toward goals, operational metrics, and cost accounting.

Even if security cannot be accurately measured, it can be monitored and supervised for governance decision-making purposes. It is also important to maintain and strengthen a battery of metrics subsequent to remarks expressed during their exploitation in reporting and oversight processes.

Chapter 10

Reporting and Oversight

Good governance relies on reports based on key indicators to assess the adequacy of information security (IS), the quality of security program management, costs or return on security investment (ROSI), and progress toward objectives. The security reports provided by the chief information security officer (CISO)/ chief security officer (CSO) are often considered too technical by management, who cannot find the relevant information for decision-making. On the other hand, management are often unable to clearly express what they need to find in a report, resulting in a certain vagueness about what a security report should contain.

The value of security is often differently perceived. For specialists, the fact of putting protection in place against certain threats is sufficient to justify investments, whereas management wants investments to report results expressible by figures or understandable ratios. The reporting method must be adapted to present security activities in business terms such as risk reduction, return on investment (ROSI), contribution to business development, etc. It is therefore essential to find a standard way to present security figures that will enable management to follow the security program and decide on investments.

We present in this chapter an approach to reporting and oversight intended for management and boards of directors based on various metrics and indicators. The development of these reports will be guided by the goal of answering questions such as "Are we more secure now than last year?", "Are our security expenditures justified?", and "What should we improve and how?"

This chapter provides answers to the following questions:

- What is the purpose of security reporting?
- What are strategic indicators?
- What are the main components of a security reporting system?

- How security costs can be presented?
- What is the difference between security report and security dashboard?

What is the purpose of security reporting?

10.1 Importance of Reporting for Governance

The ultimate responsibility for security lies with the board of directors. That is why they require reports containing stable indicators presenting the state of security at a given time. The purpose of reporting and oversight is to provide governing bodies with all the relevant information they need to judge the state of security at a particular point in time, and to provide guidance. Some essential elements for steering the security program were presented in Chapter 8 (Program Management). The information produced as part of reporting and oversight activities is sometimes called *strategic indicators*. All this information does not have to be provided in one document. These resources can be used by the CISO or management to communicate the state of security to all the stakeholders: board of directors, management, employees, customers, business units, correspondents, and auditors.

Questions such as "Are our security expenditures justified?", "How is our security?", or "What comprises our security costs?" are not only legitimate; they are part of a natural evolution toward better governance. The question of security adequacy is crucial and is one of the major concerns of every company official.

Public statistics or surveys provide few answers about the need to invest in security, because risks cannot be assessed outside the company context. Inaccurate financial justification undermines the credibility of security and weakens the relationship between security teams and the company's business lines. Therefore, reports should contain indicators along with universally accepted units of measurement such as cost, incident, risk, budget, strategy, annual targets, etc.

The need for reporting is also heightened by the fact that security officers increasingly report at a higher level in the company and often outside of information technology (IT) (see Chapter 6, Organization). It is essential that they know how to explain to management the strategy and rationale for security investments, if possible in a business language and with a holistic perspective. They report not only on costs/benefits but also on longer-term strategic axes of development by articulating the benefits for the organization.

Senior managers are accustomed to analyzing the company's high-level indicators—losses, earnings, ratios, economic events, sales targets, and so on—to make forecasts or understand a given situation. Security is part of the infrastructure or support, so they are more interested in reporting or feedback on the overall effectiveness of the countermeasures in place. They seek to understand the evolution of costs. They are less interested in operational metrics or ROSI calculations for an isolated process or component. Since their concerns are increased revenues, reduced costs, improved products or services, and cost control, security reports will only be taken into consideration if they adopt the same approach and the same language: strategic and functional alignments, achieving performance objectives, improving or controlling compliance, team performance, innovations, and added value for customers.

So, what are strategic indicators?

10.2 Components of a Security Reporting System

Strategic indicators are high-level indicators or aggregations of indicators or operational metrics that are used to report on the state of security or to manage the security program. These indicators present the security of information to governing bodies from different perspectives. Answering the question "How secure are we?" is not easy. This is why it will be answered indirectly through more specific questions whose answers provide strategic indicators or reporting elements about the state of security. These specific questions are as follows.

1. **Strategy**
   How does IS contribute to achieving company strategy?
   How are strategic initiatives progressing?
2. **Risks**
   What are our main risks, and how do they evolve?
   How is the risk mitigation program progressing?
3. **Posture**
   What is our security posture, and what are our protective capabilities?
   What processes/controls need to be improved and why?
4. **Compliance and audit**
   What are our compliance gaps?
   What are we doing to fix them?
   What is the status of fixing audit findings?
5. **Program**
   What are the basic principles of the security program?
   What is the status of projects in the program plan?
6. **Governance**
   How is our governance, and what improvements are needed?
7. **Security costs**
   What comprises our security costs?
   How do they evolve?
8. **Security objectives**
   What were our objectives, and did we meet them?
   What are the objectives for the next period?

What follows is a description of the strategic indicators needed by the IS governance body for reporting and oversight. The specific metrics and indicators will not be detailed, since they were the subject of Chapter 9. As already mentioned, there is a very strong dependence between reporting needs and the establishment of operational metrics. In fact, it is the need to report or oversee that will define the indicators needed. Let us note once again that security reporting and oversight can concern company security as a whole or only one domain, geographical unit, or business line. When the indicators are presented, all the elements or metrics that went into them must be available. This will provide additional explanations to enable the reports to be properly understood.

EXAMPLE

It cannot simply be stated that a risk has increased since the last evaluation. We must be able to explain it by key risk indicators (KRIs) or factual observations, such as an increase in the number of incidents observed in similar companies, increased threats or vulnerabilities, the introduction of new technology, etc.

Reporting elements or strategic indicators are dependent on each other. For example, the security program is directly dependent on the strategy, risks, posture, and compliance, as indicated in Chapter 8. This dependence and the primary metrics, KPIs, or other arguments used to elaborate the indicators are presented in Figure 10.1. The diagram shows how the primary metrics are used for reporting purposes (from left to right). It also shows the dependence between these elements. In other words, it answers the question "What elements are used to establish the strategic indicators of a security report?"

The purpose of every reporting and oversight process is to set objectives for the security system. These objectives include improving not only the security program and controls but also financial and governance objectives.

10.2.1 Strategy

The security strategy and the initiatives that comprise it should be reviewed every year (see Chapter 4). Strategic initiatives are also part of the "Plan" roadmap of the security program as defined in Chapter 8. Taking stock of the progress of initiatives (Figure 10.2) in the reporting framework is important, because it can influence the priorities that the governing body wants to establish. When the report is being presented, questions regarding the reasons for potential delay or lack of resources or even a change in strategic direction might arise. This is why the CISO should have readily available arguments explaining project progress during the previous period. This same type of reporting will be used as part of the security program review process, especially in the "Monitor" activity as presented in Chapter 8.

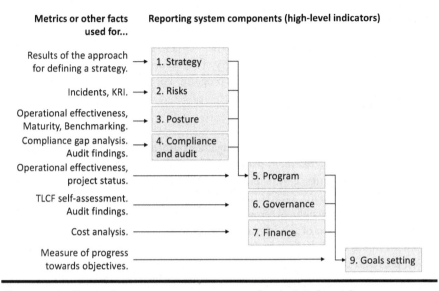

Figure 10.1   Reporting system components and associated metrics.

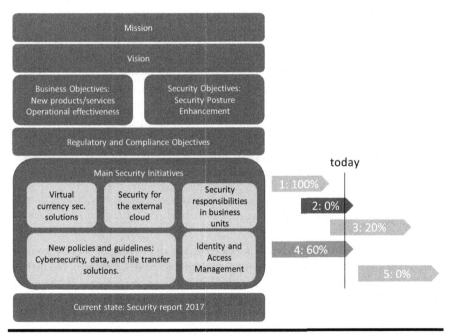

Figure 10.2   Example of key indicators on the progress of strategic initiatives.

Prerequisite

The strategy is based on a formal process that defines needs, the strategic orientations of the business units, the perceived maturity of the security processes and controls, and the imperatives of improving the security program. For more details, see Chapter 4.

10.2.2 Risks

As discussed in Chapter 7, the risk management process includes reporting to bodies responsible for risk treatment planning. The report includes a mapping of all the risks with their attributes, a heat-map, a table of factors influencing risks, and comments on the main events, trends, and changes since the last revision.

Reporting for oversight or program adaptation purposes can be made with a simplified presentation of the state of risks. In this case, we would propose a heat-map with trends or evolutions of the risks and a matrix of high risks containing an action plan and the state of progress (Figure 10.3).

This presentation highlights the most important risks, their treatment plan, and their trend. A comment may accompany this, especially if it is relevant to understanding why a high risk has a "negative" trend.

EXAMPLE

The risk of Distributed Denial Of Service (DDoS) has become very high because of numerous events in recent months and attempts to block services with ransom demands from companies in the same sector. The solution is to use a protection method with scrubbing capabilities proposed by the domain name system (DNS) provider. This solution stops the attacker's traffic before it reaches the company network. Before proceeding with this type of protection, a mini-study must be done to see whether a hybrid solution could be used (which might be cheaper), i.e. continuing to exploit the local protection tool in combination with that proposed by the DNS provider.

Prerequisite

To be able to produce this risk reporting element, the risk management process must include the development of a treatment plan as presented in Chapter 7. The metrics and KRIs used in the risk management process will not be presented in the report but will be made available if additional information is needed.

10.2.3 Posture

The report on security posture is intended to draw decision-makers' attention to weak points in the protection capacities in place. Posture can be evaluated in different ways: for example,

- By using a maturity model
- Through a benchmarking study comparing the effectiveness of controls in similar companies
- By mandating an external audit

The latter two options are recommended for the evaluation of certain processes (e.g. a cybersecurity posture audit or assessment) but are not suitable for repetitive reporting and oversight.

To present the posture and be able to reevaluate it in a repetitive way, it is preferable to use a maturity model, as presented in Chapter 9 (Metrics). The choice of the model depends on the desired level of abstraction or focus when reporting to governing bodies. A catalog of controls, as presented in Chapter 8, may already contain an assessment of current and desired maturity. In this case, it may be preferable to use these data in the report.

Likelihood \ Impact	Insignificant **1**	Minor **2**	Moderate **3**	Major **4**	Extreme **5**
Almost certain **5**	Repeatable minor incidents	10	15	20	Announced disaster
Likely **4**	4	8	12	1	20
Possible **3**	2	10	9	1	15
Unlikely **2**	4	3	2	2	10
Rare **1**	Negligible	2	3	4	Almost impossible disaster

Risk	Residual Level	Trend	Key Indicators	Actions	Status	Planned Level
External fraud	H	↗	- Number of attempts - Damage suffered - Reaction time	- Awareness - Revision of guidelines - Means of detection - External coordination	According to plan 60%	M
Third-party intrusion	H	→	- Penetration test results - External statistics	- Awareness - Elimination of vulnerabilities - Prevention improvement	According to plan 50%	M
Web server attack	H	→	- Result of penetration tests - Level of server updates	- Upgrade configurations	Late 20%	M
DDoS (Distributed Denial of Service)	E	↗	- Observations in similar industry	- Migrate to DNS provider protection	Urgent	M

Figure 10.3   Heat-map and matrix presenting the evolution of high risks.

EXAMPLE

Presentation of a maturity model bases on NIST Cybersecurity Framework (CSF).

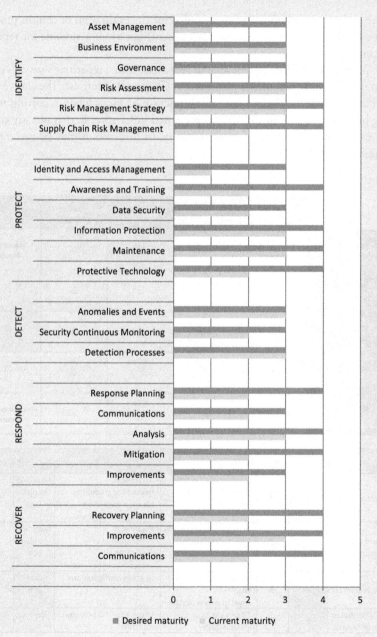

Regardless of the model chosen to present the security posture, it should be accompanied by supporting documents to better understand any differences in current and desired maturity. Thus, the compliance maturity gap in the preceding example may be due to a new regulation in a geographical area where the company is present.

We would also note that benchmarking results can influence maturity ratings. If we look at the previous cybersecurity example, a benchmarking study could indicate that the level of maturity is lower than that of the competition, which could potentially affect the company's competitiveness. Therefore, the desired level of maturity must be aligned with that of the competition.

Prerequisite

To report on security posture, we must have indicators on process effectiveness, assessments of the maturity of controls, results of audit findings, and possibly benchmarking on overall IS or on certain domains. For more details on these elements, see Chapter 9: Security Metrics.

10.2.4 Compliance and Audit

Compliance gap analyses have established priorities among the projects to fix audit findings. These projects are included in program planning, as presented in Chapter 8, and they are mandatory. Reviewing these projects or priorities should not be part of reporting and oversight, since it is the responsibility of other forums or committees. What is needed for governance reporting is the progress made in fixing these findings or possible delays. For example, high-level indicators that could be presented here include the evolution of the number of unfixed findings or delayed remedies compared with the number of new audit findings. The example in Figure 10.4 shows the evolution of delays in fixing security audit findings.

Figure 10.4   Delay in audit finding remediation.

Graphs summarizing a trend should always be accompanied by comments or explanations. In the earlier example, the delay in fixing audit findings may indicate a lack of resources, a prioritization conflict, or some other issue that governance should address when setting objectives.

Prerequisite

To report on security compliance and audit findings, we must have indicators on compliance gap analysis, progress in compliance projects, and audit findings and remediation plans.

10.2.5 Program

As shown in Chapter 8, a security program is composed of a set of operational controls and an improvement plan with a roadmap of projects. These projects mobilize resources, and their objectives must be justified (explained). Through its program, security achieves the following objectives: the deployment of strategic initiatives, risk mitigation, improvement of the posture (capacity) of the protection system, reinforcement of compliance, and the implementation of corrective measures requested by audits. As a result, the four previous elements of the report, supplemented by indicators on the effectiveness of controls and the status of ongoing projects, will make it possible to present the project portfolio along with project status. Figure 10.5 shows an example of presenting the origins of projects that are part of the security program.

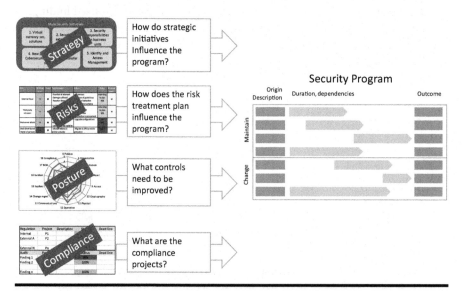

Figure 10.5 Example of presenting the origins of security program projects.

If certain projects have been triggered for reasons other than strategy, risk mitigation, maturity improvement, or compliance (e.g. securing a new subsidiary, relocations, outsourcing, new backup center, etc.), these reasons must also be mentioned.

The goal here is not to present project progress, since this is dealt with in other committees. However, if there are recurring problems in delivering the program, such as delays due to a chronic lack of resources or changes in priority, these issues must be clearly raised.

Prerequisite

Strategy, risks, posture, compliance, operational effectiveness metrics and the status of ongoing projects.

10.2.6 Governance

Presenting the strengths and weaknesses of governance when reporting is not only a sign of high maturity but also a means of communication and coordination for continuous improvement. Chapter 3 proposed different use cases of the three-level control framework (TLCF) model. The result of self-assessment could thus be used to report on the adequacy of governance practices. An example of presenting the key points of such an analysis is given in Figure 10.6.

Policies	Strategy	Organization
Needed	**Strongly needed**	**Strongly needed**
• Review the documentary framework of the policies and guidelines and provide better readability	Review the security strategy. • Align security initiatives with business objectives.	• Each business line must appoint a security delegate to participate in quarterly security project review meetings
Risk management	Program	Reporting, oversight
No improvements needed	**Strongly needed** • Set up a committee to validate IS initiatives and projects.	No improvements needed
Asset management	Compliance	Metrics
Strongly needed • Define data classes and categories and inventory them in a catalog • Identify data owners for each class/business line.	Needed Set up an employee awareness program regarding the legal and regulatory framework that impacts security.	No improvements needed

Figure 10.6   Example of governance self-assessment key findings.

Prerequisite

To report on governance, we must have a self-assessment analysis according to the TLCF framework and/or audit findings or other results of studies by specialized consultants commissioned by the board of directors or management.

10.2.7 Security Costs

Cost accounting principles in controlling security expenditures were presented in Chapter 9: Security Metrics. If the company has accepted cost distribution criteria, it can then present security expenses under different aspects. Data concerning security expenditures, possibly combined with other indicators such as turnover trends or number of employees, will enable the board of directors or governing body to better analyze the impact of security costs and propose adjustments.

Reporting on overall security costs may include the following strategic indicators:

- Breakdown of costs by category
- Evolution of the costs of each category
- Evolution of costs compared with other indicators, such as evolution of turnover, number of employees, overall budget, etc.
- Breakdown of expenses among other business or geographic units
- Distribution of expenses by service provided (IS, business continuity, security operations, physical security, identity and access management [IAM], etc.)

There follow some examples of presenting these different elements.

1. Breakdown of costs by category

Direct security costs are generated by the activities of the security teams. They can be broken down into labor, overhead, and amortization or depreciation. Indirect costs are costs attributed to security but not generated directly by security team activities. Examples are IT operations related to security (projects, infrastructure, and operations), human resources (HR) services, corporate functions, or general services. These costs are often underestimated or neglected in companies precisely because of the absence of accounting methods to highlight them. However, they sometimes represent important figures. It often happens that 100 percent of the indirect costs are out of the CISO's control, because they are generated by other units and attributed to security.

An example of security cost distribution is presented in Figure 10.7. There are different ways of allocating costs, but existing standards used for other business units in the company should be used as much as possible. Depending on the

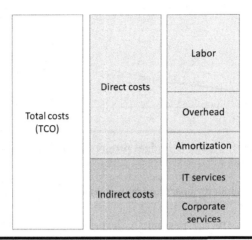

Figure 10.7 Example of breakdown of security costs.

purpose of the report, different levels of detail can also be presented. We could thus detail all the costs of different categories; for example, labor could be broken down into costs related to employee salaries and consultant fees, IT service-related expenses to the project costs of setting up controls or security infrastructure costs, etc. This breakdown will not be discussed in more details because it depends on the context of each organization.

2. Evolution of costs over several periods

Monitoring security cost trends makes it easier to analyze them and correlate them with other business costs. An explanation should be provided for each significant variation. The example in Figure 10.8 shows an increase in depreciation due probably to the implementation of an important security infrastructure.

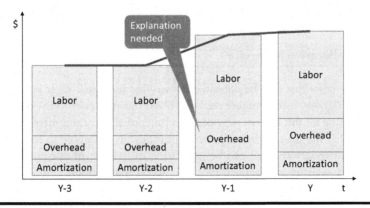

Figure 10.8 Evolution of direct costs.

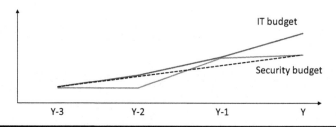

Figure 10.9   Security versus IT budget progression.

3. Evolution of security costs compared with other indicators

It is often very instructive to compare the progression of security costs with that of other categories of financial costs. For example, Figure 10.9 shows the relative progress of the security budget compared with the IT budget.

4. Reallocations of security costs to other business units

A cost allocation key can be applied to reallocate security costs to other business units (Figure 10.10). Various cost drivers exist to establish these reallocation keys: for example, the number of employees or number of workstations, possibly weighted by the criterion of security service "consumption level," etc.

> **EXAMPLE**
>
> If the HR and General Services departments have the same number of employees, the security services cost allocation keys might not be the same for both entities. Since HR is a greater "consumer" of security services (data protection, encryption, support, etc.), its consumption could be accounted using a higher weighting coefficient.

5. Cost allocation by service

Security costs can also be allocated by services provided, such as support for business initiatives, infrastructure security, IAM, business continuity, support, etc. By subdividing all the security services into functional areas and offering the same basic KPIs for the management of cost allocations, it is possible to know the cost of each security service. This can be interesting in the case of outsourcing certain services (e.g. security as a service [SecaaS], access management, etc.). The earlier reporting examples could thus be transposed unchanged to allocation of costs by IS service.

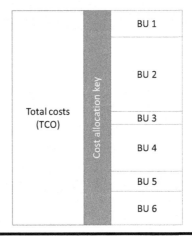

Figure 10.10 Security reallocation cost key to internal service consumers.

The presentation of security costs is quite relevant even if they cannot always be linked to the "benefits." The notion of added value is extremely important, but as noted earlier, this value is perceived through risk treatments and support for strategic initiatives. Management knows what security brings but does not always know what is included in its costs. Such a cost accounting can bring relevant answers.

Prerequisite

To be able to present real costs, cost accounting data for the security services is needed. With minor adaptations, companies that practice cost accounting will have no problem in providing these data and reports for the needs of security governance.

10.2.8 Security Objectives

The different reporting elements or strategic indicators mentioned earlier will enable the board of directors and management to assess the general evolution of IS and set objectives for the next period. This is not a review of the program, strategy, or risk management, but rather, an adjustment of all the activities following the oversight exercise.

One of the main tools for revising and setting new objectives is the IS balanced scorecard (BSC), as presented in Chapter 9: Security Metrics. Its use in the context of oversight is particularly recommended due to the strategic and holistic aspect of the objectives mentioned therein. Based on what was stated earlier, such a BSC could be presented as in Figure 10.11. Objectives and metrics to measure progress will be established at the end of the reporting session and will serve as a guide for adaptations in all areas of IS management.

Perspective	Objective	Metrics
Finance	Review how technical costs are attributed to the IS.	Cost reporting.
	Establish a breakdown of security costs per service.	Costs per security service.
	Master the gap between the budget and actual expenditures.	Security costs.
Operations	"Very high" risks must be reduced within 6 months.	Progression in risk mitigation.
	Decrease the number of exceptions and / or special permissions for mobile workers by 50%.	Number of exceptions allowed per year for mobile users.
	Reduce the time to resolve audit findings. Delays of more than 3 months should not exceed 10% of the findings.	No of delays > 3 months/No findings.
Client	Reduce delays in projects supporting business initiatives	Progress of the projects.
	Review the security strategy for better alignment with business needs.	Security strategy validated by the business units committee.
Evolution	Educate all employees about data protection.	Rate of participation in awareness sessions.
	Define the security policy adaptation plan for business units.	Result of the survey of business lines on the adequacy of the regulatory framework.

Figure 10.11   Example of a balanced scorecard for IS.

Prerequisite

Measurement of progress toward objectives established in the form of a BSC. All security report items previously presented.

10.3 Dashboard

Dashboards are often confused with reports, and it is important to distinguish between the two approaches. Reporting, with its elements as described earlier, is the process of reviewing management practices, while a dashboard is primarily a real-time monitoring tool for certain events or metrics. Both approaches are complementary. A dashboard is often consulted to track operational events, while a report is prepared for review purposes at defined frequencies.

A security dashboard can be made up of various indicators, facilitating the monitoring of the security system. It might include

- Project progress
- Evolution of incidents
- Follow-up of breaches of internal regulations
- Statistics or indicators on access rights
- Distribution of workloads by IS service (operations, projects, support, investigations, studies, etc.)
- Internal or external events or incidents that may impact risk assessment
- Number of investigations or forensic analyses
- Follow-up awareness sessions
- Follow-up of security control tests according to a pre-established plan
- Trends in threat monitoring

A dashboard is an aggregation of the indicators, generally on one or two pages, intended for the CISO or committees in charge of supervising the security program. Many examples of dashboards exist in the literature, and it is not our goal to develop them further. An example of a dashboard is shown in Figure 10.12.

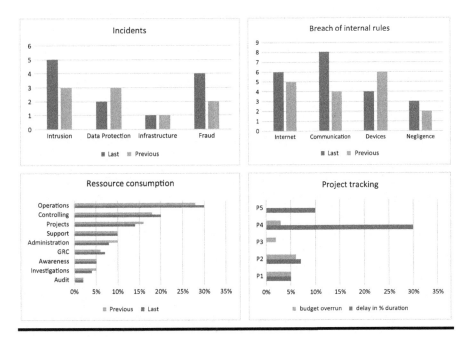

Figure 10.12   Example of security dashboard.

10.4 Conclusion

The security reporting process meets the governing bodies' security oversight needs. It also serves as a communication tool and reinforces the security culture among all the stakeholders. The few high-level indicators presented in this chapter convey overall information on the state of security and the management of the program. These indicators are based on metrics as developed in Chapter 9. Unlike reports, dashboards are used as tools to monitor operations. The two approaches are complementary, and companies can use them interchangeably, as long as they provide the necessary elements for decision-making on the evolution of the security program. However, their content must be previously accepted by the boards of directors and management, since they will become a governance tool. The method of security reporting must not deviate from established company standards for other business units. It must be integrated into the culture and provide relevant information to ensure adequate governance.

Chapter 11

Asset Management

Effective protection or adequate security is not possible without knowing precisely the objects or values to be protected. The standards and many authors mention the fact that developing an inventory of assets is the first thing to do in the context of an information security management system (ISMS). This is indeed important, although companies without an inventory often have a protection system in place. This is not recommended, of course, for reasons that we will see later. Good governance requires formal asset management, because it optimizes the protection system. The risk management process is based on threats and the vulnerabilities of corporate assets. Knowing the value of the assets and deciding how to protect them are essential prerequisites for risk assessment and treatment. Policies and standards should refer to asset classes of confidentiality and sensitivity and specify the rules that must be applied for their protection in different contexts.

Asset management needs one essential tool, and that is an inventory of assets. In many minds, this inventory is a costly and resource-intensive bogeyman of significant proportions. It should therefore be pragmatically constructed to add value to the business and security processes. It is also important to distinguish an inventory of IT infrastructure or components from an inventory of assets to be protected. As with risk management, a pragmatic approach is needed to focus on the essentials.

This chapter provides answers to these key questions:

- What is an information asset?
- Why is it important to manage assets?
- What is an inventory of assets, and what is it used for?

What is an information asset? Why is it important to manage assets?

11.1 Information Asset Management

According to the standard ISO 55000—Asset management, an asset is an "item, thing or entity that has potential or actual value to an organization." (©ISO Adapted from ISO/IEC 55000:2014 with permission of the American National Standard Institute (ANSI) on behalf of the International Organization for Standardization. All rights reserved.) From the viewpoint of information security (IS) governance, an asset is any information or means of accessing this information that the company possesses and that has value. Informational assets can exist in various forms, such as electronic data, communicated information, media on which the information resides (database, files, server, or mobile devices), the applications by which they become accessible, or the networks through which they transit. These different means should also be considered assets. Information must therefore be protected as content along with its medium or means of access as a container. This is, indeed, what IS has always done, with more or less focus on or distinction between categories or different types of assets. To better understand a company's different information assets, we can start by classifying them into categories. Without pretending to be exhaustive, we can distinguish the following categories:

- Data on all media (database, paper, office file, etc.)
- Applications or software (developed internally or acquired)
- Hardware and equipment (laptops, servers, mobile devices, USB)
- Network as a support for information flows
- Infrastructure (as a means for information availability)
- People (knowledge of employees and third parties)

All the standards in the field of IS offer recommendations concerning asset management. The International Organization for Standardization (ISO) 27001/2 standards refer to it in their control objectives and controls. For example, part A.8 Asset Management encompasses the following control objectives and controls:

Responsibility for assets (A.8.1), which objective is "To identify organizational assets and define appropriate protection responsibilities" with specific controls:

- Inventory of assets (A.8.1.1)
- Ownership (A.8.1.2)
- Acceptable use of assets (A.8.1.3)
- Return of assets (A.8.1.4)

Information classification (A.8.2), which objective is "To ensure that information receives an appropriate level of protection in accordance with its importance to the organization" with specific controls:

- Classification of information (A.8.2.1)
- Labelling of information (A.8.2.2)
- Handling of assets (A.8.2.3)

Media handling (A.8.3), which objective is "To prevent unauthorized disclosure, modification, removal or destruction of information stored on media" with specific controls:

■ Management of removable media (A.8.3.1)
■ Disposal of media (A.8.3.2)
■ Physical media transfer (A.8.3.3)

ISO has also published three other standards that set down the principles and best practices in the field of asset management in a much broader context. These are

■ ISO 55000:2014 Asset management—Overview, principles and terminology
■ ISO 55001:2014 Asset management—Management Systems—Requirements
■ ISO 55002:2014 Guidelines for the application of ISO 55001

The risk management process as proposed by the ISO 31000 and 27005 standards recommends starting from assets and then identifying the threats and the vulnerabilities that can be exploited by these threats, so as to arrive at the risks and the controls that the company should implement to mitigate them. Other chapters of the standards, especially those relating to policies, refer to company assets to define the rules of their use, responsibilities, risk appetites, handling principles, and protective measures.

Asset management is becoming increasingly important in the current environment, not only because regulations require it but also because of the imperatives of paradigm shifts in the protection approach. The necessity of making data available outside of company boundaries implies that modern protection systems should be implemented closer to the data to protect them in all circumstances while remaining flexible enough and adaptable to the changing needs of the business. Network partitioning, honeypots, and similar techniques for attack isolation are only a sample of the measures that are being used in modern protection systems (Figure 11.1). A security system based solely

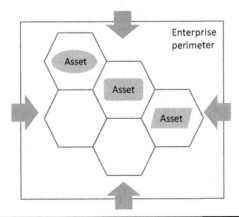

Figure 11.1   Close protection of assets.

on perimeter protection is no longer feasible. If a company carries out different businesses with segregated security policies, as discussed in Chapter 5, it is a safe bet that risk appetites and the required protection standards will also be differentiated. Under these circumstances, different security strategies cannot be implemented without knowing exactly what assets to protect, how they are classified, and in what context they are used.

Very often, organizations adapt their security policies without a feasibility study or expanding their knowledge of the assets and the real needs of protection. Assets are often not classified according to their criticality and confidentiality, which makes the task of developing security policies even more haphazard. This practice can lead to policy mismatches and potentially counterproductive effects. Understanding data is not just about identification and inventorying. To develop applicable policies, organizations need to know their data life cycle, including how they are created, what flows and processes they are involved in, where they are stored, and how they are destroyed. These analyses often prove incomplete, in particular because of a lack of clearly defined responsibilities in regard to them.

Among all the recommendations for asset protection that can be found in different standards and professional literature, three concepts are essential and deserve to be highlighted. These are asset classification, policies and standards for asset protection, and asset accountability. The following explanations in connection with these three concepts are intended to facilitate an understanding of certain pragmatic practices in the context of the governance and management of information assets.

11.1.1 Asset Classification

We have repeatedly mentioned the importance of classifying data and other company values according to different criteria. In terms of security, this means establishing different classes of asset confidentiality and criticality. Confidentiality classes are used to define the different categories of asset visibility or accessibility, while criticality classes mainly concern their availability and integrity. There is, in general, no direct correlation between the different classes of assets. "Highly confidential" data might not be considered "highly critical" and vice versa.

EXAMPLE

A client's file, as a record containing all of their personal data, is considered highly confidential in a banking institution, while it might not be very critical (available at any time), because current operations are often performed with identifiers or client numbers unrelated to their personal data. On the other hand, application servers or stock trading applications as well as data on exchange rates or transactions with third parties will be considered critical for operations, even if they are not very sensitive.

The number of classification levels a company needs depends not only on the objective criteria of the level of confidentiality, availability, integrity, legal and regulatory requirements, or value for the company, but also on the ability or willingness of the company to apply differentiated protections according to the class and type of asset. Asset classification must also reflect the company's willingness and ability to protect them in a differentiated manner according to risk appetite. If there is no need to protect "sensitive" and "very sensitive" data differently, then there is no need to maintain these two classes of confidentiality. One is enough.

11.1.2 Asset Protection Standards

Protective measures should be defined for each asset class and according to the context of asset use. For example, it is important to specify the context and need regarding when applications that are considered confidential can be used, or how and for which need removable media can be used. It is recommended to use standards such as ISO 27001/2 as an inventory of potentially applicable controls when setting policies and asset protection standards. The different recommendations that standards propose in this area can generally be grouped into five categories: data hiding, access control, disposal of assets, supervision, and availability and integrity assurance.

1. *Data hiding*: Data hiding techniques are used to make data unusable in the case of loss or theft. They include encryption or denaturing techniques that devalue the data, prevent their use by unauthorized persons, and protect the company against penalties or complaints that could ensue in the event of major incidents. The management and protection of encryption keys are vital here and must be supervised very closely by security officer.

   The ISO 27001/2 control objectives and controls that apply directly to this protection category are Cryptography (A.10), Policy of the use of cryptographic controls (A.10.1.1), and Key management (A.10.1.2).

2. *Access control*: Policies, standards, and techniques for managing access rights are intended to limit the exposure of assets solely to those who need to access them in the performance of their duties. In this way, the company prevents unauthorized access and reduces the likelihood of threats by malicious persons.

   The ISO 27001/2 control objectives that apply directly to this protection category are Information security policies (A.5), Access control (A.9), Business requirements of access control (A.9.1), User access management (A.9.2), User responsibilities (A.9.3), System and application access control (A.9.4), Secure areas (A.11.1), and Network security management (A.13.1).

3. *Disposal of assets*: Companies must have deletion policies for data that are no longer needed for operations and for legal archiving. These measures aim to limit the area exposed to incidents and reduce complaints and legal accountability.

The ISO 27001/2 control objectives that apply directly to this protection category are Information security policies (A.5), Disposal of media (A.8.3), Secure disposal or reuse of equipment (A.11.2.7), Return of assets (A.8.1.4), and Management of removable media (A.8.3.1).

4. *Supervision*: Asset use must be subject to regular supervision to identify inappropriate patterns of use. Specific measures in this area include monitoring, logging, log correlations, alerting, and protecting log information. The use of confidential assets by authorized persons may also be subject to supervision.

The ISO 27001/2 control objectives that apply directly to this protection category are Information security policies (A.5), Logging and monitoring (A.12.4), Control of operational software (A.12.5), and Incident management (A.16).

5. *Availability and integrity assurance*: Company assets must be available and free from defects to ensure the smooth running of business operations. Specific measures in this area include backups (of data and software), availability of infrastructure, disaster recovery, business continuity, and availability of premises. Recovery techniques after incidents belong to this category.

The ISO 27001/2 control objectives that apply directly to this protection category are Information security policies (A.5), Equipment (A.11.2), Backups (A.12.3), Network security management (A.13.1), Information security aspects of business continuity management (A.17), and Information backup (A.12.3.1).

The internal regulatory framework must therefore define the standards or protection rules to be applied according to the classification of the assets and the contexts of their use. Different methods can be adopted to present and document these standards. The following is an approach that could be appropriate for most businesses. Let us suppose that a company has defined three privacy classes:

1. *Confidential*: Accessible only to certain persons in the organization
2. *Internal use*: Accessible to all employees
3. *Public*: Publicly accessible

Table 11.1 shows an example (excerpt) of presenting the rules or protection standards by type of asset and class of confidentiality. The boxes at the intersection of asset type and classification may contain protection rules or references to the same rules documented elsewhere. These rules (standards) must take into account the context of asset use and propose protective measures to be applied.

Table 11.1 Rules or Protection Standards for Assets Depending on Their Classification

Type of Asset		Application	Office Document	Database	Removable Media
Class		A	B	C	D
Confidential	1	Rule A.1	Rule B.1	Rule C.1	Rule D.1
Internal use	2	Rule A.2	Rule B.2	Rule C.2	Rule D.2
Public	3	N/A	Rule B.3	N/A	N/A

EXAMPLE

Based on the presentation proposed in Table 11.1, the confidentiality rules for office documents (column B) can be summarized as follows (simplified):

Rule B.1: Office documents classified as "confidential" must be systematically encrypted or filed in protected folders. They cannot be consulted while outside the company.
Rule B.2: Documents for internal use cannot be communicated externally. They must be kept within the company, in a document library system provided for this purpose. They can be consulted outside the company.
Rule B.3: Public documents must not contain information that is for internal use or confidential. The content should have no mention of the company.

Internal policies must clearly establish asset classification criteria based on their characteristics or context of use. For example, office documents that contain confidential data must be considered confidential, computer servers are classified according to the classification of their hosted databases, and applications are classified according to the class of data processed.

11.1.3 *Roles and Responsibilities in Asset Management*

Formal responsibility for assets is a guarantee of good risk management and adequate controls set in accordance with the risk appetites and measures recommended in the policies. We are talking here about functional responsibility as opposed to technical or administrative responsibility such as database administrators (DBAs) or application support. The functional manager of an asset is more concerned with the quality and proper use of the asset in business processes than with technical questions. Data owners or application owners have semantic knowledge of the assets and are the privileged interlocutors of architects and information technology (IT) developers.

EXAMPLE

IT servers host databases and applications. In many data centers, the "server" asset is under the responsibility of system engineers whose primary concern is to ensure its availability along with the underlying applications and databases. The responsibility for the confidentiality and integrity (quality) of data and applications is often not well defined. DBAs or application developers cannot be considered the "owners" of these respective assets. They often ignore the semantics of hosted data as well as the functional aspects of the applications. The ownership for these assets must be defined by the business or the persons who use them for the needs of their operations. These functional managers must be consulted in all change projects concerning their assets (such as server virtualization, patches, application tests, or outsourcing).

Many companies have put in place or are evaluating the possibility of establishing a central data accountability function. The objective is to ensure that data are supervised and their use is controlled in the context of IT architectures, and to ensure the adequacy of policies and controls. No commonly accepted name or well-defined specifications exist for this type of profile, but it may be a chief data officer (CDO), data protection officer (DPO), data architect, or some other. When these responsibilities are assigned, it must be ensured that the person in charge has sufficient authority and independence to perform their duties. Such a profile can provide expertise and assist chief information security officers (CISOs), governing bodies, and business executives in the more effective management of assets and the security program.

An inventory is one of the main tools in asset management. The next section will present some recommendations, methods, and tools for establishing and using an asset inventory.

What is an inventory of assets, and what is it used for?

11.2 Asset Inventory

Let us say straightaway: a security program may exist even if the assets to be protected have not been formally identified. In other words, companies do not wait to identify and formally record their assets before setting up protection systems. Business leaders know implicitly what values to protect and have put controls in place. Hospital administrators know that patient data are confidential and must be protected, industrialists know that manufacturing secrets are valuable, and bankers know that client records and their reputation must be protected. Why, then, worry about identifying company assets, and why develop an inventory?

The answer is simple. Without a formal inventory of assets classified according to the degree of sensitivity (confidentiality), criticality, and other criteria, a company will not be able to optimize its protection system. A security program without an asset inventory will be either too expensive or ineffective. Without knowing exactly what assets to protect, where they are, and how they are used, protection will not be targeted and therefore not optimized. Such a system will be either very restrictive and expensive, since it is supposed to apply maximum protection to all the assets, or inefficient, since it is unsuitable to protect very sensitive assets that deserve high protection. It cannot be adapted to the economic models and technological challenges of today.

EXAMPLE

Grouping or virtualizing application servers of different criticality classes on the same physical servers does not facilitate the implementation of a differentiated availability strategy. The disaster recovery plan (DRP) will not be able to provide the operational recovery of key critical processes and applications as a priority. Recovery will be slowed down, as it will apply to the entire infrastructure, which could result in weakening of the company's resilience system.

An asset inventory or asset register is a list of all assets, as defined earlier, that have value for the organization and deserve protection. It contains the necessary information concerning each asset, facilitating risk management and the choice of mitigation measures. Volumetric data and statistics that can be derived from the contents of such an inventory also facilitate decision-making on the controls to be applied. An inventory also makes it possible to clearly establish responsibilities in asset protection and management and to meet regulatory requirements. The different technical formats of asset inventories will not be developed here, because they are unimportant from the governance viewpoint. Nevertheless, the concepts that will be mentioned may be useful in inventory compilation projects.

None of the standards specifies which attributes should accompany the assets in an inventory, since the diversity of the attributes depends on how the company wants to use them. However, if we refer to what has just been said and bear in mind the recommendations of the standards, the essential attributes could be listed as follows:

■ Unique identifier of the asset
■ Name of the asset
■ Description
■ Category or type—to be defined internally
■ Confidentiality class

- Criticality class
- Owner or accountable (person or department)
- Personal data (Y/N)
- Other sensitive data (Y/N)—to be defined
- Location
- Used by third party (Y/N)
- References to other related assets—dependency links (e.g. application linked to a server or database)
- Referencing business units and processes that use the asset

The notion of the owner of an asset is essential. Indeed, the person or unit that is responsible for it is also responsible for the attributes and maintaining the information contained in the inventory. This owner should also be responsible for updating the inventory and for the use of the assets under their responsibility. To be able to decide which classification to assign to an asset, the asset owner can produce exhaustive lists of examples (e.g. provide a list of personal data such as last name, first name, address, etc.) as well as classification rules. The classification assigned to an asset may vary depending on different criteria, such as the context, and may be time related. For example, an internal document containing a strategic decision may be classified as "confidential" until the decision is communicated, in which case it could be moved to the "limited access" category.

How should an asset inventory be compiled?

Compiling an inventory of assets is not an easy task. There are no predefined standards or templates for the content or universally recognized tools or methods for its development. The very evocation of the term *inventory* or *register* causes reactions ranging from "useless" to "indispensable" according to organization maturity. However, in the current state of evolution of threats and regulatory frameworks, the question is no longer whether or not an inventory is needed but rather, how to elaborate it in a pragmatic way, so that the security program and security governance can make the most of it. It is very likely that most organizations already have the basic elements of an inventory or rudimentary formats in the form of application lists or IT components.

Many automated tools, called ITAM (IT Asset Management), assess all the infrastructure assets (hardware, software, and databases) for configuration or licensing purposes. These solutions have the advantage of being very exhaustive in the establishment of inventories of the IT infrastructure. However, they often do not provide information on classifications, responsibilities, and the use of assets in business operations. These infrastructure inventories, also known as configuration management databases (CMDBs), could be used as a starting point for extractions to build an inventory of higher-level IS assets and then be completed by the attributes mentioned earlier. Asset inventories could also be compiled in a very pragmatic way as lists to be filled in by hand progressively as assets are identified, assigned to someone's responsibility, and given a classification.

Many companies offer tools for mapping data, applications, or other resources used in business operations. These are often solutions to satisfy the need for compliance in relation to data protection regulations. Questionnaires are sent to unit managers with the objective of recording all the assets used in their operations. The outcome of this census method is a data mapping (personal or confidential) across different company processes. It will then be used not only to identify the assets but, especially, to understand their use, which will facilitate risk analysis and the implementation of adequate protection.

Many advantages can be mentioned concerning this approach compared with traditional inventories based on the systematic inventory of IT infrastructure. A CMDB contains a lot of technical information about the infrastructure, the network, and data repositories. This is a snapshot that does not give the origin of the data, their actual use, and especially, the risks associated with their use by different business units.

EXAMPLE

Email addresses contained in a customer relationship management (CRM) used for customer tracking could also be used by the marketing department. A classical and static inventory of assets such as a CMDB will reference the CRM database but will not be able to classify it automatically or highlight the use of its data by other business units.

Personal data protection regulations or the principles of data privacy increasingly require companies to demonstrate their ability to control flows of sensitive data. The establishment of personal data mapping will have the benefit of meeting this requirement while also enabling a more accurate privacy impact assessment (PIA) and risk analysis related to the processing of personal data. It will also help to understand the data life cycle: how data are collected, from which sources, which operations are dependent on them, where they are temporarily stored, which business roles have access to them, what systems and applications use them, where they are deposited, and how they are destroyed.

EXAMPLE

Article 30 of the European General Data Protection Regulation (GDPR) requires companies to establish "records of processing activities" to understand how personal data are actually processed. The goal is to be able to answer the questions "Why are these personal data collected?" and "What processes need these data?"

This data mapping can be considered an inventory of applications or processes that use confidential or personal data with attributes such as name of the process, assets (application) used, data collected and processed, and reason or justification for use. This will then answer questions about "how" and "why" the assets of the company are used.

What is the purpose of an inventory?

Table 11.2 shows an example of how applications (as assets) are used as part of the processes in different business units. Each business function can be subdivided into several processes that are supported by different applications and used in different business units. An application can be used in several processes (e.g. enterprise resource planning [ERP]).

The information used to build this mapping can come from an asset inventory as long as the attributes of the applications contain a reference to the processes and business units that use them. This mapping of applications highlights, for example, the fact that the HR process uses the A3 application in all the business units. If this application is classified as "confidential," then it is necessary to review the criteria of its use and in particular, the adequacy of the protections associated with it (such as access rights or encryption of the underlying databases). The inventory should also contain the dependency links between the assets, making it possible to understand which assets are bound together (application, database, and server) and thus facilitate the analysis of risks or regulation impacts (Figure 11.2).

An inventory can also be used to track the current level of asset protection. If the policies and standards specify which controls should be applied to the assets according to their classification (see earlier), then we can qualify each asset in the inventory by its level of compliance with these rules. This makes it possible to better analyze the risks associated with assets considered insufficiently protected or not benefiting from adequate protection according to the requirements of the internal regulatory framework. The example in Figure 11.3 shows the positioning of insufficiently protected assets according to their classification and volume of use (frequency or number of users). This facilitates decision-making by the governing bodies or prioritization committees regarding the introduction of corrective measures. Risks related to insufficiently protected assets that are widely used and classified as confidential should be treated as a priority.

Many other examples of the use of asset inventories can be cited. Company governing bodies and management should be well aware of the benefit that security program management can gain from an inventory of information assets. They should thus sponsor and encourage the efforts of security managers to compile them. Ignorance of the benefits of such a tool is often behind the reluctance to grant the necessary budgets for their development, which in turn weakens the protection system, prevents the optimization of controls, and ultimately increases risks and security-related costs.

Table 11.2 Example of Asset (Applications)/Process Mapping

Function	Process	Business Unit 1	Business Unit 2	Business Unit 3	...	Business Unit n
Production	Purchase		A1			
	Controlling	A1				
	Stock mgmt			A1		
						A2
	Production		A2			A2
				A2		
Corporate functions	HR	A3	A3	A3	A3	A3
		A3				
	Risk	A4	A4	A4	A4	A4
	Finance			A2		
					A2	
			A2	A2		
	Legal & Compliance			A4	A4	
		A4	A4			
Relationship mgmt	CRM	A5		A5		A5
	Suppliers		A5	A5		
	Support				A5	
		A6	A6	A6	A6	A6
	Contracts	A2				
Sales	Marketing				A5	
			A5			
	Sales		A5	A5		
Etc.						

Asset inventory				
Asset	...	Class	...	Link reference
Application A		Confidential		
...				
Server S		Confidential		
...				
Database DB		Confidential		

Figure 11.2   Reference links between assets.

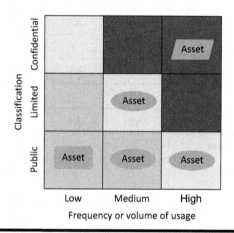

Figure 11.3   Example of distribution of inadequately protected assets.

11.3 Conclusion

The information asset management process encompasses a series of core activities in the management and governance of the security program. It may be considered a prerequisite for risk management and the establishment of security controls. This is particularly true in the current context, where the exchange of data, often confidential, goes beyond company borders or is part of new business models. An asset inventory is one of the essential tools to answer questions asked by every governing body about the use and protection of a company's main values.

This chapter provided some insight into how to effectively and pragmatically manage a company's information assets. The identification of assets and their classification by confidentiality and criticality makes it possible to compile an inventory that will quickly become an invaluable tool and source for risk analysis and impact analysis and a reference for all the stakeholders, from operations to governing bodies and auditors. Several inventory tools and methods are available on the market. It is important, however, to clearly define and keep in mind the objectives that this inventory should help to achieve. This is a prerequisite for its acceptance and effective use in the long term.

Chapter 12

Compliance

Every company operates within a legal and regulatory framework, and compliance with this framework is a major concern for company officials. It is a generally accepted fact that regulatory pressure has been increasing lately for different reasons and weighs more and more heavily on company budgets. Large businesses have entire teams in charge of compliance working in close collaboration with legal services. So, what does this have to do with the governance of information security (IS) where controls protect company assets and, as such, meet the governing bodies' needs? There are many reasons why information technology (IT) and IS are affected by the legal and regulatory framework.

Personal data flows through multiple channels. New business models are often based on the collection and exploitation of personal data, which could harm many companies. Some of them are not even aware that such practices are no longer tolerated. Laws have been passed, and people are increasingly hostile toward the misuse of their personal data. Company compliance and privacy teams are therefore concerned about the need to ensure the responsible use of data entrusted to them.

IT or automated data processing is an area that has been strongly impacted by recent regulatory changes, particularly regarding data protection, processing, and archiving. Compliance often requires an adaptation of data processing procedures, and this primarily affects IT and IS.

We will not list all the regulations that impact IS in different countries, which is beyond the scope of this book. References to these regulations can be found in other works. Our goal is to present the concepts and tools to manage and govern IS compliance that can be applied to any regulation in any company.

This chapter provides answers to these key questions:

■ What is a legal and regulatory framework?
■ What are the different categories of external regulations that apply to security?
■ How can IS compliance be managed?

What is meant by a legal and regulatory framework?

12.1 Legal and Regulatory Framework

Companies are often ignorant or misinformed about the external regulations that apply to their industry and especially those related to security in the countries in which they operate. Working in several legal frameworks in Europe, Asia, or the U.S. multiplies questions regarding the laws that apply. If we add the fact that the different countries of the European Union have their own regulations besides those that apply in the Union, the spectrum of different law enforcement options increases even further. In some cases, European laws or regulations only present the foundation on which the laws or regulations of the member countries are based. It is often difficult to interpret these local regulations, which may be stricter, because of a certain ambiguity due to their rather descriptive nature. This causes uncertainties as to how they are to be applied. Terms such as *sufficient protection* or *abusive treatment* are indeed common and compound the difficulties already present in the interpretation of different regulations.

Relying on lawyers or specialized consultants is a current practice, if only to be able to decide which law or regulation applies in which circumstances. The different categories of documents (in European legislation, for example) do not facilitate their understanding. Thus, very often, "directives" impose objectives on member countries without specifying how to achieve them, while "regulations" give more specific instructions. Furthermore, directives cannot replace local laws. This interweaving with multifarious relationships between different laws and regulations is an example of the difficulties that companies face when managing compliance in general. This situation is not only complicated in the European Union but applies to all companies that operate across borders.

Before developing the subject of managing the compliance program, let us point out the different categories of regulations that are part of the legal and regulatory framework.

The term *legal framework* refers to the laws that are applicable to a business. These laws can be general (such as codes or even constitutions) or specific for a sector of activity (such as laws on banks or the financial sector, labor law, etc.). A multinational company must respect all the laws of the different countries in which it operates.

Regulatory framework refers to all the guidelines and circulars of a business sector (e.g. regulations for financial institutions, the medical sector, transportation, etc.). This term also includes the internal regulatory framework as developed in

Chapter 5. External regulations are very often issued by the regulatory bodies of the sectors of activity. They are not considered laws but can be very restrictive and have significant repercussions for business processes.

The term *normative framework* may refer to standards and good practices commonly accepted by professional communities. Not as binding as laws, they are used as a reference of quality in the business context. The overall economic sector of a country often imposes rules of behavior that must be respected. The standards for IS mentioned throughout this book all belong to this category.

Employee knowledge of the legal and regulatory framework not only protects a company against possible sanctions; it also allows employees to better understand the constraints related to their daily activities. The measures taken to protect personal data, for example, must be understood in the broader context of the legal framework, not just in relation to internal regulations. It is therefore essential to have an internal reference system or develop an awareness program regarding the external legal and regulatory framework that applies to the organization. This referencing and explanation of the legal and regulatory framework can take different forms, e.g. posting excerpts or references on the intranet, adapting internal regulations for external references, or organizing awareness sessions on the legal and regulatory framework. Employees might then be required to be as familiar with this as they are with internal regulations.

What are the different categories of external regulations that apply to security?

12.2 Categories of External Regulations Impacting Security

Many laws and regulations include articles that impact IS. We cannot analyze them all, but it is possible to classify them in different categories that are potentially valid in many legal frameworks. There is no universally accepted classification, but following is a tentative list:

- Data protection
- Electronic signature
- Preservation and archiving
- Labor law
- Operational risk management regulations
- Common law
- Consumer rights
- Sectoral regulations

Data protection encompasses all regulations related to data protection issues and especially the protection of personal data (data privacy). To take one example, the European General Data Protection Regulation (GDPR) regulates the processing of personal data of European citizens. According to this regulation, all companies processing the data of European citizens or operating in the Union must respect the principles set out therein. Different countries also have similar regulations or laws, such as the Personal Data (Privacy) Ordinance in Hong Kong, the Personal Information Protection and Electronic Documents Act (PIPEDA) in Canada, or the Federal Act on Data Protection (FADP) in Switzerland. This category includes all the laws aimed at protecting the privacy and rights of persons as guaranteed by constitutions.

Personal data protection regulations protect the rights of those who are the subject of data processing, be they physical or legal persons. In short, they aim to institute the following principles (excerpt):

■ All data processing must be lawful in accordance with the principles of proportionality.
■ Data can only be processed for a specific purpose and as provided by law.
■ A person must be aware of the collection and purpose of the processing that is done to their data.
■ Consent must be given (and can be revoked) by the person concerned.

IS and IT are directly affected by this category of laws, as they must ensure the proper processing of data, protection against leakage, unexpected changes, and unauthorized data processing. Some laws have relatively technical requirements to ensure compliance with these protection principles, especially with regard to prohibiting access to unauthorized persons, transfer, communication, use, logging, etc. If the processing of personal data is outsourced to a third party, then it must be performed according to the same regulatory constraints as if it were executed by the process owner. This transfer can be made only if the persons, whose data are part of this outsourcing, have given their explicit consent, and provided that no other regulation prohibits it. Other requirements may exist such as, for example, the right of access of individuals to their personal data. The requirement of *privacy by design* in many regulations, stipulating that the protection of personal data must be embedded in the system, has a direct impact on software development. Organizational requirements could also be present concerning the functions of data processors, data controllers, data owners, governing bodies, or the data protection officer (DPO).

In Chapter 3, Section 3.3 *Impact on governance—a proactive approach*, we presented an example illustrating the impact of GDPR regulations on a company security system. Details of the impact analysis will be developed later on.

Electronic signature comprises laws governing recognition requirements for electronic signature certification providers as well as rules for accepting electronic signatures in transactions. IS and IT can be affected when managing public key infrastructures (PKI) or services around this technology. Regulations often specify requirements or restrictions on the use of electronic signatures.

Preservation and archiving encompasses laws and regulations that govern the recording and electronic retention of data and documents. Apart from commonly accepted accounting standards and rules, these regulations specify the conditions of preservation, especially with regard to integrity (unfalsifiable, authenticity), the need for visibility regarding attempts at data modification, documentation of the preservation procedures, availability—access to authorized persons, separation of archived data from current data, organization—roles and responsibilities in archiving domains, etc.

IT and IS are affected by these regulations mainly because of the company's obligation to ensure the availability of nonmodifiable data carriers, to make available electronic signature techniques to certify the authenticity of record proofing systems such as timestamps, log file preservation solutions to provide oversight, and migration solutions when the retention format needs to change and thus ensure accessibility to retained documents, etc.

Labor law primarily includes laws and regulations concerning protection of the personality in the workplace, protection of employee personal data, protection of human rights, health protection, personal integrity, working conditions, accessibility of premises, etc. Certain sectoral regulations may impose stricter or more specific rules, particularly with regard to the supervision or control of the workplace, rules on the use and consultation of private emails, hygiene regulations, etc. IT and IS are affected by these regulations, especially with regard to the physical protection of employees, their integrity, their health, the use and control of communications, and the monitoring of behavior in the workplace.

Operational risk management regulations impose more responsible behavior toward protecting business operation, consumers, the environment, and economic partners. Basel III and the Sarbanes–Oxley Act (SOX) are part of this. Basel III is designed to impose stricter practices in the operational risk management of banks and financial institutions. Security and IT are indirectly affected. Sectoral laws or regulations may impose stricter requirements for some organizations. For example, Finma, the financial market supervisory authority in Switzerland, has issued directives on operational risk management—"Operational Risks at Banks" (FINMA-Circular 08/21). Its Annex 3 sets out nine principles with the requirements that banks must meet to protect client identifying data (CID).

Common laws, such as constitutions, codes of obligation, civil codes, criminal codes, and others, may contain provisions that affect IS. They include articles on the protection of privacy, preservation of documents and accounting documents, unauthorized access to data and computer systems, data deterioration, computer fraud, bugging and recording communications, communication espionage, violation of telecommunications secrets, etc.

Consumer and business rights are also protected by regulations such as spam prohibition, eCommerce obligations, trade secret protection, transport and data transfer security, consumer protection, etc. The central bank of the Bahamas, for example, has published a regulation on ebanking services.

Sectoral regulations. The legal and regulatory framework includes all the directives issued by control bodies of the industrial sectors within a given country (see the example of the Financial Sector Supervisory Commission in Luxembourg). We have already mentioned some of them in the banking sector, but they exist in all other sectors, particularly in the fields of health, transport, trade and transport of raw materials, production, etc. The impact of these regulations on IS can be considerable. Some authorities also publish guidelines on good practices, which are not necessarily laws but set standards of good practice for the companies affected. For example, the Monetary Authority of Singapore has published a document entitled *Technology Risk Management Guidelines*, which aims to "promote the adoption of sound practices and processes for managing technology".

How should IS compliance be managed?

12.3 Compliance Management Process

It is often thought that security and IT compliance is a technical issue and that it is sufficient to have good tools to demonstrate that the required controls are in place. In fact, many vendors offer governance risk and compliance (GRC) solutions that can help companies move towards this objective. These are platforms that integrate the technologies and tools for compliance management, policy documentation, inventory and risk management, control referencing, and incident management. These solutions are certainly very useful, especially if they have managerial support, but they alone are not sufficient. Compliance with legal and regulatory frameworks often requires organizational adaptations, as we have already seen in many examples. The effective implementation of GRC tools is often complex precisely due to the lack of strict definitions of processes and responsibilities in these areas.

The difficulty also comes from the fact that compliance in the field of security is very often the sole responsibility of the chief information security officer (CISO) or chief information officer (CIO), who is asked not only to understand the requirements of a regulation but also to implement the compliance management process. As already mentioned in Chapter 6: Organization, a gap often still exists in legal competence, understanding, vision, and responsibility between security officers and legal officers.

Compliance rarely affects a single business unit; it touches the entire company. This is not reacting piecemeal to fill the gaps but adopting a process of continuous improvement across all the units. Compliance services must take the lead with regard not only to regulations affecting the core business but also to those directly related to security or IT. Senior managers must be kept informed and feel accountable. They must act as informed sponsors and promote effective cooperation between the different units. Companies must therefore adopt a methodical approach and a repetitive process to identify compliance risks and analyze potential impacts across the organization.

Adopting objectives from the standards that we have listed throughout this book can help companies make their IS compliant with legal and regulatory frameworks. IS is primarily concerned with compliance requirements in the following areas:

■ Management and governance to ensure continuous improvement of the security program
■ Risk management, including the risks of noncompliance
■ Protection of assets against threats by setting up the operational controls recommended by the standards
■ Management of access rights to ensure that information is available to those who are entitled to it

Compliance is often perceived as an important burden weighing on businesses. Nevertheless, taking a systematic approach to the management of compliance gaps can benefit the company image and be a means of continuous improvement. Compliance management with planning and a process approach should be able to show noticeable positive effects.

EXAMPLE

Requirements in security-related standards already include good practices that should be followed, such as baseline security configurations, risk management, asset management, data classification, access controls, policy definition, incident management, etc. A security system with a certain level of maturity of processes according to standards should not have significant compliance gaps.

The few recommendations following relate to IS management but could be applied to other areas as well. The compliance management process can be summarized in four steps:

1. Create a reference guide of the legal and regulatory framework.
2. Carry out impact assessment and gap analysis.
3. Treat the gaps.
4. Audit and monitor compliance.

Let us see this process and its tools in more detail.

12.3.1 Inventory of Regulations

Having a reference or inventory of the legal and regulatory framework directly applicable to IS facilitates communication and awareness. It can range from the simplest (Table 12.1) to more complete forms including information such as article of law, object of protection, detailed description of the regulation, company unit affected (business or geography), issuing body of the law or regulatory authority, etc.

The previous example shows the schema of a legal and regulatory framework reference for IS or IT, but a reference could also be set up for the company as a whole, in which case the applicability criteria by region and/or business unit would be included.

12.3.2 Impact Assessment and Gap Analysis

A gap analysis and an impact assessment must be carried out for each regulation and if possible, by business unit and/or geographical area. This analysis should be done with great care, and many specialists might have to be involved to accurately identify the gaps. Lawyers are used to interpreting articles of the law, and auditors know whether practices are in compliance. However, the legal and regulatory framework will need to be accessible and comprehensible to all stakeholders through simplified compliance mapping.

Table 12.1   Example of a Simplified Format of a Regulatory Framework Inventory

Domain		
ID	**Name/Description**	**Reference**
Data protection		
GDPR	European General Data Protection Regulation	https://www.eugdpr.org/
FADP LPD	Federal Act on Data Protection (FADP)	https://www.admin.ch/opc/en/ classified-compilation/19920153/ index.html
Electronic signature		
…		
etc.		
…		

EXAMPLE

GDPR gap analysis requires multiple skills. Lawyers and compliance officers should be able to respond to questions such as

- Is the company concerned?
- Are contractual documents with customers compliant?
- Is the company doing client profiling?
- Are data from suppliers or third parties affected by the regulations?

On the other hand, they will probably not be able to comment on personal data processing, data ownership, technical protection measures, etc. Other company profiles need to be solicited for this.

Having a systematic approach to gap analysis is paramount. A questionnaire can be used for each regulation, touching on its key points. This approach would allow different profiles of people to answer the practices that concern them. Asking closed questions and giving clear answers can be beneficial for several reasons. First, it makes it possible to express the degree of compliance of the practices in a very explicit way. It also allows other employees in the organization to understand regulatory practices and impacts in areas they may be less familiar with. And finally, it speeds up the process of analyzing noncompliance, which might otherwise be very imprecise and sometimes incomplete. Table 12.2 is an example of summarizing gaps on key points.

If a question cannot be answered, or if the requirement is partially satisfied, the answer may contain a special indication and suggest further investigations. The questions should refer to regulation articles and provide all the explanation needed to understand the targeted objective. If the answer to a question is negative (the practice is not in compliance), then the actions needed to remedy it should be

Table 12.2   Example of a Question to Identify a Compliance Gap (GDPR)

Key Point	Consent
Question	Can customers withdraw their previously given consent?
Explanation	According to Article 7, customers who have consented to the use of their personal data must have a clearly explained method enabling them to withdraw their consent
Response	No
Action required	Adopt a procedure for the withdrawal of consent and communicate it to the customers

mentioned. The layout of the questions, before their presentation and clarity play a very important role. They should reflect the requirements of the regulations as closely as possible while being comprehensible to a wide audience. Their division into key points or main requirements of the regulation facilitates the involvement of various profiles and a general understanding of the regulations.

Numerous consulting firms, GRC solution providers, and professional associations already propose such questionnaires or tools to facilitate gap analysis. For example, the Information Systems Audit and Control Association (ISACA) and the Capability Maturity Model Integration (CMMI) Institute offer a self-assessment and gap analysis questionnaire for the GDPR regulation.

A gap analysis can be conducted using the results of this questionnaire. The goal is to establish a list of priorities, which will then be incorporated into projects as part of the security program management, as presented in Chapter 8: Program Management. The gaps could be presented and communicated in different ways; for example, using a format similar to that shown in Table 12.2. Gap analysis also serves to identify regulatory-specific risks or risks of noncompliance such as customer or third-party risks in the case of data protection regulations.

Privacy impact assessment (PIA) is the process of identifying, analyzing, and addressing privacy risks associated with company services and products and the systems the company operates. These analyses are conducted to identify the impact of regulations or best practices on the protection of personal data (data privacy) or to make sure that personal data is processed in accordance with company policies. This practice aims to mitigate regulatory risks in the context of change or the introduction of new services. Above all, it helps to better understand what personal data is collected and used, for what purpose, and whether the data processing is in accordance with the principles of lawfulness. An example of a code of good practice is published by the Information Commissioner's Office (ICO, UK) in "Conducting privacy impact assessments: code of practice".

12.3.3 Treating Gaps

Filling the gaps may require significant adaptations and potentially impact all building blocks in TLCF. Special attention must be paid to adapting policies and standards before technical solutions are implemented, because the internal regulatory framework must reflect external requirements. An example of the impact of the GDPR regulation is given in Chapter 3: Control Framework Use Cases, Section 3.3 *Impact on governance—a proactive approach*.

Sometimes, legacy systems cannot be adapted to new regulations. For example, the concept of privacy by design will probably not be respected by legacy systems. Such exceptions should be clearly reflected in internal policies and regulations. Nevertheless, a compliance plan and additional controls should be introduced. Compliance projects should be integrated into strategic initiatives, be part of developments that bring perceived quality, and go beyond the simple measure of satisfying regulators. Exceptions clearly formulated and supplemented by additional measures will be accepted by auditors and clients.

12.3.4 Audit and Compliance Monitoring

Internal and external audits provide solid support for governance, management, and IS operations. Soliciting an external opinion and subjecting the system to an evaluation can be beneficial for obvious reasons. Referring to ISO 27014, presented in Chapter 1, audits allow the governing body to provide oversight as part of the "Assure" process. Security officers also take advantage of audit findings to improve the maturity of the information security management system in place and justify initiatives before the governing body. Finally, security operations managers use audit findings to improve controls. However, care must be taken to ensure that audit projects are planned to cover priority topics (e.g. review a potentially low-maturity security process) and that the findings that follow are discussed and accepted by the security officer and their team.

Audits can also play an important role in impact analyses and identifying gaps in the regulatory framework. Auditors may be asked to comment on compliance outside the auditing process. Indeed, an organization may seek the advice of an auditing firm as a consultant. Auditors do not have the right to advise clients during an audit, but they can if they are engaged as consultants. The added value of such a consultant lies in the advice they can offer not only as an expert on regulations but also as an expert on the evaluation criteria used in the audit process. This dual competence allows an organization to optimize compliance efforts.

12.4 Conclusion

Good IS governance requires a highly effective compliance management process. The complexity of external regulations, which will increase in coming years, requires a high level of maturity and organization in the management of compliance, especially by companies operating across borders. Different approaches can be adopted, similar to the one presented in this chapter. In any case, a repetitive process of monitoring regulations and continuous adaptation must be introduced as the only guarantee of compliance adapted to the needs of the company. Adequate compliance requires the involvement of different officers in the company as well as external experts. Ignorance or blind trust in GRC solutions rarely brings viable solutions in the long run. As with program management or security risks, compliance management needs to take a pragmatic approach. Relying on external expertise while maintaining a critical attitude toward proposed solutions and involving internal skills can pay off in the long run.

New and growing practices such as Big Data or Data Analytics present not just commercial, but also scientific and social, opportunities. In this production of new knowledge, many companies see opportunities to develop new business models. If we add the possibilities of exchange, unlimited creativity and inventiveness in the use of these data, then data privacy could become a challenge for humanity. However, new regulations in the field of data protection also offer companies new opportunities. Handling personal and confidential data with care according to the regulations in force has become a differentiating factor, as customers are more and more aware of the danger of digital transformations. Companies that are able to demonstrate their effectiveness in this area will have an economic advantage and will be sought as preferred partners.

Further Readings

Chapter 1: Security Governance

Krag Brotby, "Information Security Governance: A Practical Development and Implementation Approach", Wiley, 2009

Alexandre Fernandez-Toro, "Management de la sécurité de l'information, Implémentation ISO 27001 et ISO 27002", Eyroles, 2012

Todd Fitzgerald, "Information Security Governance Simplified", CRC Press, 2012

Richard O'Hanley and James S. Tiller, "Information Security Management Handbook", CRS Press, 2013

S.H. von Solms and R. von Solms, "Information Security Governance", Springer, 2009

Marko Cabric, "Corporate Security Management", Butterworth-Heinemann, 2015

Tony Campbell, "Practical Information Security Management", Apress, 2016

Michael E. Whitman, Herbert J. Mattord, "Management of Information Security", Cengage, 2016

Charles Sennewald and Curtis Baillie, "Effective Security Management", Elsevier, 2015

"The Global State of Information Security Survey 2018", PWC, 2018. http://www.pwc.com/gx/en/issues/cyber-security/information-security-survey.html

"The Zettabyte Era: Trends and Analysis", CISCO, 2016. www.cisco.com/c/en/us/solutions/collateral/service-provider/visual-networking-index-vni/vni-hyperconnectivity-wp.pdf

Rassoul Ghaznavi-Zadeh, "Enterprise Security Architecture—A Top-down Approach", ISACA Journal, 2017. https://www.isaca.org/Journal/archives/2017/Volume-4/Pages/enterprise-security-architecture-a-top-down-approach.aspx

Jean Jacques du Plessis, Anil Hargovan, Mirko Bagaric, "Principles of Contemporary Corporate Governance", Cambridge University Press, 2011

"Information Security Governance, Guidance for Boards of Directors and Executive Management", IT Governance Institute, 2006.

"Information Security Governance, Guidance for Information Security Managers", IT Governance Institute, 2008.

Michael Fitzgerald, "Security and Business: Financial Basics", CSO Online, 2008,http://www.csoonline.com/article/394963/security-and-business-financial-basics?page=1

Daniel E. Greer, Jr., "Economic & Strategy of Data Security", Verdasys, 2011.

Shon Harris, "Information Security Governance Guide", Tech Target, 2018. http://searchsecurity.techtarget.com/tutorial/Information-Security-Governance-Guide

Jody R. Westby and Julia H. Allen, "Governing for Enterprise Security - Implementation Guide." Software Engineering Institute, Carnegie Mellon University, June 2007.

Pauline Bowen, Joan Hash, and Mark Wilson, "Information Security Handbook: A Guide for Managers", NIST, 2006. https://csrc.nist.gov/publications/detail/sp/800-100/final

CobIT 5: A Business Framework for the Governance and Management of Enterprise IT, ISACA, 2012

Enterprise Security Architecture, White Paper, John Sherwood, Andrew Clark & David Lynas, 2009

ISO/IEC 27014: Information technology — Security techniques — Governance of information security, ISO/IEC 2013

Chapter 2: Control Framework

NIST special publication 800-53 rev 4:https://nvd.nist.gov/800-53/Rev4

ISO/IEC 27001: Information technology — Security techniques — Information security management systems — Requirements, ISO/IEC 2013

ISO/IEC 27002: Information technology — Security techniques — Code of practice for information security controls, ISO/IEC 2013

Chapter 4: Strategy

John P. Pironti, "Developing an Information Security and Risk Management Strategy", ISACA Journal, 2010

Chris McClean, "Build A Governance, Risk, And Compliance Strategy Worthy Of Business Consideration", Forrester, 2012

Ed Ferrara and Andrew Rose, "Create A Security Strategy That Builds Real Business Value", Forrester, 2014

Martin Whitworth, "Six Steps To A Better Security Strategy", Forrester, 2016

ISO/IEC 15504: Information Technology - Process Assessment, ISO/IEC 2012

"Open Information Security Management Maturity Model", The Open Group, 2011

Chapter 5: Policies

Tom Scholtz, "Best Practices for Creating an Enterprise Information Security Charter", Gartner, 2014

Chapter 6: Organization

"Mastering the New Business Executive Job of the CIO Insights From the 2018 CIO Agenda Report", Gartner, 2018. https://www.gartner.com/imagesrv/cio-trends/pdf/cio_agenda_2018.pdf

"What CISOs Worry About in 2018", A Ponemon Institute Survey, 2018. https://www.opus.com/resource/2018-ciso-survey-ponemon-institute/

Andrew Rose, "Build A Strategic Security Program And Organization", Forrester, 2013

Christopher McClean, "Build your Seccurity Practice For Success", Forrester, 2015

Taryn Aguas, Khalid Kark, and Monique François, "The New CISO Leading the strategic security organization" Deloitte Review, Deloitte, 2016

Chapter 7: Risk Management

Jack Freund and Jack Jones, "Measuring and Managing Information Risk: A FAIR Approach", Elsevier, 2015

Evan Wheeler, "Security Risk Management: Building an Information Security Risk Management Program from the Ground Up", Elsevier, 2011

"Le rôle essentiel du conseil d'administration dans la surveillance efficace des risques", Ernst & Young, 2013

Devassy Jose Tharakan, "Protecting Information - Practical Strategies for CIOs and CISOs", ISACA Journal, 2016

Christopher McClean, "Define And Articulate The Role Of Risk Management", Forrester, 2016

ISO 31000: Risk management — Guidelines, ISO 2018

"The Risk It Framework", ISACA, 2009

Chapter 8: Program Management

Mark Rhodes-Ousley, "Information Security", McGraw Hill, 2013

Jason Andress, Mark Leavy, "Building a Practical Information Security Program", Elsevier, 2017

Joseph Opacki, "Building a Security Culture: Why Security Awareness Does Not Work and What to Do Instead", ISACA Journal 2017. https://www.isaca.org/Journal/archi ves/2017/Volume-4/Pages/building-a-security-culture.aspx

Laura Koetzle and Renee Murphy, "Develop Your Information Security Management System", Forrester, 2017

Christopher McClean, "Define A Roadmap To Accelerate Your Security Program", Forrester, 2015

Chapter 9: Security Metrics

Lance Hayden, "Security Metrics: A Practical Framework for Measuring Security & Protecting Data", McGraw Hill, 2010

Andrew Jaquith, "Security Metrics: Replacing Fear, Uncertainty, and Doubt", Addison Wesley, 2007

Jeff Pollard, "Remove The Mystery From Security Metrics", Forrester, 2016

Ed Ferrara, "Measuring The Effectiveness Of Your Security Operations", Forrester, 2015

Mukul Pareek, "Standardized Scoring for Security and Risk Metrics", ISACA Journal, 2017. https://www.isaca.org/Journal/archives/2017/Volume-2/Pages/standardize d-scoring-for-security-and-risk-metrics.aspx

Sanil Bakshi, "Performance Measurement Metrics for IT Governance", ISACA Journal, 2016. https://www.isaca.org/Journal/archives/2016/volume-6/Pages/performance -measurement-metrics-for-it-governance.aspx

Andrej Volchkov, "How to Measure Security From a Governance Perspective", ISACA Journal, 2013. https://www.isaca.org/Journal/archives/2013/Volume-5/Documents/How-to-Measure-Security-From-a-Governance-Perspective_jrn_English_0913.pdf

Ed Ferrara, "Don't Bore Your Executives – Speak To Them In A Language They Understand", Forrester, 2011

Bill Brenner, "Companies on IT Security Spending: Where's the ROI?", CSO Online, 2010. http://www.csoonline.com/article/518764/companies-on-it-security-spending-where-s-the-roi-

Scot Berinato, "A Few Good Information Security Metrics", CSO Online, 2005. http://www.csoonline.com/article/220462/a-few-good-information-security-metrics

Bruce Schneier, "Security ROI: Fact or fiction?", Computerworld, 2008. http://www.computerworld.com/s/article/9114021/Security_ROI_Fact_or_fiction_

Michael Cobb, "Measuring Risk: A Security Pro's Guide", InformationWeek Reports, 2012. http://reports.informationweek.com/abstract/15/8840/Risk-Management/strategy-measuring-risk-a-security-pro-s-guide.html

"The Open Group Releases Maturity Model for Information Security Management", The Open Group, 2011. http://www.opengroup.org/news/press/open-group-releases-maturity-model-information-security-management.

ISO/IEC 15408-1:2009, Evaluation criteria for IT securityhttp://www.iso.org/iso/iso_catalogue/catalogue_tc/catalogue_detail.htm?csnumber=50341

Julia H. Allen, Pamela D. Curtis, "Measures for Managing Operational Resilience", Software Engineering Institute, 2011.

Steve Dickson, "How to Measure the ROI of Cybersecurity Investments", ITSP Magazine, 2018. https://www.itspmagazine.com/from-the-newsroom/how-to-measure-the-roi-of-cybersecurity-investments

Daniel E. Greer, Jr., "Economic & Strategy of Data Security", Verdasys, 2011.

Derek Slater, "Security Metrics: Critical Issues", CSO Online, 2012. http://www.csoonline.com/article/455463/security-metrics-critical-issues

"Forrester's Identity And Access Management Cost Model ", Forrester, 2015. https://www.forrester.com/report/Forresters+Identity+And+Access+Management+Cost+Model/-/E-RES130561#

Indicateurs Sécurité, Cigref, 2007. https://www.google.ch/search?q=indicateurs+s%C3%A9curit%C3%A9+cigref&ie=&oe=

ISO 27004 Information technology - Security techniques - Information security management - Measurement, ISO/IEC 2009

Chapter 10. Reporting and Oversight

"Connecting the dots: A proactive approach to cybersecurity oversight in the boardroom", KPMG, 2014. https://home.kpmg.com/cn/en/home/insights/2015/12/connecting-the-dots-201512.html

Ed Ferrara, "Determine The Value of Information Security Assets And Liabilities - Information Security Economics 102", Forrester, 2012

Andrew J. Sherman, "Harvesting Intangible Assets: Uncover Hidden Revenue in Your Company's Intellectual Property", AMOCON, 2012

Andrew Rose, "The CISOs Handbook - Presenting To The Board", Forrester, 2013

Chapter 11. Asset Management

"ISO 55000:2014 Asset management — Overview, principles and terminology"https://www.iso.org/obp/ui/#iso:std:iso:55000:ed-1:v2:en

"Asset inventory and security management in ICS", Home / Blog / Asset inventory and security management in ICS, INCIBE 2016. https://www.certsi.es/en/blog/asset-inventory-and-security-management-ics

"GDPR Article 30 Solutions Brief, Practical Guide for GDPR Article 30 Compliance", TrustArc, 2018. https://info.trustarc.com/gdpr-article30-solutions-brief.html

Heidi Shey, John Kindervag, "Know Your Data To Create Actionable Policy", Forrester, 2013

Dejan Kosutic, "How to handle Asset register (Asset inventory) according to ISO 27001", 27001 Academy, 2018. https://advisera.com/27001academy/knowledgebase/how-to-handle-asset-register-asset-inventory-according-to-iso-27001/

Index

Printed in the United States
by Baker & Taylor Publisher Services